THE DEL
POSTO
COOKBOOK

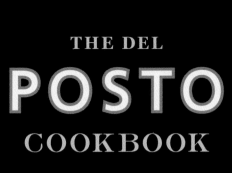

THE DEL
POSTO
COOKBOOK

MARK LADNER

WITH

MICHAEL R. WILSON

—

FOREWORDS BY

MARIO BATALI AND JOE BASTIANICH

FOOD PHOTOGRAPHY BY PAULETTE TAVORMINA

GRAND CENTRAL
Life & Style
NEW YORK • BOSTON

Grand Central Life & Style
Hachette Book Group
1290 Avenue of the Americas
New York, NY 10104
grandcentrallifeandstyle.com
twitter.com/grandcentralpub

First Edition: November 2016

Grand Central Life & Style is an imprint of Grand Central Publishing.
The Grand Central Life & Style name and logo are trademarks of Hachette Book Group, Inc.

The publisher is not responsible for websites (or their content) that are not owned by the publisher.

The Hachette Speakers Bureau provides a wide range of authors for speaking events.
To find out more, go to www.hachettespeakersbureau.com or call (866) 376-6591.

Food photography copyright © 2016 by Paulette Tavormina

Restaurant interior photographs copyright © 2016 by G. Girlado

Print book interior design by Gary Tooth / Empire Design Studio

Library of Congress Cataloging-in-Publication Data has been applied for.

ISBNs: 978-1-4555-6154-4 (Hardcover); 978-1-4555-6153-7 (E-book)

Printed in the United States of America

WOR

10 9 8 7 6 5 4 3 2 1

FOR JASPER

CONTENTS

MARIO BATALI

I FIRST MET MARK LADNER when I was working in the kitchen at Pó in the early '90s. He came in to check out the restaurant with a friend. The two of them asked for different, separate tasting menus. (She must have been a vegetarian, the 1994 equivalent of vegan/gluten-intolerant/heretic.) It was something I simply never did in my one-man hotline kitchen. But for the intriguing, super-friendly comrade in arms and "up and coming chef" Mark Ladner, I made it happen, for that one and only time. It may have struck a note.

We became friends and associates and a few years later I had the luck to hire him to be sous chef at Babbo. Soon thereafter, he became the executive chef/partner at Lupa, then a partner and chef at OTTO, and ultimately executive chef at Del Posto. He is the archetype of a New York City chef. Constantly thinking, perfecting, shopping, tweaking, and changing, Mark's style has evolved from classic white-tablecloth ristorante cooking, through rustic down-and-dirty osteria, to modern flexitarian pizzeria, and then on to cucina alta at Del Posto, which was awarded the first modern four-star review for an Italian restaurant by the *New York Times*. At each stop along his path, the core to the dining experience at Mark's tables has always been the fundamental joy of delicious pleasure and guest satisfaction.

At Del Posto today, Mark will prepare six distinct tasting menus for a six top on a Saturday night at 8:30pm: two vegans, one vegetarian (plus fish), one person who's allergic to lemongrass, and one person who prefers not to eat lamb. It is a testament to the control Mark has over one of the largest kitchens in New York and over each antique Ginori plate he sends into the dining room that every individual in the behemoth space can have a distinct experience. And that each diner experiences an equally heightened level of hospitality and unique, yet recognizable, flavor.

In a time when nearly all of the restaurants celebrated on the "world's best restaurants" lists predominantly serve a unique menu to all guests, with no options, Mark stays the course of a true restaurateur, offering options and variations to the delight and whimsy of a vast and varied clientele. This bucks the trend of awarding absolute monarchy to the chef, much to the joy of a whole world of customers who prefer to choose what they'd like to eat when they go out to dinner.

In stark contrast to many 21st-century chefs who dream of utilizing high technology to modify the texture and appearance of fine ingredients, Mark's cooking is decidedly low-tech, which makes it quite simple to translate into the home kitchen. Even in a world filled with sous vide equipment, immersion circulators, and liquid nitrogen, Mark's food is extremely relevant in all aspects of presentation to the guest. For this and a million other reasons, Del Posto simultaneously exudes old-school style and contemporary innovation, in spite of Mark's seemingly antithetical assertion of traditional definitions of hospitality and luxury.

This book in your hands delves into Mark's mind, his kitchen, and his entire ethos. Do not let his extreme precision deter you from simply cooking delicious and provocative, thoughtful food. In the same way that Mark spends hours every day teaching young chef-disciples his strategy and techniques, you can learn them on your own time, in your own kitchen, at your own pace, whenever you'd like, much like a diner enjoying Mark's expertise and joy at the fantastic temple that is Del Posto.

In 2004, THE CORNER OF 10th Avenue and 16th Street on the far west side of New York City's Meatpacking District was very different than it is today. A proverbial no-man's-land, the High Line was still a good five years away, and the surrounding area was much more likely to be a haven for ladies of the night than home to the multimillion-dollar relocation of the Whitney Museum.

But there was me, and Mario and Lidia, chasing another fortuitous real estate deal that was simply too good to pass up. Like all our previous endeavors, it started with a space. In this case, a mind-boggling 28,000-square-foot plot, huge by any city's restaurant standards, especially in Manhattan. Looking at the giant raw space, we envisioned a restaurant defined by its grandeur. Given our ambitions for Del Posto, the plan for the restaurant soon became clear—create a place to rival the best continental fine-dining restaurants of the world. And it would be Italian, of course.

It wasn't just the location or the sheer size that navigated us into uncharted territory, the concept of luxury Italian fine-dining in New York was something we had to completely invent from scratch. But one thing was certain, it had to be 100 percent authentic Italian cuisine. Taking the simple and down-to-earth cooking of an Italian grandmother and elevating it to the highest and most elegant standards possible was a gamble for a restaurant the size of Del Posto, but we were committed to the idea.

Reinvention was not exactly a foreign concept to Mario and me by the time we'd stumbled upon the 10th Avenue space. Even with Babbo and some of our other prior conceptions, we were creating new categories of restaurants that other dining groups would come to populate. At OTTO we put an enoteca (wine bar) inside a pizzeria, something you will never see in Italy—they don't even drink wine with pizza, they drink beer. The concept of an urban pizzeria with 500 wines on the list was innovative and experimental, but it was exactly what Italian food and wine lovers in New York City were hungry for—they just didn't know it yet.

Like the restaurant, the wine program at Del Posto has always been audacious, with an elaborate collecting philosophy and a huge cellar. It is arguably one of the most comprehensive Italian wine lists in the country, and can probably lay claim to having one of the biggest Champagne lists in New York City. At one point we even had our own labeling program.

Del Posto was not conceived as a restaurant that would follow trends. It was, and still remains, a restaurant almost defined by its impracticality, and is meant to endure. There hasn't been a flood of high-end Italian restaurant concepts to follow Del Posto, primarily because it is not that easy to do and requires an insane amount of resources. In the fall of 2010, after almost five years of hard work and evolution, the restaurant received a four-star review from the *New York Times* (the first Italian restaurant to do so in almost 40 years), which was a most welcome validation.

The impact of Del Posto's success is clear, but not so much in outright duplication of the restaurant. Our old-world style of cooking and service, with contemporary touches, continues to influence the culture of Italian dining in America. If you want to invent the future, you can't be afraid of reinterpreting the past. Tapping into what people want to experience today, while remaining true to the essence of Italian sensibility, has always been the driving force behind all of our restaurants, but Del Posto is by far our best example of this philosophy.

MARK LADNER

HEN DEL POSTO OPENED MORE THAN A DECADE AGO, I had no idea that we might be able to create a new style of sophisticated Italian-American cuisine. This was never the goal, nor did I think we were capable of such a feat. Every restaurant is a work in progress, and we are still developing. What I can say for certain is that I have been dedicated to building a bridge between the classic, regional cuisine of Italy and America's culinary ingenuity. Over the last decade, I have completely committed myself and our kitchen to harnessing every ounce of potential that traditional Italian cooking has to offer fine dining in America. Del Posto considers New York to be Italy's (unofficial) 21st region. We have created our own regional Italian cuisine, based on what has been available here, as well as New Yorkers' expectations. It didn't come easy, but it has been extraordinarily rewarding.

In the fall of 2003, I sat down with Joe Bastianich and Mario Batali at OTTO, our New York City pizzeria, to discuss my prospects of being the first executive chef of their newly conceived colossal 24,000-square-foot restaurant.

At that time, I had two successful partnerships with Mario and Joe, creating affordable Italian concepts, and I wasn't concerned with elegant or ambitious dining. They envisioned Del Posto to be the end-all of high-end Italian restaurants. I was quite surprised and overwhelmed by the offer, but mostly not interested in working on a fancy restaurant of that size. Nearly five years prior, I had given up plating dishes as anything more than dumping pastas from sauté pan to plate, and I was enjoying the freedom of this simple approach immensely. But, upon further consideration, I came to understand that such a large-scale proposition comes around only once, and the shelf life for this sort of offer is very short.

I took the job. And...I was unprepared. Naively, I imagined the restaurant as a chance to cook less covers with a larger staff. I thought we would just take the food I had already been making—rustic cooking informed by regional Italian recipes— delicately sprinkle it on more elegant plates, and *presto!* The rest would be history. However, the ambition of the project and the trajectory of Mario's and Joe's explosive careers, as the most successful of a new breed of American restaurateurs, drove their decisions. They put the game plan for the restaurant on a fierce steroids regimen— calling for a restaurant paved in marble with fields of imported linens, silver coffers, and crystal decanters. Their plans included a lounge, a baby grand piano, an enoteca, and private banquet rooms that could seat 200 people or more. The service would include carts delivering tableside preparations of large haunches of meat and whole fish for tables of two, four, and even six.

During the early planning, Mario's guidance for the food was based on the delicious Italian recipes in his award-winning cookbook, *Molto Italiano*. But it was early 2004, and the best and the brightest in the industry at that time were changing the tides of culinary thinking with new technology and techniques that would come to be known as modernist cuisine. I was reading the books and blogs, watching videos, and trying my best to understand this contemporary wave that was changing the landscape of my profession. But we were setting out to make classical, regional Italian food at a very high price point. We decided that the kitchen was going to be old-school and low-tech—no combi, no sous vide, and no powders.

We opened the restaurant in the winter of 2005 and it was sloppy. I was in the position of trying to create, curate, and manage a team of 150 people, 60 of whom were in the kitchen. It took too much time to cook, plate, coordinate, serve, or explain the food. The cuisine oscillated between being too contrived and not contrived enough. We'd serve a perfectly stacked pyramid of lamb shoulder croquettes, followed by a plate of bucatini you might find at our pizzeria but that was three times the price. I was frustrated—the food and the experience were not cohesive. I felt the cuisine didn't have a distinct style that was recognizably mine. For every winning dish, there was a dud. For every satisfied diner, one was upset.

Del Posto had no precedent—an Italian restaurant of its size, level of ambition, and price point had never existed in New York City before. Who could possibly be interested in eating food this expensive and convoluted on any given night? Really, how many, when places like Buddakan and Spice Market were around the corner and dominating the restaurant scene in New York with their casual, abbreviated dining experiences—where high-quality food was served family-style in party-like atmosphere with hip music. We had no gimmick or any particularly compelling new angle. But we firmly believed that traditional cooking, familiar flavors,

and recognizable food will never go out of fashion, and we wanted to present it with old-world, choreographed service.

Even though we had loads of talent on both sides of the swinging doors, we had a long way to go. I needed to be a better leader and allow the restaurant and the staff to claim their full potential and create a more compelling and unified culture. I needed to properly take advantage of the resources, the facilities, and the support that Joe, Mario, and Lidia had given us. I needed to get myself together.

In 2009, I committed us to a very ambitious tasting menu that I referred to as Le Collezione. I invested nine months into planning and plotting the content of this tasting menu. It would prove that we could push ourselves very hard and that we could produce and present an elaborate, nine-course menu that involved 126 service implements per diner—I forged working and lasting relationships with Italian design houses Richard Ginori, Alessi, and Ruffoni. Given the complexity of the menu, it was a service nightmare, but it turned out to be a training miracle. With wildly, lavishly, inappropriate service, we proved to ourselves that we had the resources to do almost anything. We sat the entire staff down to eat Le Collezione. What better way to integrate and train our staff? The sommelier, a dishwasher, a bartender, and a receptionist were a perfect four top, and the best team-building exercise. Staff tastings became our research and development. An abbreviated version of Le Collezione became the first successful Del Posto tasting menu. We discovered that by really focusing on age-old Italian cooking techniques, we could push the boundaries even further.

We harnessed a forgotten, traditional technique for vitello tonnato from Lombardy. Rather than relying on mayonnaise in the tuna sauce for the roasted veal, we gently cook veal and tuna together, making a rich sauce from the rendered juices. Then we introduce unusual garnishes—croutons stained black from olives, lime cells and lemon basil together to simulate an effervescence similar to Sprite soda,

and an unknown preserved caper shoot from the small island of Pantelleria.

We applied our new style of cooking to Jota, a pasta and bean soup from Friuli, traditionally thick enough to hold a spoon and warm a farmer's tired bones. Our Jota became light and lively in comparison by using beans from the most recent harvest, before the skins have had time enough to become tough, simmered with just water and vegetables until soft, and then emulsified with a light and fresh olive oil from Liguria. Complemented by baseball-stadium-style sauerkraut, BBQ-style smoked pork shoulder, and puffed rice penne (gluten-free), our Jota became a unique American-inflected Italian recipe that was served to guests as a precursor to the pasta course rather than a hearty winter meal in a bowl.

We spiced Long Island duck in the style of a recipe made popular by the school of gourmands, Apicius (documented in the book *De re coquinaria* from the fifth century), that celebrated the ancient Roman spice trade. The duck is paired with charred celery and Savor, a condiment created by our friend and figurehead of contemporary Italian cooking, Massimo Bottura. His distinctive accompaniment, made of quince paste, chestnuts, apples, and pumpkin seeds, is a lovely combination of sweet and savory elements, and a modern foil for ancient duck.

In 2008, I found artist and flavor savant Brooks Headley. We had been unlucky with our pastry department in the past, and we were looking for a new direction. We needed someone willing to take chances and change the perception Italian pastry had in America. The first thing Brooks made for us was a chocolate-and-ricotta tortino. It hit all the right spots. Great, rich Tuscan chocolate, lactic curds of fluffy cow's milk. A Devil Dog, cloaked in a shell of high-quality Sicilian pistachios. His desserts use salts and acids as weapons to tame sugar. His ideas, many of which are in this book, fiercely respect tradition while also turning it on its head. Together we were able to create a completely coalesced meal for the first time. We were in business.

We retrained the entire front of house staff. Our general manager and service director were focusing on purposed communication with our guests in order to create a real dialogue about our intentions and their expectations. The kinks were being worked out, and we started to feel good. The team was strong and proud. We were integrating other mediums into our thinking—art, literature, design, language, and desire.

We were making proper, solid, old-fashioned-technique cuisine. It was not pretentious stuff, but the food your mom might make given the support of Lidia, Joe, and Mario, and a gentle hand. Who on God's green earth has the time or interest in torturing vegetables for five hours on the flicker of a flame until they liquefy? We did. Because low-and-slow tech is lovely—like a nap in the sun.

We pour cloudy liquid chocolate into a bucket of ice because we like sculptures. Why tease a pile of flour and eggs into a loose amoeba? Because Todd English once told me gnocchi should be light as an angel's kiss. We were doing our best work and momentum was building.

Over the years the critics have been mostly kind. In the early days, 2006, we were given three stars in the *New York Times* and, somehow, received two Michelin stars. I say *somehow* because I was not happy with what we were doing then. In 2010, Del Posto was the first Italian restaurant to be awarded four stars by the *New York Times* in nearly 40 years. The previous recipient had been a boutique restaurant with a short life—a true labor of love by the chef. But Del Posto was massive, a factory, and there were certainly no restaurants like it in Italy, where one service per table a night is the norm.

Years ago, during the early days of Del Posto, I was having dinner at Rao's with Patrick Martin from Heritage Foods and Alice Waters from Chez Panisse. Alice and I got to talking about my over-

whelming difficulties in trying to run such an enormous restaurant. Alice in her infinite wisdom suggested I break the kitchen departments into separate "restaurants," with separate chefs. This would allow them each to have the opportunity and autonomy to evolve organically and independent of one another. Honestly, I thought she was crazy. But she was absolutely right.

Del Posto is a 400-seat restaurant with 200 employees. Needless to say, it takes a village. This book represents our passion for Italian cooking and fine dining. The recipes here are the work of a large team of talented people, all of whom have contributed something to each of these dishes.

There is no better way for me to share the true spirit of our recipes than to have you make them at home and learn how to use the techniques we have refined over the years. While the recipes may seem long and intimidating, we have worked tirelessly to cover every detail of their process so that you can successfully make our food in your kitchen.

THE ITALIAN MENU, SERVIZIO DEL VINO & THE LARDER

THE DEL POSTO MENU

DEL POSTO IS AN ENORMOUS RESTAURANT on 10th Avenue in Manhattan, with double-height ceilings, balconies, multiple private dining rooms, an expansive wine cellar, a bar, and a lounge, that serves up to 400 people each night. A dining room buzzing with activity is part of the New York City experience, but the restaurant also works tirelessly to provide subtle, refined service that makes fine dining special. Antique and custom-made Italian

china plates with underliners and silver chargers and crystal services for truffles and caviar are all part of an old-world atmosphere that celebrates our Italian and American heritages. Del Posto is not a temple of food, but rather like going to an Italian nonna's house for supper, if Nonna's house were a grand palazzo.

We strongly believe an Italian meal should never be austere, and that fine dining is a form of pampering, where guests decide about every aspect of their experience and feel as though they are breathing rarefied air. A number of years ago we decided to get rid of the Chef's Tasting Menu, a multitude of dishes prepared in specific sequence, showcasing the kitchen's best dishes. It is a style of dining that most high-end restaurants have as a staple offering. But offering a menu driven by the kitchen rather than the guest never made sense for Del Posto. Instead, we present the option of the Captain's Menu, empowering the captains in the dining room to work directly with guests to build customized meals.

A classic Italian menu starts with the antipasto of light vegetables, fish, or meat preparations, transitions to the pasta or rice primo, then onto heavier proteins in the secondo course, and concludes with dolce, or dessert. This well-balanced succession of preparations is known as the *Quattro Piatti*, or Four Plates. Del Posto is dedicated to this traditional-style menu, and the recipe chapters in this book provide a varied collection of dishes for each of these four courses, along with a chapter for small bar snacks, assaggi, and a chapter for cookies and candies.

SERVIZIO DEL VINO

DEL POSTO RESTS ON THE SHOULDERS of its wine cellar, physically and figuratively. The wine program at Del Posto is central to the dining experience, as it should be at any Italian restaurant.

Building a comprehensive Italian wine cellar is no small task considering that Italy boasts more than a thousand varietals of winemaking grapes, which is astounding compared to France's few hundred. No country produces as diverse a collection of wines as Italy does, due in large part to its wildly varied topography and weather systems. The country packs two major mountain ranges, coastlines from five different seas, arid plateaus, lush riverbeds, and high-altitude lakes into an area only three-quarters the size of California. Its ancient territory spans 20 regions, all of which grow different grapes and make wines differently.

The Del Posto cellar was built from the ground up and contains more than 50,000 wines, only a third of which are represented on the menu. The other two thirds are aging as part of a collecting program started when the restaurant opened more than a decade ago, and includes wines that date back to the 1930s. The cellar has been referred to as the Metropolitan Museum of Italian Wines because it aims to be an all-encompassing collection but focuses intensely on the masters—most of which are procured from private collections.

The cuisine at Del Posto breathes new life into age-old regional traditions, and the wines in the restaurant's collection are selected because they come from similar places and traditions. There is an adage among sommeliers that the first rule of wine pairing is "If it grows together, then it goes together." Unlike most restaurants in Italy, Del Posto presents dishes influenced by regional cooking from many different parts of Italy, and also unlike many restaurants in Italy, we are able to offer wines from equally as many regions.

The American palate for wine continues to evolve at a rapid pace. You never used to find fish paired with red wine, or an entire meal accompanied by different courses of sparkling wines, for example, but this happens regularly now. This new enthusiasm and knowledge makes pairing wines really exciting for us because Italian wines are so varied.

Having access to a collection as extensive as this one is really not just about the wines, but also about having access to the knowledge that goes along with collecting them. Throughout this book we share this knowledge with a selection of suggested wine pairings that express the diversity and vitality of Italian winemaking.

THE LARDER

MANY OF THE RECIPES in this book call for special Italian-made products. Cornerstones of Italian cooking, these distinctive ingredients come from centuries-old regional traditions. While most of these products are discussed in recipes through-out the book, the following are workhorse ingredi-ents in the Del Posto kitchen, included in multiple recipes, and require some special attention here.

CAPERS

Capers are sun-dried, pickled flower buds from the thorny caper plant, and a staple in Mediterranean pantries—from southern France to Syria. The best Italian capers are cultivated in the arid and rocky climates of the Aeolian islands, just northwest of Sicily, and the small island of Pantelleria, located between Sicily's south coast and North Africa. Good capers are delicate, tangy, vegetal, and slightly piquant. Those packaged and sold in salt are far better than those jarred in liquid. Generally, the smaller the caper, the better they are—anything bigger than a raisin is likely flavorless. When choosing Italian capers look for small, dark-green buds from Lipari or Pantelleria, tightly packed in salt. Before cooking with salt-packed capers, they should be rinsed of their salt with lukewarm water, soaked for 10 to 15 minutes, rinsed again, and then dried off.

PARMIGIANO-REGGIANO

Grana means "grain" in Italian and is the nickname for the many types of hard, craggy cheeses grated for pastas and risottos. Parmigiano-Reggiano is one of the country's greatest culinary achievements and the king of grana. Made in the Emilia-Romagna region from local cow's milk, it is produced in large 80- to 85-pound smooth-rind wheels. While imitated around the world (known as Parmesan), there is absolutely no substitute for its nutty notes, hay-like fragrance, and creamy texture studded with crunchy calcium deposits. The Italian government carefully regulates Parmigiano-Reggiano, and the authentic versions are stamped with a registration number and date of production. Like most cheeses, its flavor strengthens and its acidic qualities mellow with age. It's called *giovane* if it's aged for at least 12 months (the minimum amount of time), *vecchio* when more than 24 months, *stravecchio* when 36 months, and *stravecchione* when upward of 48 months. There are many artisan producers who go above and beyond the government regulations for their Parmigiano-Reggiano, making incredible versions of the cheese. A few of these artisans produce a version called *Vacche Rosse,* which means "red cows." Until the middle of the 20th century, Parmigiano-Reggiano was made from the milk of the native Reggiana cow—the cheese's namesake and a breed distinguished by its red coat. During the last 60 years, the red cows have become virtually extinct, as they have been replaced by less expensive breeds. Recently, a few producers have revitalized the Reggiana, or Vacche Rosse, in order to make traditional Parmigiano from its milk, which is very high in the butterfat required for cheese to age well. The finest Parmigiano is best simply drizzled with aged balsamic, or complemented by fruit compotes and spicy mostardas. Depending on how it's used in our recipes, we call for different ages of Parmigiano-Reggiano. When grating Parmigiano at home, we strongly suggest using the star holes of a

box grater rather than a Microplane or any other type of shredder.

PECORINO ROMANO GENUINO

Pecora is the word for "sheep" in Italian, and pecorino is a sheep's milk cheese made throughout Italy. Pecorino Romano comes from Lazio and has been made in the farmlands surrounding Rome for more than two millennia—it was included in the rations for ancient Roman legionaries. This hard, smooth-rind cheese is pungent, briny, and slightly piquant. It is an essential cheese for many Roman pasta dishes such as cacio e pepe, but should be used sparingly because it can be very salty. Americans have come to call this style of cheese simply romano.

Pecorino Romano is now produced in many regions of Italy, but those labeled *Genuino* are made in Lazio with the milk from designated herds of sheep that graze in fields outside Rome. The Genuino is the highest quality of Pecorino Romano, with gamy aromatics and a crumbly texture that becomes creamy when warmed.

PECORINO FIORE SARDO

Pecorino Fiore Sardo is a white and pale yellow smooth-rind cheese with slightly smoky notes made from sheep's milk on the island of Sardinia (hence the Sardo) in both fresh and aged varieties. The fresh younger cheese is milky and sweet with a tinge of acid. The aged mature cheese hardens and concentrates its salt. This version is much more common, and is good for grating over pastas and salads, providing a dose of tangy, creamy salt. Essentially, this is Sardinia's version of Lazio's Pecorino (Romano) and tends to be slightly softer and less salty than its Roman cousin.

BALSAMICO TRADIZIONALE

Balsamic vinegar is one of Italy's most widely available products, and also one of its most precious. But trying to navigate the world of this cooked-grape vinegar can be daunting. Basically, there are two types of balsamic vinegar: the highly regulated, crown jewel of vinegars, aceto balsamico tradizionale, and the hundreds of other balsamics that range in quality and can be labeled as balsamico di Modena or condimento balsamico.

The tradizionale is produced by hand in small quantities by a centuries-old method in the provinces of Modena and Reggio nell'Emilia, where every aspect of its production is regulated by DOP standards, allowing it to be labeled tradizionale. Juice from local white Trebbiano grapes is simmered in large copper cauldrons for 24 hours or more. Once concentrated to a syrup called *mosto cotto* in Italian, it is aged for a minimum of 12 years in a *batteria*, a series of five wooden barrels. The barrels are made from a variety of woods—from acacia to juniper—and are fitted with openings covered with fabric, which allows oxygen to reduce and concentrate the liquid inside. As it ages and reduces, the vinegar is moved to progressively smaller barrels until it finishes in the fifth and smallest barrel—at which point its sugars have highly concentrated and become the consistency of molasses. This artisanal process and its resulting flavors justify the high cost of aceto balsamico tradizionale. A few of the recipes in this book call for a drizzle of tradizionale, which is used at the restaurant. But don't be discouraged if tradizionale isn't available; there are many high-quality aged balsamic vinegars, labeled simply as condimento or aged balsamic, that make fine substitutes.

OLIVE OIL

Exploring the world of Italian olive oils can be just as immersive as discovering the country's wines. There are dozens of olive varietals grown in Italy for making olive oil, each with their own unique characteristics. In northern regions the taggiasca olive produces light fine oils with delicate almond notes, while stronger, fruitier oils are made from the casaliva, leccino, and moraiolo olives. In Tuscany and central Italy, the frantoio and moraiolo olives produce spicy and herbaceous oils. The gentile di Chieti is found in Abruzzo, the cima di Bitonto in Puglia, and the nocellara del Belice in Sicily. Throughout the country, oils pressed from these

olives can be blended by producers for balance and complexity of flavors, or sold as monovarietal oil, which means the oil was produced from one type of olive grown in one specific place. And like wine, the monovarietal oils aren't necessarily better than blended oils—quality oils come from quality olives and quality producers. Unlike wine, olive oil doesn't get better with age; its flavors dull with time and it should be used as fresh as possible. Del Posto uses a large collection of cold-pressed, extra-virgin oils in the kitchen, but we use four basic types of oil from different parts of the country for the dishes in this book. These styles of oil are noted in the recipes and readily available in the United States.

Ligurian

Oils made in coastal Liguria are predominantly pressed from taggiasca olives, but also can include oils from rignola and colombara olives. This part of coastal Italy has a climate similar to southern Italy, where sun-soaked groves of olive trees are cooled by sea air blowing off the coast. We turn to Ligurian oils for their lively almond and artichoke notes, slightly buttery texture, and smooth finish, which won't overtake subtle flavors in delicate salads, pestos, and sauces. There are many producers of fine Ligurian oil, and we often use Ceppo Antico, which is a taggiasca blend.

Tuscan

A vast number of olive oils are made in Tuscany, each with their own style and personality. The three main production areas are near Chianti, Siena, and Lucca, and most Tuscan oils are blended from a multitude of different olives. We use a robust, muscular style of Tuscan oil for finishing heavy dishes such as roasted meat. These oils have a particularly spicy finish and strong aromas of fresh-cut grass. Tenuta di Capezzana and Frantoio Franci are two oils used at Del Posto for finishing touches on heartier dishes.

Sicilian

Sicily has been cultivating olives for oil since the Phoenicians occupied the Island in the eighth century BC. There are at least seven major growing areas on the island, and ten times as many styles of oil. We call for two styles of Sicilian oils in our recipes: delicate and intense, often labeled *delicato* or *intenso*. The Sicilian delicatos are fruity, with hints of bitterness and spice on the finish, and good with seafood and vegetable preparations. Lu Trappitu is one great producer of delicato. The intenso style of Sicilian oil is luscious, darker in color, and slightly bitter in flavor. Its piquant notes are not as strong as Tuscan oils, but its grassy notes can provide similar accent on the palate. Frantoi Cutrera Primo is a high-quality intense Sicilian selection.

PIENNOLO DEL VESUVIO TOMATOES

Canned and jarred tomatoes are found in just about every Italian kitchen, and Del Posto is no different. There are many wonderful canned summer tomatoes available, and San Marzano, a variety of plum tomato, are the most ubiquitous. However, jarred piennolo cherry tomatoes from Mount Vesuvius in the Campania region provide the base for the tomato sauces at Del Posto. Casa Barone is the best producer of jarred piennolo tomatoes available here. Their organic tomatoes grow in the lava-enriched soil of the Mt. Vesuvius National Park. Jarred in their own juices, the bright red Barone piennolos are at once fresh-tasting and incredibly sweet. They don't really need to be cooked or reduced because they are unusually rich.

TRUFFLES

Truffles are synonymous with luxurious Italian dining, especially in northern Italy. A mainstay in the Del Posto kitchen, their intoxicating aromas epitomize extravagance and celebration.

Quality truffles are nearly impossible to cultivate and truffle hunting involves luck and special dogs, trained to sniff out even the smallest of these "diamonds of the kitchen." During the fall months, the tartufai—truffle foragers—scour the forests of northern and central Italy for this elusive tuber, which grows underground (as much as two feet) in the root system of certain trees. Ranging in size from a marble to a baseball, good fresh truffles are quite expensive—fetching more than $150 per ounce, depending on market rates. Their availability and quality vary from year to year. The Italian white truffles are the most prized and are found between October and December. They boast strong aromas with hints of garlic, hay, and cheese. The fresh black truffle (Périgord or black winter truffle) arrives between and November and March with intense aromas of what can only be described as the forest floor. The black summer truffle is almost flavorless and dull on the nose, and is found between May and August.

Fresh truffles are extremely perishable; their aromas dissipate with every hour they are out of the ground. Fresh white and black truffles arrive during fall and winter at specialty grocers. Look for firm, heavy truffles with intense aromas; in some cases they should have a slight ammonia scent. Avoid storing them in rice, which dries them out. Keep them wrapped in paper or cloth and then in a plastic box. When purchasing truffle oil, look for one made with real truffles; many products on the market are only synthesized to smell like truffles. Canned and jarred truffle peelings can be bought at a fraction of the cost of fresh truffles. Look for those from French or Italian black winter truffles. These often come in truffle juice, which is used in a few of the recipes in this book. Truffle juice is also sold on its own and should come from European black winter truffles. All of these products can easily be purchased at gourmet stores and online.

ASSAGGI

When guests arrive at Del Posto, they are greeted
with a collection of small tastes, *assaggi* in Italian. Savory creations
presenting some of the kitchen's best techniques, the assaggi highlight
staple ingredients from Del Posto's Italian larder. These exciting
snacks prime the palate for the meal ahead and pair well with
aperitivo cocktails and sparkling wines. Changing with the seasons,
a wide variety of assaggi are prepared daily at the restaurant, but this
selection of nine classic recipes makes for a festive, elegant cocktail
party or welcoming bites before a meal.

From left to right on table:
*Which Came First: Chicken and Egg
Salad Tramezzini (page 9); Marinara
Soup with Caper Salt (page 5); Veal
Tartar and Potato Chip Club (page
10); Baccalá Croquettes with Red
Pepper Jelly (page 6); Supplì di
Marchesi with gold dust (page 4); and
Tuna and Truffle Sfere (page 8)*

From left to right on stand:
*Ceci Farinata (page 8); Mini Lobster
and Corn Crostatas (page 11); and
Palline di Pane (page 7)*

SUPPLÌ DI MARCHESI

Chef Gualtiero Marchesi is considered the father of modern Italian cooking, creating *nuovo cucina* in the 1980s. He was the first Italian to win three Michelin stars and has influenced an entire generation of chefs. Drawing great inspiration from 20th-century painters, Marchesi often reconstructs classic recipes in new ways. One of his most iconic dishes, risotto oro e zafferano, is a classic saffron risotto alla Milanese topped with a square of edible gold leaf. As homage to Marchesi's enduring vision for contemporary Italian cooking, these risotto balls are fried until molten in the center, then sprinkled with edible gold dust.

Makes 36 (1-inch or 2.5-centimeter) suppli

SUPPLÌ

1 tablespoon (15 milliliters) extra-virgin olive oil

1 tablespoon (15 grams) minced shallot

2 tablespoons (1 gram) saffron threads

¾ cup (145 grams) vialone nano, carnaroli, or arborio rice

1 teaspoon (4 grams) kosher salt

½ cup (118 milliliters) dry white wine

2 tablespoons (30 grams) unsalted butter, cut into small cubes

3 tablespoons (13 grams) freshly grated Parmigiano-Reggiano cheese (see Larder, page xxiv)

1 (8-ounce or 225-gram) block robiola cheese, cut into small cubes (leaving rind on)

PUFFED RICE

Kosher salt

1 cup (190 grams) vialone nano, carnaroli, or arborio rice

About 1½ quarts (scant 1½ liters) vegetable oil, for frying

2 cups (200 grams) rice flour

TO SERVE

4 large eggs

Kosher salt

Edible gold luster dust, for dusting (optional, see note)

SPECIAL EQUIPMENT: a candy / fry thermometer

For the suppli: In a medium saucepan, bring 3 cups (710 milliliters) of water just to a boil, then remove from the heat.

In a medium saucepan, heat the olive oil over medium-low heat. Add the shallot and cook, stirring occasionally, until softened, about 3 minutes. Remove the pan from the heat and stir in the saffron, then stir in the rice and salt. Over medium heat, cook the rice, stirring to coat it with the oil mixture, until it is aromatic and lightly toasted, about 1 minute. Add the wine and cook, stirring occasionally, until the liquid has evaporated, then add about ½ cup of the hot water. Cook, stirring frequently, until the liquid is mostly absorbed.

Continue adding the water in ½-cupfuls, stirring frequently and allowing each addition of liquid to mostly absorb before adding the next, until you have a very tender, overcooked risotto. (The risotto will take 28 to 30 minutes of cooking from the time you begin adding liquid; you may have water left over.) Stir in the butter, Parmigiano-Reggiano, and robiola. Spread the risotto in an even layer in a large baking dish and chill, uncovered, until the risotto is set, at least 1 hour or overnight. Cover and refrigerate until ready to use.

For the puffed rice: Bring a medium pot of well-salted water to a boil. Line a baking sheet with paper towels. Boil the rice, stirring occasionally, until tender, about 18 minutes. Drain and rinse well under cold running water (to rinse off any residual starch), then spread onto the prepared baking sheet. Pat dry well with additional paper towels.

Pour enough of the vegetable oil into a heavy 5-quart (4.7-liter) saucepan to come up 1½ inches (3.8 centimeters). Heat the oil to 400°F (204°C). In a large bowl, toss together the plain cooked rice with 1 cup (100 grams) of the rice flour to coat. Then, over a second large bowl, sift to remove the excess flour (the rice granules should be separate and evenly coated with flour).

Working in ½-cup (70-gram) batches, fry the coated rice until lightly golden, 1 to 2 minutes per batch (the oil will bubble up when the rice is added). Using a small mesh strainer, transfer to paper towels to drain. Season generously with salt while warm. Let cool completely. Remove the oil from the heat and reserve it for frying the suppli.

To serve: Reheat the vegetable oil to 350°F (177°C). Meanwhile, place the remaining 1 cup (100 grams) rice flour in a large shallow bowl. In a second shallow bowl, beat together the eggs. In a third shallow bowl, place the puffed rice.

Roll the supplì mixture into 1-inch (2.5-centimeter) balls. In batches, dredge the balls in the flour, shaking off excess. Dip into the egg, letting the excess drip off, then roll in the puffed rice to generously coat, pressing gently to help the rice adhere.

In batches of 3, fry the supplì until a light crust forms on the outside and the cheese inside is hot and melted (test one to check for doneness), about 1 minute. Using a slotted spoon, transfer to paper towels to drain. Season with salt while hot. If desired, use a fine-mesh strainer to dust the supplì with gold luster dust. Serve immediately.

NOTE: *Edible gold luster dust can be purchased at gourmet stores and online. These supplì can be made without the decorative gold luster dust; the flavors will not change.*

MARINARA SOUP
with Caper Salt

At Del Posto, this soup is served in small, custom-made porcelain cups. Any small, espresso-sized cup or shot glass can be used instead.

Makes 16 (1-ounce or 30-milliliter) portions

CAPER SALT

1 cup (188 grams) salt-packed capers, rinsed with warm water

1 cup (236 milliliters) red wine vinegar

SOUP

1 cup (236 milliliters) jarred piennolo tomatoes with their juices (see Larder, page xxix)

1 tablespoon (15 milliliters) extra-virgin olive oil

1 garlic clove (4 grams), gently smashed and peeled

Pinch dried oregano

Pinch red chili flakes

1 cup (236 milliliters) Tomato Broth (see Cool Summertime Minestra, page 24)

Kosher salt

Sugar

3 basil leaves

TO SERVE

Very good extra-virgin olive oil, preferably intense Sicilian (see Larder, page xxix)

SPECIAL EQUIPMENT: parchment paper; a food mill or blender

For the caper salt: In a nonreactive bowl, soak the capers in the vinegar. Cover and refrigerate overnight.

Heat the oven to 200°F (93°C). Line a baking sheet with parchment paper. Drain the capers, then spread in a single layer on the prepared baking sheet (discard the vinegar). Bake until dry and crisp, 2 to 2½ hours. Let the capers cool completely, then finely grind in a spice grinder. (Caper salt keeps in an airtight container at cool room temperature for up to 1 month.)

For the soup: Pass the piennolo tomatoes (with their juices) through the fine-holed disk of a food mill or purée in a blender, then force through a medium-mesh sieve to extract the seeds.

In a medium saucepan, combine the oil and garlic. Heat over medium heat until fragrant, about 2 minutes. Remove from the heat. Stir in the oregano and red chili flakes. Let stand 10 seconds, then add the puréed tomatoes and the tomato broth. Return to medium heat and bring to a simmer. Cook, stirring occasionally, until the flavors marry, 3 to 5 minutes. Remove from the heat. Stir in a generous pinch each of salt and sugar. Adjust the seasoning to taste, then stir in the basil.

To serve: Spread the caper salt on a small plate. Dab the rim of a small soup cup on a wet paper towel to dampen, then dip into the caper salt to rim the edge. Repeat with the remaining cups. Remove and discard the garlic and basil from the soup, then ladle the soup into the cups. Add a drop or two of Sicilian extra-virgin olive oil to each cup.

BACCALÀ CROQUETTES
with Red Pepper Jelly

Makes about 24 (1-inch or 2.5-centimeter) croquettes

BACCALÀ

Scant 1 cup (60 grams) kosher salt, plus more for seasoning

1 tablespoon plus 2 teaspoons (total 20 grams) sugar

½ pound (225 grams) skinless cod fillet

RED PEPPER JELLY

¼ cup (50 grams) sugar

½ teaspoon (2 grams) powdered fruit pectin

1¾ pounds (800 grams) red bell peppers

2 tablespoons (20 grams) drained, seeded, and finely chopped B&G hot cherry peppers (from a jar), plus 1 tablespoon (15 milliliters) of the pickling liquid

3½ tablespoons (52 milliliters) white wine vinegar

1 teaspoon (4 grams) kosher salt

CROQUETTES

2 cups (473 milliliters) whole milk

1 heaping cup (300 grams) ½-inch (1.25-centimeter) cubes peeled russet potato

Scant ⅓ cup (60 grams) mayonnaise, preferably Hellman's, Best Foods, or Kewpie

1 tablespoon (15 grams) Gulden's spicy brown mustard

TO SERVE

1½ quarts (scant 1½ liters) vegetable oil, for frying

½ cup (60 grams) rice or potato flour

4 large eggs, beaten

2 cups (110 grams) uncooked Hungry Jack instant mashed potato flakes

Kosher salt

SPECIAL EQUIPMENT: a candy / fry thermometer; a ricer or food mill

For the baccalà: In a small baking dish, stir together the salt and sugar, then put the cod in the dish and pat the salt mixture all over it. Chill, covered, overnight.

For the red pepper jelly: In a small bowl, mix together the sugar and pectin. Set aside. Dice enough of the bell peppers to yield 1¾ cups (250 grams). Cut the remaining bell peppers into small cubes and place in the bowl of a food processor. Purée to form a pulpy "juice."

In a medium saucepan, combine the diced bell peppers, the pepper "juice," the B&G peppers and pickling liquid, vinegar, and salt. Bring to a gentle simmer and cook until the peppers are tender but still hold their shape, about 15 minutes. Stir in the reserved sugar mixture, increase the heat to high, and bring to a boil. Reduce to a simmer and cook, stirring occasionally, until the mixture is thickened and reduced by about a third, about 25 minutes. Transfer the jelly to a heatproof jar. Cover and refrigerate and let chill, about 2 hours. (The jelly can be made up to 2 weeks ahead and kept covered and refrigerated.)

For the croquettes: Remove the cod from the salt mixture. Rinse well under cold running water. In a medium saucepan, heat the milk just to a simmer. Add the cod. Gently simmer until the cod flakes easily, 5 to 8 minutes. Using a slotted spoon, transfer the cod to a plate. Add the potatoes to the milk and simmer until tender, about 12 minutes. Strain the potatoes and, while hot, pass through a ricer or food mill into a medium bowl. Let cool completely.

Add the mayonnaise and mustard to the potatoes; stir well to combine. Gently break up the cod into small flakes (but not so small that the flakes become stringy), then very gently fold into the potato mixture to just combine.

To serve: In a heavy 5-quart (4.7-liter) saucepan, heat the vegetable oil to 350ºF (177ºC). Place the flour in a large shallow bowl. In a second shallow bowl, beat together the eggs. In a third shallow bowl, place the potato flakes.

Roll the cod mixture into 1-inch (2.5-centimeter) balls. In batches, dredge the balls in the flour, shaking off the excess. Dip into the egg, letting the excess drip off, then gently roll in the potato flakes to generously coat (the flakes are delicate; do your best not to crush them or work them into the cod mixture). In batches of 5, fry the croquettes until lightly golden, about 1½ minutes. Using a slotted spoon, transfer to paper towels to drain. Season with salt while hot, then dollop with pepper jelly. Serve immediately.

NOTE: *Leftover pepper jelly keeps, covered and refrigerated, for up to 2 weeks. Use the leftovers on meats, cheeses, fish, sandwiches, and more.*

PALLINE DI PANE

For the tomato marmellata: In a small saucepan, heat the oil and garlic over medium-low heat until fragrant, 1 to 2 minutes. Add the onion and cook, stirring occasionally, until tender, about 7 minutes. Stir in the bomba, remove the pan from the heat for 30 seconds, then add the vinegar. Return to medium-low heat and cook, stirring occasionally, until the liquid is mostly evaporated. Add the tomato sauce and cook, stirring occasionally, until the mixture is flavorful, about 3 minutes. Stir in the sugar and salt. Transfer to a heat-proof container and let cool completely. (The marmellata keeps, covered and refrigerated, for up to 1 week. Let come to room temperature before serving.)

For the palline di pane: Rinse and spin dry the escarole, leaving a few drops of water on the leaves. In a large wide saucepan, cook the oil and garlic over medium-low heat until fragrant, 1 to 2 minutes. Add the shallot and cook, stirring occasionally, until tender, about 5 minutes. Stir in the red chili flakes, then add the escarole. Cook, stirring occasionally and adding water by the tablespoon as necessary to keep the pan from becoming completely dry, until the escarole is very tender, about 1 hour. Remove and discard the garlic. Transfer the escarole to a colander to drain and cool. Squeeze tightly to remove as much liquid as possible, then finely chop.

In a large bowl, combine the breadcrumbs and milk. Let stand until the breadcrumbs have absorbed the milk, about 5 minutes. Add the chopped escarole and the prosciutto, pecorino, Parmigiano, and egg. Mix just to combine.

In a wide heavy saucepan, heat the vegetable oil to 350°F (177°C). Meanwhile, roll the escarole mixture into 1-inch (2.5-centimeter) balls, then roll in the breadcrumbs to generously coat, pressing gently to help the breadcrumbs adhere. In batches of 5, fry the palline di pane until lightly golden, about 1½ minutes. Using a slotted spoon, transfer to paper towels to drain. Season with salt while hot. Spoon the marmellata on top. Serve immediately.

NOTE: *Calabrian bomba (or bomba Calabrese), a local specialty from the southern region of Calabria, is a spicy chili spread made from peperoncino, tomato, and other local vegetables. Jarred bomba can be purchased at Italian gourmet stores and online.*

Makes about 28 (1-inch or 2.5-centimeter) bread balls

TOMATO MARMELLATA

2 teaspoons (10 milliliters) extra-virgin olive oil

1 garlic clove (4 grams), finely chopped

3½ tablespoons (50 grams) finely chopped yellow onion

1 tablespoon (15 grams) Calabrian bomba (see note)

1 tablespoon (15 milliliters) red wine vinegar

¾ cup (180 milliliters) Del Posto Tomato Sauce (see 100-Layer Lasagne, page 98)

1 teaspoon (4 grams) sugar

Generous pinch kosher salt

PALLINE DI PANE

1 (1-pound or 453-gram) head escarole, trimmed and coarsely chopped

1 tablespoon (15 milliliters) extra-virgin olive oil

1 garlic clove (4 grams), gently smashed and peeled

1 tablespoon (15 grams) finely chopped shallot

Pinch red chili flakes

About 1 cup (55 grams) plain coarse breadcrumbs, plus ½ cup (27 grams) more for frying

⅓ cup (75 milliliters) whole milk

1 (6-ounce or 175-gram) hunk of prosciutto, cut into cubes, then finely ground in a food processor

¼ cup plus 2 tablespoons (total 25 grams) freshly grated Pecorino Romano Genuino cheese (see Larder, page xxv)

¼ cup plus 2 tablespoons (total 25 grams) freshly grated Parmigiano-Reggiano cheese (see Larder, page xxiv)

1 large egg, beaten

1½ quarts (scant 1½ liters) vegetable oil, for frying

Kosher salt

SPECIAL EQUIPMENT: a candy / fry thermometer

CECI FARINATA

Makes about 24 (1-inch or 2.5-centimeter) fried chickpea balls

1 (15-ounce or 425-gram) can chickpeas

1 tablespoon (15 milliliters) extra-virgin olive oil

1½ teaspoons (8 milliliters) fresh lemon juice

Kosher salt

1 large egg

1 tablespoon (15 milliliters) black truffle oil (see Larder, page xxix)

1 tablespoon (15 milliliters) whole milk

¼ pound (113 grams) fontina cheese, grated on the large holes of a box grater

2½ tablespoons (20 grams) finely chopped drained canned black truffle peelings (see Larder, page xxix)

1½ teaspoons (2 grams) finely chopped flat-leaf parsley

¼ cup (25 grams) chickpea flour (also called garbanzo bean flour or ceci flour)

1½ quarts (scant 1½ liters) vegetable oil, for frying

SPECIAL EQUIPMENT: a ½-ounce (15-milliliter) mini ice cream scoop for the farinata batter (optional)

In a colander set over a bowl, drain the chickpeas, reserving their liquid. In a blender, combine ⅓ cup (75 milliliters) of the chickpea liquid, 1 cup (174 grams) of the chickpeas, the olive oil, lemon juice, and ¼ teaspoon (1 gram) salt. Purée until smooth. Adjust the seasoning to taste.

In a large bowl, whisk together the egg, truffle oil, and milk. In a second bowl, using your hands, mash the remaining ½ cup (78 grams) chickpeas. To the egg mixture, add the mashed chickpeas and a generous ⅓ cup (85 grams) of the chickpea purée, along with the cheese, truffles, and parsley. (Reserve the remaining chickpea purée for serving.) Stir together to combine, then stir in the flour until just combined.

In a wide heavy saucepan, heat the vegetable oil to 375ºF (190ºC). In batches of 5, using a mini ice cream scoop or tablespoon, carefully drop 1-tablespoon (15-gram) spoonfuls of the batter into the oil and fry until the farinata balls are lightly golden and the cheese inside is hot and melted (test one to check for doneness), about 1 minute. Using a slotted spoon, transfer to paper towels to drain. Season with salt while hot.

Swoosh the reserved chickpea purée onto serving plates. Arrange the warm farinata balls on top. Serve immediately.

TUNA AND TRUFFLE SFERE

Makes 24 (1-inch or 2.5-centimeter) tuna balls

¾ pound (345 grams) well-chilled sushi-grade ahi tuna steak

Generous ⅓ cup (48 grams) finely diced celery

Scant ¼ cup (45 grams) mayonnaise, preferably Hellman's Best Foods or Kewpie

Kosher salt

1½ ounces (45 grams) fresh black truffle (see note)

SPECIAL EQUIPMENT: a truffle shaver, mandoline, or other manual slicer

Dice the tuna into small cubes and place in a bowl. Add the celery and mayonnaise, stirring to combine. Chill in the refrigerator while you shave the truffle.

Onto a baking sheet, thinly shave the truffle, letting the pieces fall in a single layer (some overlapping is OK, but try to keep the shavings separate). Using a spoon, scoop and then form the tuna mixture into 1-inch (2.5-centimeter) balls. Gently roll the balls in the truffle shavings, lightly pressing to help the truffle shavings adhere. Serve immediately.

NOTE: *Fresh black truffles can be purchased at Italian or gourmet markets, or mail-ordered online (see Larder, page xxix).*

Which Came First:

CHICKEN AND EGG SALAD TRAMEZZINI

These mini sandwiches recall the soft white-bread tramezzini found in bars and lunch counters throughout Italy. Similar to English tea sandwiches, tramezzini are made with slices of Pullman loaf, crusts trimmed. Here, chicken salad and egg salad are fused together in small, triangular white-bread sandwiches, then drizzled with olive oil.

For the chicken salad: In a large bowl, mix together the chicken, celery, mayonnaise, vinegar, and chervil. Season to taste with salt and pepper.

For the egg salad: Place the eggs in a medium saucepan. Add water to cover by 2 inches. Bring the water just to a boil over high heat. Remove the pan from the heat, cover, and let stand 10 minutes. Drain the eggs, then submerge in a bowl of ice water to cool.

Crack and peel the eggs, then finely chop and place in a large bowl. Stir in the mayonnaise and vinegar. Season to taste with salt and pepper.

To serve: Spread the chicken salad on 4 slices of the bread. Spread the egg salad on top. Top with the remaining bread slices. Cut off and discard the crusts, then cut the sandwiches on the diagonal into 4 pieces each. Arrange the tramezzini on serving plates with a cut side facing up. Drizzle with the Sicilian oil. Serve immediately.

Makes 16 small tramezzini

CHICKEN SALAD

1 cup (135 grams) chopped cooked chicken (boneless skinless breast boiled in chicken stock works well)

3 tablespoons (24 grams) finely diced celery

2 tablespoons (24 grams) mayonnaise, preferably Hellman's, Best Foods, or Kewpie

1 teaspoon (5 milliliters) red wine vinegar

1 teaspoon (1 gram) finely chopped chervil

Kosher salt and freshly ground black pepper

EGG SALAD

3 large eggs

2 tablespoons (24 grams) mayonnaise, preferably Hellman's or Kewpie

½ teaspoon (3 milliliters) red wine vinegar

Kosher salt and freshly ground black pepper

TO SERVE

8 slices white sandwich bread, such as Pepperidge Farm

Very good extra-virgin olive oil, preferably delicate Sicilian (see Larder, page xxix)

BLACK TRUFFLE VINAIGRETTE

2 tablespoons (30 milliliters) truffle
juice (see note)

¾ teaspoon (3½ milliliters) sherry vinegar

¼ teaspoon (1¼ milliliters) tamari

¼ teaspoon (1¼ milliliters) Tabasco sauce

Pinch sugar

Pinch kosher salt

1½ tablespoons (23 milliliters) grapeseed
or vegetable oil

1 tablespoon (15 milliliters) truffle oil
(see note)

1½ teaspoons (5 grams) finely chopped
fresh or canned black truffle (see note)

**RUSSET POTATO CHIPS WITH
CAPER SALT**

2⅓ cups (550 milliliters) vegetable oil,
for frying

1 small russet potato (225 grams),
scrubbed under running water and
patted dry

Caper Salt (see Marinara Soup, page 5),
for seasoning

VEAL CRUDO

8 ounces (225 grams) trimmed veal
tenderloin, well-chilled

2 teaspoons (10 grams) minced shallot

Generous 1 tablespoon (10 grams)
salt-packed capers, rinsed and soaked
(see Larder, page xxiv)

1½ tablespoons (5 grams) finely chopped
flat-leaf parsley stems, plus 1 teaspoon
(1 gram) finely chopped flat-leaf parsley
leaves

1 teaspoon (5 milliliters) extra-virgin
olive oil

¼ teaspoon (1¼ milliliters) fresh
lemon juice

1 teaspoon (4 grams) kosher salt

Pinch freshly ground black pepper

SPECIAL EQUIPMENT: a candy / fry
thermometer; a mandoline or other
manual slicer

VEAL TARTAR AND POTATO CHIP CLUBS

For the vinaigrette: Place the truffle juice in a small saucepan. Bring to a simmer and cook until reduced to 1½ tablespoons (22 milliliters). Transfer to a blender and let cool completely. Add the vinegar, tamari, Tabasco sauce, sugar, salt, and 1½ tablespoons (22 milliliters) water and purée to combine. With the machine running, add the grapeseed and truffle oils in a slow and steady stream. Transfer to a bowl and stir in the chopped truffle. Set aside.

For the potato chips: In a heavy medium skillet, heat the vegetable oil until a candy / fry thermometer registers 350°F (177°C). Meanwhile, using a mandoline or other manual slicer, cut the potatoes lengthwise into paper-thin slices (about 1 millimeter thick). Submerge the slices in a bowl of cold water and let stand 5 minutes.

Wash the potato slices in the water (to help release the starch), then drain and blot completely dry in a single layer between layers of paper towels.

Working in batches of 8 to 10 slices, fry the potatoes, turning once or twice, until golden, about 1½ minutes per batch, making sure the oil returns to 350°F (177°C) before adding the next batch. Using a slotted spoon, transfer the fried chips to paper towels to drain. Season with a pinch of caper salt while warm (optional).

For the veal crudo: Finely chop the veal and place in a large bowl. Add the shallot, capers, parsley stems and leaves, oil, lemon juice, vinaigrette, salt, and pepper. Stir together to combine.

Sandwich small spoonfuls of the crudo between the potato chips. Serve immediately.

NOTE: *Truffles, truffle juice, and truffle oil can be purchased at gourmet markets or ordered online (see Larder, page xxix).*

MINI LOBSTER AND CORN CROSTATAS

For the crostata dough: In a large bowl, stir together the flour, polenta, and salt. Using your fingers, work in the butter until the mixture resembles coarse crumbs with some larger pieces remaining. In a slow and steady stream, add the cold water, mixing with your hands to combine. Turn out the dough onto a clean work surface and shape into a flattened disk. Wrap in plastic wrap and chill in the refrigerator for at least 1 hour or overnight. (The dough can be frozen for up to 1 month. Thaw in the refrigerator overnight before using.)

Lightly coat 30 (1⅜-inch or 3.4-centimeter) plain round petit four molds with nonstick cooking spray, then arrange on a baking sheet. On a clean, lightly flour-dusted work surface, roll out the dough to ⅛ inch (.3 millimeter) thick. Using a 1⅜-inch (3.4-centimeter) round cutter, cut out 30 rounds. Fit the rounds into the petit four molds, then nestle an empty petit four mold on top of each filled mold. Gently but firmly press each of the top molds until you see the dough come just barely above the top edge of the bottom mold. Chill in the refrigerator for 30 minutes. (Leave both molds in place throughout the chilling and the baking processes.)

Heat the oven to 350°F (177°C). Transfer the baking sheet to the oven and bake the tart shells until light golden, 10 to 12 minutes. Remove from the oven and let the shells cool completely in the molds, then unmold.

For the custard: In a medium bowl, beat together the egg yolks; set aside. In a blender or mini food processor, purée the canned corn until smooth. In a small heavy-bottomed saucepan, combine the corn purée, cream, sugar, and salt. Bring just to a bare simmer over medium-low heat, then remove from the heat.

While vigorously whisking the yolks, slowly add about 2 tablespoons (30 milliliters) of the warm corn mixture. Repeat once, then add the yolk mixture back to the pot with the corn mixture and whisk to combine.

Return the saucepan to medium-low heat and, whisking constantly, cook until the custard is thickened, about 3 minutes more. Using a rubber spatula, force the custard through a medium-mesh sieve into a small bowl (you may see bits of creamed corn left behind in the sieve; you may also skip this step and simply whisk in the butter), then whisk in the butter. Cover the surface of the custard with plastic wrap and refrigerate until cold, at least 30 minutes or up to 3 days.

To serve: In a bowl, stir together the lobster and the tomato marmellata. Spoon the lobster filling into the tart shells. Dollop the custard on top. Garnish with the summer savory.

NOTE: *The 1⅜-inch (3.4-centimeter) round cutter and 1⅜-inch (3.4-centimeter) plain round petit four molds can be purchased online or at specialty kitchen supply stores.*

Makes 30 (1⅜-inch or 3.4-centimeter) crostatas

CROSTATA DOUGH

⅔ cup (85 grams) unbleached all-purpose flour

1½ tablespoons (8 grams) instant polenta

Pinch kosher salt

4 tablespoons (57 grams) cold unsalted butter, cut into small pieces

2 tablespoons (30 milliliters) very cold water

Nonstick cooking spray

CORN CUSTARD

2 large (36 grams) egg yolks

⅓ cup plus 1 tablespoon (total 100 grams) canned creamed corn

3½ tablespoons (52 milliliters) heavy cream

1 teaspoon (4 grams) sugar

Pinch salt

1 teaspoon (5 grams) unsalted butter

TO SERVE

¾ cup (115 grams) coarsely chopped cooked lobster meat

3 tablespoons (45 grams) Tomato Marmellata (see Palline di Pane, page 7)

Summer savory for garnish

SPECIAL EQUIPMENT: a (1⅜-inch or 3.4-centimeter) round cutter; 60 (1⅜-inch or 3.4-centimeter) plain round petit four molds (see note)

ANTIPASTI

Traditionally, the antipasto is an eclectic
collection of small tastes, designed to whet the appetite before
the meal begins. Casual shared plates, served cool or at room
temperature, the antipasti often include cured meats, crostini,
a variety of marinated vegetables, and light seafood creations.
It is common to find an assortment of antipasti set out on a display
table or buffet at restaurants in Italy.

At Del Posto, the antipasto course is the opening act of a structured
menu, rather than an informal prelude to the meal. Salad, vegetable,
and seafood preparations, inspired by recipes from typical Italian
antipasto spreads, are conceived as plated dishes that represent the
season. This chapter offers a diverse selection of recipes for both warm
and cool weather ingredients.

The antipasto course also marks the beginning of the wine service.
The leafy greens, poached shellfish, and acidic dressings in the
cool or ambient-temperature dishes call for dynamic white, light red,
and sparkling wines. Greatly influencing the development of recipes
at Del Posto, the wine pairings progress in tandem with the
flavors of the menu—starting with light, crisp white wines for
the antipasto and transitioning to robust reds for the heavier primi
and secondi courses.

SNIPPED HERB AND LETTUCE SALAD
with Peach Citronette

Set on the Grand Canal in Venice, Harry's Bar has been a watering hole for the international jet set since Hemingway made it his home away from home in the 1950s. Harry's Bar is the birthplace of the Bellini—a mix of fresh white-peach purée and a small amount of effervescent Prosecco from the Veneto. Stirred in a glass pitcher and served in a diminutive, stemless glass, the Bellini is uniquely frothy, sweet, and slightly tart. Named for the luxurious pink hues found in the 15th-century paintings of local Venetian artist Giovanni Bellini, the drink has become ubiquitous the world over. Inspired by the Bellini at Harry's, this summer salad hopes to capture the drink's refreshing balance of sweet-peach and acidic flavors, along with the breezy spirit and understated elegance of Italy's greatest barroom.

Use the freshest, sweetest peach possible, and the best available lettuces. Avoid bruising the lettuce leaves by gently tossing the salad in a large bowl. Substitutions can be made for the lettuces, but use delicate, mild-tasting varieties. Herbs can also be varied: Add or substitute with chervil, basil, or tarragon.

For the citronette: In a blender, combine the peach and 1 tablespoon (15 milliliters) water. Purée until smooth. Transfer the purée to a medium bowl. Add the vinegar, oil, salt, and sugar, then vigorously whisk together to combine well. Adjust the salt and sugar to taste (the citronette should have a nice sweet-tart balance).

For the salad: In a large bowl, combine the Bibb lettuce, mesclun, and mâche. Whisk together the citronette, then drizzle it over the top. Add a pinch of salt and pepper. Gently toss together the salad until the greens are just lightly coated with the dressing. Divide among serving plates, then sprinkle with the celery leaves and herbs.

NOTES: *If fresh peaches are not in season, frozen peach purée or peach nectar may be used instead. A 1:1 ratio of fresh orange juice to bottled yuzu juice (or champagne vinegar) can be blended as a substitute for the citron vinegar.*

Serves 4 to 6

PEACH CITRONETTE

½ medium pitted overripe peach (85 grams), cut into ½-inch (1.25-centimeter) pieces (see note)

⅓ cup (85 milliliters) citron vinegar (see note)

⅓ cup (85 milliliters) grapeseed oil

½ teaspoon (2 grams) kosher salt

¼ teaspoon (1 gram) sugar

SALAD

2 heads Bibb lettuce (180 grams), trimmed and leaves separated

6 loosely packed cups (90 grams) mesclun greens

2 loosely packed cups (30 grams) mâche or other delicate microgreens

Kosher salt and freshly ground black pepper

¼ cup (4 grams) celery leaves (from the inner heart of the bunch)

1½ tablespoons (4 grams) snipped chives

¼ cup (4 grams) mint leaves

¼ cup (4 grams) flat-leaf parsley leaves

RADICCHIO AND LETTUCES
with Lemon-Ginger Balsamic Dressing

Serves 4 to 6

LEMON-GINGER BALSAMIC DRESSING

¼ cup plus 3 tablespoons (total 105 milliliters) extra-virgin olive oil

3 tablespoons (45 milliliters) balsamic vinegar

1 teaspoon (⅓ gram) lemon zest

2 tablespoons (30 milliliters) fresh lemon juice

1½ tablespoons (20 grams) finely grated fresh ginger

½ teaspoon (2 grams) kosher salt

SALAD

1 small head (175 grams) tardivo di Treviso (see note), trimmed and leaves separated, outer leaves reserved for another use

1 head (150 grams) castelfranco (see note), trimmed and leaves separated

2 small heads baby red romaine (90 grams), trimmed and leaves separated

2 small heads baby green romaine (90 grams), trimmed and leaves separated

1 head frisée (50 grams), root end and dark green parts trimmed and discarded, remaining leaves coarsely torn

1 small head baby lollo rosso (40 grams), trimmed and leaves separated

Kosher salt and freshly ground black pepper

Radicchios are known as northern Italy's *fiori d'inverno,* or flowers of winter, and cool-weather salads become particularly compelling when they arrive in November and December. This recipe highlights tardivo di Treviso, the most regal variety of radicchio, grown around the city of Treviso in the Veneto region. Distinguished by long bone-white ribs and narrow crimson leaves, tardivo comes from an esoteric, centuries-old farming practice: After the plants surface in the fall, they are left in the ground for two frosts, and their leaves are glazed with ice. As the plant begins to die from frostbite, its sugars concentrate in the root system and its inner leaves curl toward the delicate heart of the plant. Before the soil freezes entirely, the tardivo is urgently removed from the ground by hand and held in cold storage for a month. After this incubation period, in a process called *imbianchimento,* the outer leaves of the plant are removed and discarded. The heart of the plant is then rejuvenated in naturally warmed springwater from the region's Sile River, revealing pearlescent semisweet stalks edged with dark-red, bitter leaves.

For the dressing: In a medium bowl, vigorously whisk together the oil, vinegar, lemon zest and juice, ginger, and salt to combine well.

For the salad: In a large bowl, combine the tardivo, castelfranco, red and green romaine lettuces, frisée, and lollo rosso. Whisk together the dressing, then drizzle it over the top. Add a pinch of salt and pepper. Gently toss together the salad until the greens are just lightly coated with the dressing.

NOTE: *Tardivo and castelfranco are members of the radicchio family. Endive, frisée, or other chicories can be substituted if castelfranco and tardivo are not available.*

INSALATA PRIMAVERA
della Terra with Citron Vinaigrette, Italian Ricotta, and Rosemary Crumbs

Serves 4 to 6

PARSNIP-ROSEMARY CAKE CRUMBS

½ pound (226 grams) unsalted butter, at room temperature, plus more for greasing

2 cups plus 2 tablespoons (total 280 grams) unbleached all-purpose flour

¾ cup (115 grams) instant polenta

1¾ teaspoons (9 grams) baking powder

1¼ teaspoons (7 grams) baking soda

¾ teaspoon (3 grams) kosher salt

½ cup (107 grams) packed light brown sugar

¼ cup (50 grams) granulated sugar

¼ cup (60 milliliters) extra-virgin olive oil

2 large eggs (100 grams)

1 pound (453 grams) parsnips, trimmed, peeled, and shredded on the large holes of a box grater or food processor

3 tablespoons (12 grams) finely chopped fresh rosemary

PEA PURÉE

1⅓ cups (165 grams) frozen peas

4 small flat-leaf parsley leaves

½ teaspoon (2 grams) sugar

Kosher salt

COOKED VEGETABLES

6 baby beets (110 grams), trimmed

6 baby carrots (65 grams), trimmed

6 medium stalks green asparagus (90 grams), trimmed

Extra-virgin olive oil, for grilling or roasting

Kosher salt and freshly ground black pepper

CONTINUED

In celebration of the spring harvest, this mix of fresh, grilled, and blanched vegetables brings together many different ingredients and techniques to create a salad with real depth and complexity. As is the case with most spring salad recipes in Italy, this one allows for personal variation and is structured with flexibility in mind. The vegetables and garnishes are not limited to those in the ingredient list, and the recipe can be used as a guide for micro-seasonal ingredients. The vinaigrette and rosemary cake crumbs go well with anything that is bright and fresh at the market.

For the cake: Heat the oven to 325°F (163°C). Grease a 9 x 13-inch (23 x 33-centimeter) baking pan with butter.

In a medium bowl, sift together the flour, polenta, baking powder, baking soda, and salt; set aside. In the bowl of a stand mixer fitted with the paddle attachment, beat together the butter, brown sugar, and granulated sugar on medium speed until light and fluffy, 3 to 4 minutes. Drizzle in the oil, then add the eggs and continue mixing, occasionally scraping down the sides and bottom of the bowl, until pale yellow and fluffy, 4 to 5 minutes. Add the flour mixture and mix just until incorporated (do not overmix or the cake will be dense), then fold in the shredded parsnips and rosemary (the batter will be thick).

Transfer the batter to the prepared baking pan, spreading it evenly with a rubber spatula. Bake, rotating the pan once halfway through, until the edges are golden brown and the cake bounces back to a light touch, 45 minutes to 1 hour. Transfer to a wire rack and let the cake cool completely in the pan. Cut and crumble enough of the cake to yield 1 cup of crumbs (see notes).

For the pea purée: Cook the peas and parsley in a small saucepan of well-salted boiling water until the peas are tender, about 1 minute. Drain, then run under cold water to cool completely. In a blender, combine the pea mixture, 2 tablespoons (30 milliliters) water, the sugar, and ¼ teaspoon (1 gram) salt; purée until smooth. Using a rubber spatula, force the purée through a medium-mesh sieve into a small bowl. Cover the surface of the purée with plastic wrap (to preserve its bright green color) and chill until ready to use.

For the cooked vegetables: Prepare or heat a grill to medium-high. Loosely wrap the beets in a foil packet with 2 tablespoons (30 milliliters) water. Drizzle the baby carrots and green asparagus with oil to lightly coat and season with salt and pepper. Grill the beet packets and the vegetables until crisp-tender, 5 to 15 minutes, depending on the vegetable. Once the beets are crisp-tender, remove them from the foil packet, then cook for a final few minutes on the grill. Transfer the vegetables to a plate as each is ready. Set aside.

Bring a large saucepan of well-salted water to a boil. In turns, separately cook the turnips, snap peas, and green beans, just until crisp-tender, 1 to 3 minutes, depending on the vegetable. As each vegetable is ready, use a fine-mesh sieve or slotted spoon to transfer to a colander to drain, then

6 baby turnips (275 grams), trimmed, cut in half if large

12 snap peas (40 grams), trimmed and strings removed

12 green beans (40 grams), trimmed

ITALIAN RICOTTA

7 ounces (200 grams) fresh ricotta cheese

2 teaspoons (10 milliliters) extra-virgin olive oil

Kosher salt and freshly ground black pepper

CITRON VINAIGRETTE

½ cup (120 milliliters) extra-virgin olive oil

¼ cup (60 milliliters) citron vinegar (see notes)

½ teaspoon (2 grams) kosher salt

RAW VEGETABLES

About 3 medium radishes (50 grams), preferably a mix of varieties, very thinly shaved

½ small fennel bulb (120 grams), trimmed and thinly shaved lengthwise

6 stalks white asparagus (90 grams), trimmed and thinly shaved lengthwise

TO SERVE

1 loosely packed cup (15 grams) assorted tender microgreen leaves such as watercress, mâche, baby pea shoots, and/or baby red sorrel

12 small mint leaves

Maldon sea salt

SPECIAL EQUIPMENT: an adjustable-blade slicer

submerge in a bowl of ice water to cool. Drain and pat dry. Cut the snap peas and green beans in half lengthwise.

For the Italian ricotta: In a small bowl, gently stir together the cheese, oil, ½ teaspoon (2 grams) salt, and a pinch of pepper. Set aside.

For the vinaigrette: In a bowl, vigorously whisk together the oil, vinegar, and salt. Set aside.

For the raw vegetables: Prep the radishes, fennel, and asparagus.

To serve: Dollop and swoosh the pea purée onto each serving plate. Dollop the Italian ricotta onto the plates. Arrange the cooked and raw vegetables on each plate. Whisk together the vinaigrette, then drizzle it over the vegetables. Garnish with the micro-greens, mint, and cake crumbs. Sprinkle with Maldon sea salt.

NOTES: *A 1:1 ratio of fresh orange juice to bottled yuzu juice (or champagne vinegar) can be blended as a substitute for the citron vinegar. The leftover rosemary cake can be kept, covered, at room temperature for up to 3 days, or frozen for up to 1 month—it's wonderful toasted.*

❧ WINE PAIRING ❧

The combination of raw, blanched, and roasted vegetables in this spring salad yearns for a glass of Kerner. One of the unique grapes of Italy, the Kerner is grown in the mountainous region of Alto Adige in northern Italy, and is the love child of the white Riesling grape and the red Schiava grape. Much like the complexity of flavors in this salad, the Kerner grape produces a wine that is aromatic with flowers and ripe fruit, but balanced by earthy notes and good minerality. The fresh mountain air of its high-altitude growing region gives it ample acidity, making it perfectly suited for this antipasto course. Kerner is in fairly limited supply, since not much of it is being grown, but Franz Gojer, Köfererhof, and Abbazia di Novacella are three of the best producers.

ROOTS AND FRUITS
with Robiola Sformato and Quince Viniagrette

The autumnal cousin of the Insalata Primavera (page 18), this vegetable antipasto features as much available produce as cooler months allow. Here, fruits are treated as savory rather than sweet, and the soft robiola sformato and cooked mushrooms contrast the crisp raw apple, fennel, and crunchy granola. By incorporating a wide variety of root vegetables and fall fruits, this winter salad feels fresh in a season when ingredients are limited.

For the cooked roots and fruits: Heat the oven to 425ºF (218ºC) with the rack in the middle. Line a rimmed baking sheet with parchment paper.

Heat a large skillet over medium-high heat until hot. Add 1 tablespoon (15 milliliters) of the oil, then add the squash pieces and cook, turning once and seasoning with salt, until golden, 3 to 4 minutes per side. Transfer to the prepared baking sheet.

Return the skillet to medium-high heat. Cook the remaining vegetables in the same manner, adding more oil, seasoning with salt as you go and adjusting the cooking time by a minute or two, as needed, just until the vegetables are golden on two sides (the apple and pear cubes will require 1 to 2 minutes on one side only and should be transferred to a plate and set aside).

Roast the browned vegetables until crisp-tender: the mushrooms for about 5 minutes; the baby carrots for about 10 minutes; and the remaining vegetables 15 to 20 minutes, transferring the vegetables to a plate as they are ready. Set aside.

For the granola: Reduce the oven temperature to 325ºF (163ºC). Line a rimmed baking sheet with parchment paper. In a medium bowl, whisk together the oil, sugar, salt, cayenne pepper, and allspice. Add the pumpkin seeds, almonds, coconut flakes,

and syrup and stir to evenly coat. Spread on the prepared baking sheet and bake until the coconut and almonds are golden, 15 to 17 minutes. Let cool completely on a wire rack.

For the robiola sformato: Place the egg yolks in a medium heatproof bowl and set aside. Break the cheese (including the rind) into small pieces and place in a small saucepan. Add the cream and salt. Heat the mixture over medium heat, whisking frequently, until the cheese is melted (you may have small pieces of unmelted rind; this is OK), then remove from the heat. Whisking the egg yolks constantly, slowly add about ¼ cup (60 milliliters) of the hot cheese mixture. Repeat twice, then add the egg mixture back to the pot with the cheese mixture, whisking to combine. Heat the mixture over medium-low heat, whisking constantly, just until small bubbles break the surface, about 1 minute. Strain the hot mixture through a fine-mesh sieve into a bowl. (If the mixture appears slightly curdled, purée it in a blender until smooth.) Cover the surface of the sformato mixture with plastic wrap and let stand at room temperature until ready to use.

For the quince vinaigrette: In a small saucepan, bring the verjus, quince paste,

Serves 4 to 6

COOKED ROOTS AND FRUITS

¼ cup plus 2 tablespoons (total 90 milliliters) extra-virgin olive oil

1 small butternut squash (700 grams), bottom half trimmed, seeded, and cut lengthwise into ½-inch-thick (1.25-centimeter-thick) pieces (save remaining piece for another use)

Kosher salt

1 medium celery root (300 grams), peeled and cut into 1-inch (2.5-centimeter) cubes

6 baby beets (175 grams), unpeeled, trimmed (tops reserved, if you have them)

12 shiitake mushrooms (170 grams), stems removed and discarded

½ large sweet potato (160 grams), cut into ½-inch-thick (1.25-centimeter-thick) rounds

6 baby carrots (100 grams), unpeeled, trimmed (tops reserved, if you have them)

½ large Fuji or Honeycrisp apple (110 grams), peeled, cored, and cut into 6 (¾-inch or 2-centimeter) cubes (save the unpeeled remaining ½ apple for the Raw Roots and Fruits)

½ large Anjou or Comice pear (110 grams), peeled, cored, and cut into 6 (¾-inch or 2-centimeter) cubes (save the unpeeled remaining ½ pear for the Raw Roots and Fruits)

GRANOLA

1 tablespoon (15 milliliters) extra-virgin olive oil

1½ teaspoons (8 grams) packed dark brown sugar

¼ teaspoon (1 gram) kosher salt

⅛ teaspoon (½ gram) cayenne pepper

CONTINUED

and sugar to a simmer over medium-low heat. Whisking frequently, cook just until the quince paste and sugar have dissolved, 1 to 2 minutes. Transfer the mixture to a bowl and chill in an ice bath or in the refrigerator, then whisk in the oil, cider, and salt.

For the raw roots and fruits: Prep the apple, pear, pomegranate seeds, and beet tops.

To serve: Use large serving plates. Dollop and swoosh 3 tablespoons (39 grams) of the sformato onto each plate. Arrange the roasted and raw roots and fruits on each plate. Whisk together the vinaigrette, then drizzle it over the salads. Sprinkle with the granola and a pinch or two of Maldon sea salt.

⅛ teaspoon (½ gram) allspice

⅓ cup (50 grams) raw pumpkin seeds

⅓ cup (50 grams) raw almonds

⅓ cup (50 grams) unsweetened coconut flakes

1 tablespoon (15 milliliters) maple syrup

ROBIOLA SFORMATO

3 large egg yolks (50 grams)

7 ounces (200 grams) robiola cheese

¾ cup (177 milliliters) heavy cream

1¼ teaspoons (5 grams) kosher salt

QUINCE VINAIGRETTE

2 tablespoons (30 milliliters) verjus (see note)

1 tablespoon (15 grams) quince paste

1 teaspoon (4 grams) sugar

3 tablespoons (45 milliliters) extra-virgin olive oil

1 tablespoon (15 milliliters) apple cider

¼ teaspoon (1 gram) kosher salt

RAW ROOTS AND FRUITS

½ large Fuji or Honeycrisp apple (110 grams), cored and cut into 6 wedges

½ large Anjou or Comice pear (110 grams), cored and cut into 6 wedges

¼ cup (30 grams) pomegranate seeds

1 loosely packed cup (15 grams) baby beet tops, red sorrel, or microgreen leaves, small flowering fresh thyme or edible flowers, and/or snipped baby carrot tops

TO SERVE

Maldon sea salt

SPECIAL EQUIPMENT: parchment paper

TOMATO BROTH

5 pounds (2¼ kilograms) very ripe plum or vine-ripened tomatoes, quartered and cored

1 (35-ounce or 1-kilogram) jar piennolo tomatoes (see Larder, page xxix)

1 tablespoon (15 milliliters) sherry vinegar

1 tablespoon (12 grams) kosher salt

1 teaspoon (4 grams) sugar

TORTELLINI

About 11½ loosely packed cups (180 grams) basil leaves

2½ loosely packed cups (25 grams) flat-leaf parsley leaves

Generous ⅓ cup (80 milliliters) extra-virgin olive oil, plus more for drizzling

About 1 ice cube (22 grams)

½ medium garlic clove (2 grams), peeled

½ teaspoon (2 grams) sugar

½ teaspoon (2 grams) kosher salt

1 cup (100 grams) freshly grated Parmigiano-Reggiano cheese (at least 24-month aged; see Larder, page xxiv)

½ batch Fresh Egg Pasta Dough (page 103)

Semolina flour for dusting

TO SERVE

Kosher salt

2 teaspoons (10 milliliters) extra-virgin olive oil, plus more for drizzling

⅔ pound (300 grams) assorted seasonal vegetables (at least 5 different types), such as summer squash, zucchini, baby carrot, baby turnip, asparagus, Persian cucumber, snap peas, green beans, and/or red bell pepper, cut into ½-inch (1.25-centimeter) cubes or pieces

8 ounces (227 grams) burrata cheese, torn into small pieces

Small Thai or Genovese basil leaves for garnish

SPECIAL EQUIPMENT: cheesecloth; a 1½-inch (3.8-centimeter) round cutter, preferably fluted; a food mill or blender

COOL SUMMERTIME MINESTRA
with Basil Pesto Tortellini and Burrata

This light minestra replaces a classic minestrone's hearty root vegetables and stewed tomatoes with an assortment of crisp-tender vegetables and a light broth made from tomato water. Capturing the essence of summer, this fresh soup is also a nod to an insalata Caprese—sliced tomatoes, basil, and mozzarella. Here, the basil becomes pesto, encapsulated in delicate tortellini, and the creamy pieces of burrata bleed into the fresh tomato broth.

For the tomato broth: In a food processor or blender, purée the plum tomatoes until smooth. Line a large fine-mesh sieve with a doubled 12-inch (30-centimeter) square of cheesecloth, then set the sieve over a large, tall nonreactive bowl or other container. Pour the tomato purée into the prepared sieve. Gather the cloth around the mixture and loosely tie together the corners. Put a small plate on top of the sack, then set a heavy weight (like a large can of beans) on top. Chill for 24 hours.

Remove the bowl with the tomato water from the refrigerator. Very gently squeeze the sack to extract any remaining liquid, then discard the sack. Transfer 6¾ cups (1.6 liters) of the tomato water to a large saucepan (save any remaining tomato water for another use).

Pass the piennolo tomatoes (with their juices) through the fine-holed disk of a food mill or purée in a blender, then force through a medium-mesh sieve to extract the seeds. Add the puréed tomatoes to the pot with the tomato water. Bring the mixture just to a simmer, then remove from the heat. Skim the foam from the top. Chill the tomato broth in an ice bath or in the refrigerator, then whisk in the vinegar, salt, and sugar. Keep chilled until ready to use.

For the tortellini: Bring a small saucepan of well-salted water to a boil. Add the basil and parsley leaves and cook until the herbs are bright green and tender, 1 to 2 minutes. Drain, then rinse under very cold running water. Squeeze the herbs to remove excess liquid, then transfer to a blender. Add the oil, ice cube, garlic, sugar, and salt, then purée to form a smooth pesto. Transfer the pesto to a bowl and fold in the cheese. Cover the surface of the pesto with plastic wrap and set aside. (The pesto can be prepared ahead and refrigerated for up to 3 days, or frozen for up to 1 month. You will need only about 2½ tablespoons (37 grams) pesto for the tortellini. Save the remaining pesto for another use).

Roll out the pasta dough (as instructed on page 103) until you can just see your hand through the pasta sheets, 1 to 2 millimeters thick. From the sheets, using the round cutter, cut out 42 rounds. Working in batches of 12 and keeping the remaining pasta rounds covered with a clean kitchen towel as you work, place a pea-sized mound of pesto in the center of each pasta round. Using a finger dipped into water or a water-filled spray bottle, lightly dab or mist all the rounds to dampen, then fold the dough around the

stuffing on each piece to form half-moons, gently pressing the edges to press out any air and seal, then draw together the two corners to form a rounded bonnet shape. Set aside on a semolina-dusted baking sheet, and cover with a clean kitchen towel for up to 2 hours until ready to use. (The pasta can be made and frozen in a single layer on a parchment-lined baking sheet, then transferred to a sealed bag with the air pressed out and kept frozen for up to 1 week. Frozen tortellini will take 1 to 2 minutes longer to boil than fresh. Do not thaw before boiling.)

To serve: Cook the tortellini in a large pot of generously salted water until tender, about 4 minutes. Using a slotted spoon, transfer the pasta to a colander to drain, then divide among shallow serving bowls.

Heat the oil in a large skillet over medium heat. Add the vegetables and 1 teaspoon (4 grams) salt. Cook, tossing occasionally, until the vegetables are crisp-tender, about 2 minutes. Remove from the heat. Divide the vegetables among the serving bowls. Pour the chilled broth over the top. Top with the burrata. Garnish with basil leaves and a drizzle of oil.

❧ WINE PAIRING ❧

Coastal Liguria is home to clean and crisp white wines made from the Pigato, Vermentino, Bosco, and Albarola grapes. It is also home to basil pesto, a classic summertime condiment along the northwestern Italian coastline. Laura Aschero and Bisson are two favored producers in this small region. Bisson's Pigato is clean, vibrant, and crisp, with citrus and floral hints. Its palate gives way to saline and fresh herbs, which work in concert with the tomato broth in the cool soup and play off the intensity of the basil pesto inside the tortellini.

LIVE LARGE SCALLOP CRUDO

with 'Nduja, Asparagus, Mushrooms, and Grilled Scallions

Live scallops have unique sweet notes and a distinct meatiness not found in any other shellfish. Their surprisingly substantial flavor pairs here with 'nduja, a raw, spicy sausage from the region of Calabria. 'Nduja is a spreadable pork cure made with hot pepper and paprika, which give it a fiery flavor and color. (Del Posto makes its own 'nduja; see recipe on page 54.) Rather than overpowering the live scallop, 'nduja adds a piquant depth to the sweet shellfish and the briny vinaigrette made with the juices from inside the scallop shells.

For the scallops and scallop vinaigrette: Using a small paring knife, cut between the muscle and top shell of one scallop to release and pop open the shell. Pour any juices into a small bowl. Cut out and set aside the body (scallop), then scrape the stomach sack (black pouch), skirt (brown frill), and muscle into a small saucepan (the orange roe, which you will also have, can be saved as a cook's treat). Rinse the cleaned scallop under cold running water, then cover and refrigerate until ready to use. Discard the shells. Repeat with the remaining scallops.

Measure the scallop juices; you need 2 tablespoons (30 milliliters). If you do not have enough (or any) juices, add 1 cup (236 milliliters) water to the saucepan with the scallop scraps. Gently simmer for 15 minutes to create a broth. Strain the broth or reserved liquid through a coffee filter–lined sieve into a bowl, then chill in an ice bath.

In a medium bowl, whisk together 2 tablespoons (30 milliliters) of the scallop juices or broth and the citron vinegar, oil, and salt. Set aside the vinaigrette.

For the vegetables: Heat a grill or grill pan to medium-high. Brush the asparagus and scallions with about ½ tablespoon (7 milliliters) of the oil and season with salt and pepper. Grill until crisp-tender, 2 to 5 minutes per side. Cut each asparagus spear on the bias into 3 pieces. Leave the scallions whole.

Clean the mushrooms and pat well dry with paper towels. Return the grill or grill pan to medium-high heat. Add 2 table-spoons (30 milliliters) of the remaining oil and half of the mushrooms. Cook (do not stir or season) until the edges are deep golden brown, about 3 minutes, then continue to cook, tossing occasionally, until just tender, about 2 minutes more. Season the mushrooms with salt to taste, then transfer to serving plates. Repeat with the remaining mushrooms.

To serve: Slice the scallops crosswise into 3 or 4 slices per scallop. Arrange the scallop slices on the serving plates with the mushrooms. Smear a small dollop of the 'nduja onto each scallop slice. Arrange the aspara-gus and scallions on the plates. Whisk together the vinaigrette, then drizzle over the scallops and vegetables. Sprinkle with a pinch or two of Maldon sea salt.

CONTINUED

Serves 4 to 6

SCALLOPS AND SCALLOP VINAIGRETTE

4 very fresh large live diver scallops (see notes)

2 tablespoons (30 milliliters) citron vinegar (see notes)

2 tablespoons (30 milliliters) extra-virgin olive oil

¼ teaspoon (1 gram) kosher salt

VEGETABLES

8 medium stalks asparagus (180 grams), trimmed

6 scallions (150 grams)

¼ cup plus ½ tablespoon (total 67 milliliters) extra-virgin olive oil

Kosher salt and freshly ground black pepper

½ pound (226 grams) hen of the woods or other wild mushrooms

TO SERVE

6 tablespoons (90 grams) 'nduja sausage (see notes)

Maldon sea salt

NOTES: *Since the scallops for this dish are served raw, be sure to purchase extremely fresh product, buy them on the day you plan to serve them, and keep them properly chilled. A 1:1 ratio of fresh orange juice to bottled yuzu juice (or champagne vinegar) can be blended as a substitute for the citron vinegar. You can make your own version of 'nduja sausage with Del Posto's recipe for this spicy, spreadable Calabrian pork sausage (page 54), or purchase the sausage at Italian markets or online.*

❧ WINE PAIRING ❧

Seafood crudo brings the elegance of naked ingredients to the plate, and sommeliers
are more than excited to pair raw shellfish with wine. The sweet and salty raw
scallop with a kiss of heat from full-flavored 'nduja sausage, alongside the
herbal notes of asparagus, earthy mushrooms, and pungent scallions in this recipe,
add up to a pairing of Greco. A white grape found throughout southern
Italy, Greco is aromatic and bright, but provides a structure that others do not.
It tends to be best when grown in the volcanic soils of the Campania and Calabria
regions. Its vibrant tropical fruit notes, balanced by hints of fresh herbs
and minerality, merge seamlessly with each component of the recipe. When Greco
is paired with these raw scallops, it becomes a much more interesting wine.
Quintodecimo, a young producer near the town of Tufo in the Campania region,
is setting the qualitative mark with their Greco di Tufo, particularly the 2013 vintage.
Also, from the same year, Statti's Greco is one of the best examples from Calabria,
the birthplace of 'nduja sausage.

SEARED SCALLOPS, SUNCHOKE PURÉE,
Puntarelle, and Grapefruit with Black Truffle Vinaigrette

This late-fall antipasto brings citrus, chicory, black truffle, and sunchokes together with lightly seared sweet bay scallops. Puntarelle is an intensely flavored wild chicory exclusive to Roman cuisine, where it is tossed with an anchovy vinaigrette (see the Puntarelle Salad recipe on page 153). Puntarelle's crunchy ribs contrast the tender bay scallops and creamy sunchoke purée. While this dish makes use of the distinctly Italian aroma of black truffles from central Italy, it also highlights the sweet notes of bay scallops from Nantucket and the Peconic Bay in the Northeast.

For the puntarelle: Cut the puntarelle core into individual stalks. Cut the stalks in half lengthwise, then cut or whittle into long thin slices. Submerge the slices in a bowl of ice water for 15 to 20 minutes, then drain. Repeat the soaking process twice, using fresh ice water each time (this crisps and curls the puntarelle and removes some of the bitterness). Meanwhile, prepare the sun-choke purée and the vinaigrette.

For the sunchoke purée: Peel and thinly slice the sunchokes, then immediately place in a small bowl of water to prevent browning. In a medium saucepan, heat the oil over medium heat. Add the shallot and cook, stirring frequently, just until tender, about 4 minutes (do not brown). Drain the sunchokes and pat dry, then add them to the pan, along with a generous pinch of salt. Cook, stirring occasionally, until the sunchokes begin to soften, about 5 minutes. Add water to just cover, bring to a gentle simmer, and cook until very tender, about 10 minutes.

Reserving the cooking liquid, drain the pan contents and transfer to a blender. Add the cream and 15 milliliters (1 tablespoon) of the cooking liquid. Purée until smooth, then transfer to a small bowl. Adjust the seasoning to taste.

For the vinaigrette: Place the truffle juice in a small saucepan. Bring to a simmer and cook until reduced to 1½ tablespoons (22 milliliters). Transfer to a blender and let cool completely, then add the vinegar, tamari, Tabasco sauce, sugar, salt, and 1½ tablespoons (22 milliliters) water; purée to combine. With the machine running, add the grapeseed and truffle oils in a slow and steady stream. Transfer to a bowl and stir in the chopped truffle.

For the scallops: Remove the tough abductor muscle from the side of each scallop (some scallops are sold with the muscle already removed). Pat the scallops dry with paper towels.

Heat a large skillet over medium-high heat for 1 to 2 minutes. Add half of the oil and heat until very hot but not smoking. Add half of the scallops and cook undisturbed until one side is golden brown, 2 to 4 minutes. Using tongs, turn the scallops and cook 10 seconds more. Transfer to a large plate and season with salt to taste. Repeat with the remaining oil and scallops.

To serve: Drain the puntarelle and pat dry. Dollop the sunchoke purée onto serving plates. Whisk together the vinaigrette. In a bowl, toss together 15 milliliters

Serves 4 to 6

PUNTARELLE

1¾ ounces (50 grams) puntarelle core (the inner stalks of the bunch; see notes)

SUNCHOKE PURÉE

¾ pound (340 grams) sunchokes

2 teaspoons (10 milliliters) extra-virgin olive oil

2 tablespoons (13 grams) finely chopped shallot

Kosher salt

2 tablespoons (30 milliliters) heavy cream

BLACK TRUFFLE VINAIGRETTE

¼ cup (60 milliliters) truffle juice (see notes)

1½ teaspoons (7 milliliters) sherry vinegar

½ teaspoon (2½ milliliters) tamari

½ teaspoon (2½ milliliters) Tabasco sauce

Generous ¼ teaspoon (1.5 grams) sugar

¼ teaspoon (1 gram) kosher salt

3 tablespoons (45 milliliters) grapeseed or vegetable oil

2 tablespoons (30 milliliters) truffle oil (see notes)

1 tablespoon (10 grams) finely chopped fresh or canned black truffle (see notes)

SCALLOPS

1 pound (453 grams) bay scallops

3 tablespoons (45 milliliters) grapeseed or vegetable oil

Kosher salt

TO SERVE

Kosher salt

6 pieces (75 grams) sectioned grapefruit (see notes)

Maldon sea salt

(1 tablespoon) of the vinaigrette with the puntarelle and a pinch of kosher salt. Arrange the puntarelle and the scallops on the plates. Gently pull apart the grapefruit sections into small pieces and arrange on the plates. Drizzle with the remaining vinaigrette to taste, then sprinkle with Maldon sea salt.

NOTES: *The dark outer leaves from the puntarelle head can be saved for another use. If puntarelle isn't available, this recipe can be made without this unique ingredient. Truffle juice, truffle oil, and canned truffles can be purchased at Italian or gourmet markets, or mail-ordered (see Larder, page xxix). To section the grapefruit, use a sharp paring knife to cut the peel and white pith from the fruit; then, holding the fruit in one hand, cut between the sections and the membranes to release the sections.*

LOBSTER ALLA CAESAR
with Pickled Onions and Breadcrumbs Oreganata

It is no secret that Caesar salad hails from Mexico, not Italy. It was invented by an Italian-American restaurateur in Tijuana during the 1920s and made its way north of the border to become a staple of Italian-American cuisine. Del Posto is an Italian restaurant in New York after all, and features a few dishes that satisfy the city's craving for proud Italian-American recipes. Like the Caesar salad, American lobster is vastly different from any shellfish found in Italy and it is an unbeatable addition to this wildly popular Italian-American salad.

For the lobster: In an 8- to 10-quart (7.5- to 9.5-liter) pot, combine 6 quarts (5½ liters) water and the vinegar, onion, carrot, celery, salt, and bay leaves. Bring just to a boil, reduce to a simmer, and cook 15 minutes to make a court bouillon. Meanwhile, chill the lobsters in the freezer for 15 minutes to slow their metabolism and partially desensitize their nervous systems.

Place 1 lobster on a cutting board upside down (with its legs facing up). Kill the lobster by placing the point of a chef's knife between the lobster's hindmost legs with the blade facing the head, then thrust the knife down through the body and head (this method, including the first step of freezing, is deemed the most humane way to kill a lobster).

Separate the claws (with the knuckles attached) and the tails from the bodies. (Discard the bodies, or wrap and freeze them for up to 3 months to make lobster stock.) Insert a metal skewer or the stem end of a teaspoon between the meat and the top side of the tail shells to keep the tails straight while cooking (straight tails are easier to remove meat from once the lobsters are cooked).

Drop the claws and tails into the simmering court bouillon. Cook, partially covered, removing the tails 5 minutes and the claws 9 minutes after the time they enter the water, and transferring the pieces to an ice bath immediately when done to halt cooking. When completely cool, drain; then crack the shells and remove the meat from the tails, claws, and knuckles. Discard the tomalley, any roe, and shells (or save for another use). Cut the meat into ¾-inch (2-centimeter) pieces. Chill until ready to use.

For the quick-pickled red pearl onions: In a small nonreactive saucepan, bring 1 cup (236 milliliters) water, the vinegar, sugar, and salt just to a boil. Combine the onions, coriander seeds, and fennel seeds in a medium heatproof bowl or jar, then pour the hot liquid over them. Cover and let cool to room temperature, then refrigerate until ready to use. (You will have extra pickles; see notes.)

For the dressing: In a small saucepan, combine the vegetable oil and garlic cloves. Bring to a very gentle simmer over very low heat and cook until the garlic is softened and sweet, with a touch of golden color, about 20 minutes (lift the pan from the heat occasionally, as needed, to keep the garlic from taking on color before it is softened). Remove the pan from the heat and let the

Serves 4 to 6

LOBSTER
½ cup (118 milliliters) white wine vinegar

1 large yellow onion (360 grams), coarsely chopped

1 medium carrot (75 grams), coarsely chopped

1 celery rib (80 grams), coarsely chopped

2 tablespoons (24 grams) kosher salt

2 bay leaves

3 (1½-pound or 680-gram) live lobsters (see notes)

QUICK-PICKLED RED PEARL ONIONS
½ cup (118 milliliters) apple cider vinegar

1 tablespoon (12 grams) sugar

2 teaspoons (8 grams) kosher salt

12 small red pearl onions (80 grams), peeled, halved, and layers separated

1 teaspoon (2 grams) whole coriander seeds

½ teaspoon (1 gram) whole fennel seeds

CAESAR DRESSING
Scant ½ cup (100 milliliters) vegetable oil

9 medium garlic cloves (36 grams), gently smashed and peeled

2 large egg yolks (36 grams)

8 flat anchovy fillets (23 grams)

1 tablespoon (15 milliliters) red wine vinegar

1 tablespoon (15 milliliters) fresh lemon juice

Kosher salt and freshly ground black pepper

CONTINUED

OREGANATA BREADCRUMBS

1½ tablespoons (22 milliliters) extra-virgin olive oil

1 medium garlic clove (4 grams), peeled

1 teaspoon (1 gram) red pepper flakes

1 teaspoon (1 gram) Sicilian dried oregano

1 cup (60 grams) breadcrumbs or panko (Japanese breadcrumbs)

1 tablespoon (3 grams) finely chopped flat-leaf parsley

¼ teaspoon (1 gram) kosher salt

TO SERVE

4 heads baby romaine (225 grams), trimmed, keeping root ends of heads intact, heads cut in half lengthwise

Extra-virgin olive oil for grilling

Kosher salt and freshly ground black pepper

¼ cup (16 grams) freshly grated Parmigiano-Reggiano cheese (at least 24-month aged; see Larder, page xxiv)

½ cup (36 grams) shaved Parmigiano-Reggiano cheese

mixture cool to room temperature. Using a slotted spoon and reserving the oil, transfer the garlic cloves to a blender. Add ¼ cup (60 milliliters) water, the egg yolks, anchovies, vinegar, lemon juice, and a generous pinch each of salt and pepper. Purée until smooth. With the machine running, drizzle in the reserved oil. Purée the dressing until it is smooth, thick, and creamy.

For the breadcrumbs: Place the oil in a medium skillet. Using a Microplane or other fine-holed grater, grate the garlic into the skillet. Cook over low heat, gently moving the pan back and forth over the heat, just until the garlic is fragrant, about 1 minute. Stir in the red pepper flakes and oregano, then add the breadcrumbs and cook, stirring frequently, until the bread has absorbed the oil, 1 to 2 minutes more. Remove from the heat, then stir in the parsley and salt. Transfer the crumbs to paper towels to drain.

To serve: Heat a grill or grill pan over medium-high heat. Brush 6 of the baby romaine halves with oil and season with salt and pepper. Grill, cut sides down, until charred but still crisp-tender at the core, about 2 minutes. Turn and grill 30 seconds more. Transfer the pieces to serving plates, cut sides up. Sprinkle with the grated cheese.

Separate the leaves from the remaining romaine halves; set aside the smaller inner leaves (save the larger remaining leaves for another use). Drain 3 or 4 pickled onion pieces for each serving.

In a large bowl, toss together the lobster meat and ¼ cup (60 milliliters) of the dressing, then arrange on the serving plates. Garnish with the fresh lettuce leaves, pickled onion, and shaved cheese. Drizzle with the remaining dressing to taste (see notes), then sprinkle with the breadcrumbs.

NOTES: *One pound of cleaned lobster meat can be purchased in place of live lobsters if you prefer not to cook and clean the lobsters at home. Leftover pickled onions will keep, covered and chilled, for up to 3 months; serve them in cocktails, on cheese plates, or in salads, sandwiches, and more. Leftover dressing will keep, covered and chilled, for up to 1 week.*

✿ WINE PAIRING ✿

From its humble beginnings, lobster has come to represent luxurious American dining. Champagne, one of the most sophisticated wines to make, also conjures feelings of luxury and revelry. Its high acidity, crisp palate, and lively texture help balance the rich notes of the anchovy and egg in the Caesar dressing while preserving the inherent sweetness of the lobster. Del Posto's Champagne list is one of the largest in the United States, highlighting the best of this non-Italian wine. Champagne comes in many styles—this dish calls for leaner, brighter, and more youthful examples. Rather than a lingering rich finish found in aged Champagnes, younger Champagnes feature a very clean finish, along with tight bubbles and green apple notes. Mouzon Leroux et Fils, L'atavique Brut non-vintage is an excellent example and a stunning pairing.

LOBSTER SALAD
with Burrata and Fermented Broccoli Rabe

Lobster usually calls for a heavy dose of butter or mayonnaise. Because this antipasto is served at cool or ambient temperature, burrata adds a silken creaminess to the shellfish in place of butter. Even though the Italians shun eating seafood with cheese, combining mozzarella or burrata with shellfish is a delectable exception to the rule. Lobster is synonymous with summer dining, but in the Northeast its best season runs through the end of November, when it can be accompanied by the earthy, acetic flavors of fermented broccoli rabe. Making fermented broccolini is not challenging but requires at least two days of fermenting time. While it won't taste entirely the same, this recipe can also be made on the fly with a quick blanch of the broccoli rabe (see notes).

For the fermented broccoli rabe: Trim, then thoroughly clean the broccoli rabe under cold running water, making sure to rinse away any trace of dirt. Trim and discard any wilted leaves, then coarsely chop the broccoli rabe. (For safe preparation of fermented vegetables, work with very clean hands, utensils, and cutting boards.)

In a medium saucepan, combine a scant 4 cups (1 liter) water and the salt. Bring the water to a boil, then continue to boil for 3 minutes. Remove the pot from the heat and let the water cool to room temperature (the pan can be set into an ice bath to speed the cooling process). Transfer the cooled water to a very clean, nonreactive 2½-quart (2-liter) container with a tight-fitting lid. Using very clean tongs, submerge the broccoli rabe in the cooled, salted water. Using clean hands, place a clean paper towel on the surface of the water. Cover the container with the lid and let stand at cool room temperature in a dark room for 48 hours, then refrigerate until ready to use. (The fermented broccoli rabe will keep, covered and refrigerated, for up to 1 week.)

For the lobster: In an 8- to 10-quart (7.5- to 9.5-liter) pot, combine 6 quarts (5½ liters) water and the vinegar, onion, carrot, celery, salt, and bay leaves. Bring just to a boil, reduce to a simmer, and cook 15 minutes to make a court bouillon. Meanwhile, chill the lobsters in the freezer for 15 minutes to slow their metabolism and partially desensitize their nervous systems.

Place 1 lobster on a cutting board upside down (with its legs facing up). Kill the lobster by placing the point of a chef's knife between the lobster's hindmost legs with the blade facing the head, then thrust the knife down through the body and head (this method, including the first step of freezing, is deemed the most humane way to kill a lobster). Separate the claws (with the knuckles attached) and the tails from the bodies. (Discard the bodies, or wrap and freeze them for up to 3 months to make lobster stock.) Insert a metal skewer or the stem end of a teaspoon between the meat and the top side of the tail shells to keep the tails straight while cooking (straight tails are easier to remove meat from once the lobsters are cooked).

Serves 4 to 6

FERMENTED BROCCOLI RABE (SEE NOTES)

⅓ pound (162 grams) broccoli rabe

⅓ cup (45 grams) kosher salt

LOBSTER (SEE NOTES)

½ cup (118 milliliters) white wine vinegar

1 large yellow onion (360 grams), coarsely chopped

1 medium carrot (75 grams), coarsely chopped

1 celery rib (80 grams), coarsely chopped

2 tablespoons (24 grams) kosher salt

2 bay leaves

3 (1½-pound or 680-gram) live lobsters

MEYER LEMON VINAIGRETTE

3 tablespoons (45 milliliters) extra-virgin olive oil

1 tablespoon (1 gram) freshly grated Meyer lemon zest

1½ tablespoons (22 milliliters) fresh Meyer lemon juice

½ teaspoon (2 grams) kosher salt

½ teaspoon (1 gram) Aleppo pepper

TO SERVE

7 ounces (200 grams) burrata cheese

1 tablespoon (15 milliliters) heavy cream

½ teaspoon (2 grams) kosher salt

6 raw broccoli rabe florets (18 grams)

18 raw broccoli rabe leaves (12 grams)

Maldon sea salt

¼ cup (15 grams) Panne Grattato (page 55)

Extra-virgin olive oil, for drizzling

Drop the claws and tails into the simmering court bouillon. Cook, partially covered, removing the tails 5 minutes and the claws 9 minutes after the time they enter the water, and transferring the pieces to an ice bath immediately when done to halt cooking. When completely cool, drain; then crack the shells and remove the meat from the tails, claws, and knuckles. Discard the tomalley, any roe, and shells (or save for another use). Cut the meat into 1-inch (2.5-centimeter) pieces. Chill, covered, until ready to use.

For the vinaigrette: In a medium bowl, vigorously whisk together the oil, lemon zest and juice, salt, and Aleppo pepper. Set aside.

To serve: In a medium bowl, break the burrata into small pieces. Add ½ cup (66 grams) finely chopped fermented broccoli rabe and the cream and salt. Fold together to combine well. Let stand at room temperature for 15 minutes to allow the flavors to mingle and the mixture to come to room temperature.

Whisk together the vinaigrette, then add the lobster meat and toss to combine. Arrange the lobster pieces on the serving plates, reserving the remaining vinaigrette in the bowl. To the bowl, add the broccoli rabe florets and leaves and a pinch of Maldon sea salt, then toss to lightly coat with the vinaigrette. Top the lobster with the burrata mixture, then arrange the dressed fresh broccoli rabe pieces on top. Sprinkle with the panne grattato and a pinch or two of Maldon sea salt. Drizzle with oil.

NOTES: *If you are uncomfortable making fermented broccoli rabe at home, or lack the time to do so, simply blanch the broccoli rabe, then plunge it into ice water to stop cooking. Drain and pat dry, then season with salt and a drizzle of red wine vinegar. One pound of cleaned lobster meat can be purchased in place of live lobsters if you prefer not to cook and clean the lobsters at home.*

FRIED CALAMARI
with Spicy Caper Butter Sauce

Del Posto's fried calamari marries Italian-style fritto di mare with Rhode Island's classic recipe that includes hot cherry peppers. The squid are fried with a tempura-style, gluten-free, rice-flour batter, which makes for light and crunchy calamari that hold sauce without becoming soggy. The silken butter sauce is distinctively spicy, tangy, and rich, made with capers, reduced wine, and B&G hot cherry peppers and their pickling juice.

For the calamari: In a medium bowl, whisk together the flour, baking powder, and salt. In a slow and steady stream, whisk in the club soda to form a mixture that is the consistency of pancake batter. Stir in the parsley. Cover and chill until ready to use, at least 30 minutes or up to 4 hours.

Rinse the squid under cold water, then pat dry between paper towels. Halve any large tentacles lengthwise. Cut the bodies crosswise into ½-inch-wide (1.25-centimeter-wide) rings. Chill, covered, until ready to use.

Add enough oil to a large high-sided skillet or wide heavy saucepan to come 1 inch (2.5 centimeters) up the side of the pan. Heat the oil to 375°F (190°C). While the oil is heating, prepare the butter sauce.

For the spicy caper butter sauce: In a small heavy saucepan, boil the wine until it is syrupy and reduced to about 1 tablespoon (15 milliliters), about 4 minutes. Add the cream and boil, whisking frequently, until reduced by about half, 2 to 3 minutes. Reduce the heat to medium-low and, whisking constantly, add a few tablespoons of the butter. Add the remaining butter a few pieces at a time, whisking constantly, adding more pieces before the previous ones have completely liquefied (the sauce should maintain the consistency of hollandaise)

and lifting the pan from the heat occasionally to cool the mixture.

Remove the pan from the heat, then, in a slow and steady stream, whisk in the oil, then the cherry peppers, pickling liquid, capers, and salt. Keep the sauce off the heat but in a warm place until ready to use.

To fry the calamari: Remove the batter and calamari from the refrigerator. Whisk together the batter well, then add the calamari and stir to coat. Working in batches, lift the calamari pieces from the batter, letting excess batter drip back into the bowl, then drop pieces one by one into the hot oil. Fry the calamari, adjusting the heat as needed to maintain a 375°F (190°C) temperature, gently agitating the pieces with a slotted spoon to keep them from sticking together, until crisp (they will not turn golden), about 3 minutes. Using the slotted spoon, transfer the fried calamari to paper towels to drain.

To serve: Place the hot calamari on plates, drizzle with the butter sauce, and serve with the lemon wedges on the side.

Serves 4 to 6

CALAMARI

1 cup (160 grams) rice flour

1 teaspoon (5 grams) baking powder

1½ teaspoon (6 grams) kosher salt

¾ cup (178 milliliters) chilled club soda

2 tablespoons (6 grams) finely chopped flat-leaf parsley

1½ pounds (682 grams) cleaned medium squid (bodies and tentacles)

Vegetable oil, for frying

SPICY CAPER BUTTER SAUCE

¼ cup (60 milliliters) dry white wine

¼ cup (60 milliliters) heavy cream

9 tablespoons (128 grams) cold unsalted butter, cut into small pieces

2 tablespoons (30 milliliters) very good extra-virgin olive oil, preferably intense Sicilian (see Larder, page xxix)

2 tablespoons (10 grams) finely chopped B&G hot cherry peppers (from a jar), plus 2 teaspoons (10 milliliters) of the pickling liquid

2 teaspoons (5 grams) salt-packed capers, rinsed and soaked (see Larder, page xxiv)

¼ teaspoon (1 gram) kosher salt

TO SERVE

1 medium lemon (150 grams), cut into wedges

SPECIAL EQUIPMENT: a candy / fry thermometer

Del Posto's fried calamari feature a rich butter sauce, infused with spicy peppers and briny capers, which calls for a wine with acidity and ample fruit. Look to the wines from the slopes of Mt. Etna, the active volcano on the northeastern tip of Sicily, where grapes have been cultivated for more than 1,000 years. Nerello Mascalese, a red grape with deep smoky and bright fruit flavors, is well suited for this recipe. Nerello Mascalese makes for elegant pink wine, or rosato, with vibrant acidity and soft fruit notes of strawberry and tart cherries. Graci Etna Rosato 2014 is bright pink (the Norello grapes are left on their skins for less than 24 hours), irresistible, and leaps out of the glass.

CHARRED OCTOPUS

with Ceci, Celery Hearts, and 25-Year Balsamic Vinegar

Serves 4 to 6

OCTOPUS

2½ to 3 pounds (1⅛ to 1⅓ kilograms) cleaned octopus

1 medium yellow onion (265 grams), peeled and cut in half

1 medium carrot (80 grams), peeled and coarsely chopped

1 celery rib (80 grams), trimmed and coarsely chopped

½ head garlic (34 grams), cut in half crosswise

1 bay leaf

½ cup (120 milliliters) dry red wine

3 tablespoons (45 milliliters) extra-virgin olive oil

Kosher salt and freshly ground black pepper

CHICKPEAS

1 (15-ounce or 425-gram) can chickpeas, rinsed and drained

1 tablespoon (15 milliliters) extra-virgin olive oil, plus more as needed

1 teaspoon (5 milliliters) fresh lemon juice

½ teaspoon (2 grams) kosher salt

TO SERVE

2 celery ribs from the inner heart (80 grams), thinly sliced on the bias, plus 3 tablespoons (6 grams) coarsely chopped celery leaves

Very good extra-virgin olive oil, preferably intense Sicilian (see Larder, page xxix), for drizzling

25-year aceto balsamico tradizionale (see Larder, page xxvi), for drizzling

Maldon sea salt

It may be hard to imagine now, but when Del Posto opened its doors, octopus was an adventurous order for most diners in New York. Octopus, or *polpo,* and its smaller cousins, *polpessa* and *moscardino,* have been part of coastal cuisine in Italy since ancient times. From Liguria to Sicily, it's still common to find fishermen along the shoreline pounding fresh-caught octopus on the rocks to tenderize the tentacles as soon as they come out of the water. The bigger the octopus, the better the flavor, but the tougher the meat—requiring it to be properly tenderized by pounding or braising.

We can trace the roots of the combination of octopus and chickpeas to Italy's proximity to the Middle East, where the legume was first grown. Along with wheat, barley, and peas, chickpeas were among the first of the domesticated plants, known as the "founder crops," and date back 10,000 years. The coastal cultures in Italy embraced the chickpea and its flour, imported by their maritime merchants, and devised all manner of recipes, from baked goods to stews. During the 13th century the Sicilians picked up arms against the French rule of their island, massacring anyone who couldn't pronounce *ciciri,* or chickpea, with the distinctive Sicilian accent. Surprisingly, canned chickpeas are a phenomenal provision, as they are always cooked perfectly and retain consistent, quality flavor in the can.

For the octopus: In a 5- to 6-quart (4.7- to 5.6-liter) Dutch oven or wide heavy saucepan with lid, combine the octopus, onion, carrot, celery, garlic, bay leaf, and wine. Add water to cover by 1 inch (2.5 centimeters). Bring to a simmer over medium-high heat, then reduce to a very gentle simmer. Cover with a piece of parchment paper and the lid, and gently simmer until the octopus is tender, 30 minutes to 1½ hours, depending on whether you have 1 large octopus or 2 small ones. The tip of a sharp knife slipped into the thickest part of the octopus will slide out easily when the octopus is done. Remove the pot from the heat and let the octopus cool completely in the braising liquid. While the octopus is cooling, prepare the chickpeas.

For the chickpeas: Set aside ¼ cup (40 grams) of the chickpeas. In a blender, combine the remaining chickpeas and the oil, lemon juice, and salt. Add ¼ cup plus 3 tablespoons (105 milliliters) water, then purée until smooth. Transfer the purée to a bowl. Cover and set aside.

To char the octopus: Drain the octopus and pat dry, then cut off the tentacles at the natural dividing points at the top of the body. Discard the body. In a large skillet, heat the oil for the octopus. Season the

octopus with salt and pepper, then carefully cook in batches (the octopus will cause the oil to spit), turning once halfway through and adding more oil as needed, until golden and crispy, about 5 minutes.

To serve: Arrange the warm octopus on serving plates. Dollop with chickpea purée, then sprinkle with the reserved chickpeas, celery, and celery leaves. Drizzle with oil and balsamic, and sprinkle with Maldon sea salt.

❧ WINE PAIRING ☙

Grown in the shadow of Mt. Vesuvius in the Campania region, Fiano di Avellino is one of the most exceptional white grapes in all of Italy. Fiano grapes from Avellino produce wines with brooding and smoky notes that come from the volcanic soil of the region and possess a palate that is also vibrant and pure, with a finish that is *per sempre*. Fiano di Avellino's cool, high-altitude growing area on the side of Mt. Vesuvius combined with Campania's warm climate creates a tension between fruitiness and minerality in the wine. Producer Pietracupa's Fiano di Avellino is one of the greatest examples of this—the 2013 vintage is pure and spritely, while the 2008 shows more smoke. By accentuating the char on octopus with smoke and rounding out the chickpea purée with fruity notes, Fiano di Avellino is a must for charred octopus.

VITELLO TONNATO

with Olive Crostone, Fried Capers, Chives,
and Lime Cells

Vitello Tonnato is a classic recipe from the North of Italy. The Piedmont region claims ownership of the dish as cooled, slow-roasted veal, thinly sliced and then coated with a purée of cooked white tuna, eggs, capers, and sometimes mayonnaise and anchovy.

However, the most flavorful and elegant executions of the dish are not found in Piedmont, but in the nearby Lombardy region. There, the recipe was influenced by the French techniques that dominated the sophisticated kitchens of the region's capital city of Milan during the 19th and 20th centuries. Del Posto's recipe is inspired by a version made at Ristorante Ambasciata in the southeastern corner of the region. A restaurant clad in layers of Persian rugs and illuminated by sterling silver candelabras, Ambasciata boasts a clientele of famous northern-Italian sofisticati. This recipe treats the roasted veal and the tuna sauce as one unified element by including the tuna, anchovy, and aromatics in the cooking braise for the veal. The fat from the meat and the seafood render together, building the cornerstone of a deeply flavored emulsion, which then becomes the tonnato sauce.

Serves 4 to 6

OLIVE CROSTONE

1 baguette

½ cup (60 grams) pitted Niçoise olives

¾ teaspoon (6 grams) squid ink
(see notes)

VEAL AND TONNATO SAUCE

2 medium lemons (300 grams)

1½ tablespoons (22 milliliters)
extra-virgin olive oil

1 medium yellow onion (350 grams),
coarsely chopped

2 medium carrots (150 grams),
coarsely chopped

½ cup (118 milliliters) dry red wine

2 cups (490 milliliters) veal stock or
chicken stock, preferably homemade

2 (10½-ounce or 300-gram) jars
high-quality tuna in oil, drained

12 flat anchovy fillets (42 grams)

1 pound (453 grams) boned veal,
eye of round or shoulder

1 tablespoon plus 1 teaspoon
(total 20 milliliters) fish sauce

2 large hard-boiled egg yolks
(30 grams)

Kosher salt

3½ tablespoons (52 milliliters) very good
extra-virgin olive oil, preferably intense
Sicilian (see Larder, page xxix), plus more
for drizzling

2 tablespoons (30 milliliters) Agrumato
lemon oil (see notes)

CONTINUED

For the crostone: Cut a 7-inch (18-centimeter) length of bread from the baguette (save the remaining bread for another use). Cut and discard the crust from the baguette piece, making sure to cut away as little of the inner loaf as possible. Place the bread in a resealable plastic bag, then place the bag in a small bowl and fold the top of the bag back, so that the bag stays upright and open.

In a blender, combine the olives, squid ink, and ¼ cup (60 milliliters) water and purée until smooth. Transfer the mixture to the bag with the bread. Remove the bag from the bowl, then press out the air and seal. Using your hands from the outside of the bag, gently but firmly press the olive mixture into the bread to fully saturate the bread. Chill in the refrigerator, for at least 12 hours or up to 1 day, to allow the bread to absorb the flavor and color of the olive mixture.

Heat the oven to 225°F (107°C). Remove the bread from the bag, tear into 12 (1-inch or 2.5-centimeter) pieces, and place on a baking sheet. Bake until the crostone are dry and crunchy, about 1 hour. Remove from the oven and let cool completely. (The crostone can be prepared and kept in an airtight container at cool room temperature for up to 3 days.)

For the veal and tonnato sauce: Heat the oven to 225°F (107°C). Cut a round of parchment paper to fit the diameter of a 5- to 6-quart (4.7- to 5.6-liter) Dutch oven or wide heavy saucepan with a lid. Cut a small hole in the center of the parchment round.

Using a sharp peeler or paring knife, cut the peels from the lemons in large wide strips, avoiding the white pith. Wrap the

peels in a square of cheesecloth and secure with kitchen twine. Set aside the parchment paper and the wrapped peels (save the lemons for another use).

In the Dutch oven or saucepan, heat the oil over medium heat until hot but not smoking. Add the onion and carrots and cook until tender and lightly golden, 12 to 14 minutes. Add the wine and continue cooking until the liquid is reduced by about half. Add the wrapped lemon peels and the veal stock, tuna, and anchovies; increase the heat to high and bring the liquid just to a boil, then remove the pot from the heat. Nestle the veal in the pot. Add boiling water, if needed, just to cover the meat, then cover with the prepared parchment paper and the lid. Transfer the pot to the oven and bake for 6 to 7 hours, or until the meat is tender but still light pink in the center.

Transfer the veal and the braising liquid (including the solids) to a large nonreactive bowl; cover and allow the meat to cool completely in the refrigerator. Once cool, remove the meat from the braising liquid (reserve the liquid and solids) and refrigerate, covered, until ready to use.

Remove and discard the lemon peels from the braising liquid. Transfer the remaining liquid and solids to a blender and purée until smooth (this is the tonnato sauce base). Transfer all but 1 cup (250 milliliters) of the base to a resealable bag or airtight container and freeze for later use. (The leftover base can be frozen for up to 3 months and used to make a quick version of this recipe using roasted veal tenderloin cooked to rare in place of the braised veal.)

To the tonnato sauce base in the blender, add the fish sauce, egg yolks, and ½ teaspoon

(2 grams) salt, then purée to combine. With the machine running, add the extra-virgin olive oil and the Agrumato lemon oil in a slow and steady stream. Purée the sauce until it is smooth and creamy. Refrigerate, covered, until thickened and chilled, at least 1 hour or up to 2 days.

To serve: Pat dry the capers with paper towels. In a small skillet or saucepan, heat the oil until hot but not smoking. Carefully fry the capers (the oil will splatter) until crispy, 1 to 2 minutes, then drain on dry paper towels. Cut the veal against the grain into ⅛-inch-thick (3-millimeter-thick) slices and arrange on serving plates. Spread the chilled sauce over the veal. Garnish the plates with the olive crostone, fried capers, panne grattato, basil, and chives. Press the lime cells from the finger limes onto each plate. Drizzle with oil and sprinkle with a pinch or two of Maldon sea salt.

NOTES: *Squid ink can be purchased at Italian food markets or fish markets, or online. Agrumato lemon oil can be purchased at Italian food markets or online. If Agrumato is not available, it can be substituted with a 2:1 ratio of olive oil and fresh lemon juice. If finger limes are not available, segment 1 standard lime, then, using your fingers, gently break apart the segments to form small clusters of lime cells (they are the little clear cells inside the segments that encapsulate the lime juice). Drop the cell clusters directly onto the serving plates after breaking apart the segments.*

TO SERVE

⅓ cup (40 grams) salt-packed capers, rinsed and soaked (see Larder, page xxiv)

¼ cup (60 milliliters) extra-virgin olive oil, plus more for drizzling

3 tablespoons (11 grams) Panne Grattato (page 55)

6 basil leaves, torn in half or thirds if large, or lemon basil if available

2 tablespoons (2 grams) snipped chives

3 (9 grams) finger limes (see notes), cut in half crosswise

Maldon sea salt

SPECIAL EQUIPMENT: parchment paper, cheesecloth, and kitchen twine

BEEF AND TRUFFLE CARPACCIO

with Sage Grissini and Artichokes alla Romana

Harry's Bar, the famous watering hole for the international glitterati in Venice, created Carpaccio in 1950 as an alternative to chopped beef tartare. Thin slices of raw beef, striped with a mayonnaise sauce, the dish was named after the red and cream colors of the 15th-century paintings of the Venetian artist Vittore Carpaccio (student of artist Giovanni Bellini, for whom another of Harry's Bar creations, the Bellini cocktail, was named). Del Posto's version of this Venetian recipe is a regional mosaic, with butter-bathed black truffles from Piedmont pounded into the marbling of the meat, then topped with Roman-style artichokes.

For the artichokes: Reserving their cooking liquid, transfer the artichokes to a cutting board. Trim and reserve all but ½ inch of the stems. Cut the hearts into ½-inch (1.25-centimeter) wedges. Place half of the heart pieces and all of the stems in a blender. (Set the remaining heart pieces aside for serving.) Add the cream, salt, and ¼ cup (60 milliliters) of the reserved cooking liquid to the blender and purée to combine. Transfer the purée to a bowl. Cover and set aside. (See p. 50.)

For the carpaccio: Shave the truffle into thin rounds, about 1 millimeter thick. Arrange the pieces in a single layer in a medium saucepan; set aside. In a small saucepan, heat the butter over medium heat, stirring often, until deep nutty brown (do not burn), about 6 minutes. Immediately pour the browned butter over the truffles. Set aside until the butter has cooled just to room temperature.

Cut the steak against the grain into 4 to 6 equal pieces (depending on how many portions you are serving). Using the smooth surface of a meat pounder, pound one portion between two sheets of plastic wrap to about ⅛ inch (3 millimeters) thick. Lift up the top sheet of plastic wrap.

Remove a few of the truffle slices from the butter and place on top of the pounded beef, then top with the plastic wrap to seal. Press out the air and seal the plastic wrap at the edges, then gently tap with a meat pounder. Repeat with the remaining portions. Chill the sealed carpaccio servings in the refrigerator. (The carpaccio can be prepared up to 12 hours ahead.) Meanwhile, prepare the grissini.

For the grissini: In a large bowl, stir together the sugar, yeast, and a scant ½ cup (110 milliliters) of warm water (105° to 115°F or 40° to 46°C) and let stand until foamy, about 5 minutes. (If the mixture doesn't foam, start over with new yeast.)

In a medium bowl, whisk together the flour, salt, and baking powder. Add the flour mixture to the yeast mixture. Using your hands, mix together the dough until it comes together into a ball, then continue to knead the dough in the bowl, incorporating all of the flour, until it is smooth and elastic, about 5 minutes. In a clean bowl, very lightly coat the dough with oil, then cover the bowl with plastic wrap and let the dough rise in a draft-free place at warm room temperature until doubled in bulk, about 1 hour.

Serves 4 to 6

ARTICHOKES

1 batch Artichokes alla Romana (page 50)

2 tablespoons (30 milliliters) heavy cream

¼ teaspoon (1 gram) kosher salt

CARPACCIO

¾ ounce (22 grams) black truffle (see notes)

½ cup (115 grams) unsalted butter

8 ounces (225 grams) dry-aged boneless Delmonico steak

SAGE GRISSINI

1 teaspoon (4 grams) sugar

½ teaspoon (1 gram) active dry yeast

⅓ cup plus 2 tablespoons (total 200 grams) bread flour

1 teaspoon (4 grams) kosher salt

¼ teaspoon (1 gram) baking powder

Extra-virgin olive oil

5 ounces (150 grams) beef fat trimmings (see notes), cut into ⅓-inch (1-centimeter) pieces

1 tablespoon (12 grams) Maldon sea salt

2 large sage leaves, dried (see notes)

TO SERVE

Extra-virgin olive oil, for drizzling

Mint leaves, for garnish

SPECIAL EQUIPMENT: a truffle slicer or an adjustable blade slicer

Meanwhile, combine the fat and ½ cup (120 milliliters) water in a small saucepan. Heat over low heat, stirring occasionally, until the fat has rendered, 30 to 45 minutes. Remove and discard any cracklings, then remove the pan from the heat and cover to keep warm.

Heat the oven to 350°F (177°C). Line a baking sheet with parchment paper.

Turn out the grissini dough onto a lightly floured surface. Press and roll out the dough into a roughly 8-inch (20-centimeter) oval, about ¼ inch (.6 centimeter) thick, then cut it lengthwise into ¼-inch-wide (6-millimeter-wide) strips. Arrange the strips ½ inch (1.25 centimeters) apart on the prepared baking sheet. Bake, rotating the pan once halfway through, until the grissini are lightly golden and crisp, about 30 minutes. Meanwhile, in a small bowl, crumble together the Maldon sea salt and sage.

Transfer the pan with the grissini to a rack, then brush the warm grissini with the rendered beef fat and sprinkle with about two-thirds of the sage salt (reserve the remaining sage salt for serving).

To serve: Remove the bottom sheet of plastic wrap from one serving of carpaccio, then place the carpaccio, truffle side up, on a chilled plate and remove the plastic wrap from the top. Repeat with the remaining servings. Dollop each carpaccio with the artichoke purée, then arrange the reserved artichoke pieces on top. Sprinkle each plate with a pinch or two of the remaining sage salt, then drizzle with oil and garnish with mint. Serve with the grissini.

NOTES: *If fresh black truffle is not available, frozen or canned black truffle pieces can be substituted (see Larder, page xxix). Beef fat trimmings are available from most high-quality butchers. To quickly dry fresh sage, pick the leaves from the stems, then place on a paper towel on a microwave-safe plate. Place a second paper towel on top. Microwave on high at 10-second intervals until the leaves are dry.*

---

2 medium lemons (300 grams)

½ cup (119 milliliters) dry white wine

1 small yellow onion (100 grams), cut in half and peeled

½ small fennel bulb (50 grams)

2 leafy thyme sprigs

6 mint leaves

1 bay leaf

4 medium globe artichokes with about 2-inch-long (5-centimeter-long) stems (900 grams)

ARTICHOKES ALLA ROMANA

For the artichokes: Fill a medium saucepan half full with cold water. Through a mesh strainer, squeeze the juice from the lemons into the pot; discard the lemon seeds. Add the lemon halves, wine, onion, fennel, thyme, mint, and bay leaf to the pot.

Trim away the tough outer leaves of one artichoke to expose its tender pale green interior. Using a serrated knife, cut off the top third of the artichoke, then, using a vegetable peeler, remove the tough outer layers around the base and stem. Cut the artichoke in half lengthwise, then use a melon baller or small spoon to dig out the hairy choke in the center. Place the pieces into the pot. Repeat with the remaining artichokes.

Bring the liquid to a simmer over medium-high heat, then reduce to a gentle simmer and cook until the artichokes are tender, 15 to 20 minutes. Remove from the heat and let the artichokes cool completely in their liquid.

WARM COTECHINO
with Lentils and Prosecco Zabaglione

Rumored to bring good luck and wealth in the coming year, cotechino and lentils is a long-standing New Year's Day tradition turned superstition, served throughout Italy during the winter holidays. The coin-shaped lentils represent a promise of wealth, and the pig, from which the cotechino sausage is made, is an animal that eats while moving forward, symbolizing good luck in the future.

Cotechino sausage dates to the early 16th century when Pope Julius II laid siege to the French-aligned city of Mirandola, near Modena in the Emilia-Romagna region. With their food supplies cut off and larders dwindling, the city's butchers stuffed pig innards with a mixture of ground pork, pork rinds, fatback, and spices. Thus, cotechino was born and remains a specialty in the Emilia-Romagna, protected as a regional product with IGT status. Often served as a main course, or secondo, in Italy, this rich dish is reimagined as a shared antipasto at Del Posto. The Prosecco zabaglione, inspired by a Lorenza de' Medici recipe, balances the salty, cooked-pork sausage and the earthy lentils with a light, sweet acid.

For the cotechino: Heat the oven to 300°F (149°C). Place the cotechino in a 5- to 6-quart (4.7- to 5.6-liter) Dutch oven or wide heavy saucepan with lid. Add the chicken broth and 1 cup (236 milliliters) water. Measure out and set aside ½ cup (118 milliliters) of the Prosecco for the zabaglione; add the remaining Prosecco to the pot. Over medium-high heat, bring the liquid just to a boil, then cover and transfer to the oven. Braise until an instant-read thermometer inserted into the center of the meat registers 150°F (65°C), about 1 hour. Meanwhile, prepare the lentils.

For the lentils: In a medium saucepan, combine 1½ cups (355 milliliters) water with the broth, lentils, thyme, bay leaf, and ½ teaspoon (2 grams) salt. Bring to a simmer and cook, stirring occasionally, until the lentils are just tender, 25 to 30 minutes.

Meanwhile, in a small skillet, heat 2 teaspoons (10 milliliters) of the oil over medium-high heat. Add the onion, carrot, celery, and a pinch of salt. Cook, stirring occasionally, until just tender, 1 to 2 minutes. Remove from the heat and set aside.

Reserving the cooking liquid, strain the lentils through a fine-mesh sieve over a bowl; discard the thyme and bay leaf. In a blender, combine 1 cup (150 grams) of the lentils (reserving remaining lentils) with ¾ cup (177 milliliters) of the cooking liquid, then purée until smooth. Add the mustard and vinegar. With the machine running, drizzle in the remaining 1 tablespoon (15 milliliters) oil. Transfer the mixture to a bowl, then fold in the reserved lentils and the onion mixture. Set aside.

Remove the cooked cotechino from the oven and let stand, uncovered, while you prepare the zabaglione.

Serves 6 to 8

COTECHINO

1½ pounds (680 grams) uncooked cotechino sausage (see note)

3½ cups (830 milliliters) chicken broth, preferably homemade

1 (750-milliliter) bottle Prosecco

LENTILS

2 cups (475 milliliters) chicken broth, preferably homemade

1½ cups (235 grams) brown lentils

1 thyme sprig

1 bay leaf

Kosher salt

1 tablespoon plus 2 teaspoons (total 25 milliliters) extra-virgin olive oil

3 tablespoons (30 grams) finely chopped yellow onion

2 tablespoons (15 grams) finely diced carrot

2 tablespoons (15 grams) finely diced celery

2 tablespoons (20 grams) Dijon mustard

1 tablespoon (14 milliliters) sherry vinegar

PROSECCO ZABAGLIONE

½ cup (118 milliliters) Prosecco (reserved from the bottle for the cotechino)

7 large egg yolks (130 grams)

2 tablespoons (30 milliliters) heavy cream

1 tablespoon (12 grams) sugar

Kosher salt

CONTINUED

3 tablespoons (9 grams)
finely chopped flat-leaf parsley

3 tablespoons (8 grams)
finely chopped chives

For the Prosecco zabaglione: In a small saucepan, boil the ½ cup of Prosecco until reduced by half, about 4 minutes. Transfer to a medium metal bowl and let cool to room temperature.

Fill a medium saucepan with about 2 inches (5 centimeters) of water and bring to a gentle simmer over medium-low heat. Add the egg yolks, cream, sugar, and a pinch of salt to the bowl with the wine. Place the bowl over (but not touching) the simmering water and cook, whisking constantly and vigorously, and clearing the bottom of the bowl so that the eggs do not scramble, until the mixture is thick, foamy, and tripled in volume, 4 to 6 minutes. Remove the bowl from the heat and whisk 30 seconds more.

To serve: In a small skillet, gently heat the lentil purée over medium heat just until warm, adding water as needed to loosen the purée a bit. Fold in the parsley and chives. Spoon the purée onto a serving platter. Spoon the zabaglione over the top. Remove the cotechino from its broth and cut it crosswise into rounds, then arrange on top of the lentils. Spoon about 2 tablespoons (30 milliliters) of the broth over the meat.

NOTE: *Italian cotechino sausage can be purchased at Italian gourmet stores and online during the holidays.*

Makes 1 pound

1 tablespoon plus 1 teaspoon
(total 8 grams) smoked paprika

1 tablespoon plus 1 teaspoon
(total 8 grams) Hungarian paprika

2 teaspoons (4 grams)
cayenne pepper

1½ teaspoons (6 grams) kosher salt

1 teaspoon (5 grams)
Prague Powder #2 (see note)

½ pound (225 grams) ground
pork shoulder

SPECIAL EQUIPMENT: food-safe
rubber gloves

DEL POSTO 'NDUJA SAUSAGE

Calabria, the southern region that makes up the foot of Italy's boot,
is known for its pork products, particularly fresh sausages. 'Nduja,
pronounced *een-DOO-ya,* is a soft, spreadable cure of pork and spices and
a cousin to French andouille sausage. In Calabria, it often incorporates
beef tripe; pork liver, lard, lungs, skin, and ground shoulder; and hot
pepper and paprika. Del Posto's house 'nduja is easily made by simply
using ground pork shoulder in a short cure of just a couple of days.

In a large bowl, whisk together the smoked
and Hungarian paprikas, cayenne, salt, and
Prague Powder. Using your hands and wear-
ing food-safe rubber gloves, add the pork
and mix the spices into the sausage, then
continue to mix until the sausage begins
to feel tacky, about 2 minutes.

Transfer the mixture to an airtight
container, cover, and allow to cure at least
3 days or up to 2 weeks in the refrigerator.
('Nduja's flavor will deepen as it cures. Keep
it refrigerated for up to 2 weeks, or frozen
for up to 1 month.)

NOTES: *Prague Powder #2—also known as
Instacure #2, pink curing salt, and Sel Rose—
is composed of 6.75 percent sodium nitrite,
4 percent sodium nitrate, and 89.25 percent
sodium chloride. It is used in the curing process to
prevent botulism and to provide the characteristic
flavor and red color associated with curing.
Prague Powder #2 can be purchased online.*

PANNE GRATTATO
(FRIED BREADCRUMBS)

Many Del Posto dishes are finished with these breadcrumbs, or some variation of them. A fairly large batch of breadcrumbs can be toasted ahead (they will keep for several weeks) and then fried as needed for the recipes. Once fried, use the same day.

Makes ½ cup

¼ cup plus 2 tablespoons (total 90 milliliters) extra-virgin olive oil

½ cup (30 grams) plain coarse breadcrumbs (see note)

Finely grated zest of 1 lemon

Kosher salt

Line a small bowl with a double layer of paper towels; set aside. In a small skillet, heat the oil over medium-high heat until hot but not smoking. Fry the breadcrumbs until golden, 30 seconds to 1 minute. Using a slotted spoon, transfer the crumbs to the paper towels to drain. Let stand for 1 minute, then remove the paper towels, leaving behind the warm crumbs in the bowl. Toss the crumbs while warm with the zest and a generous pinch of salt.

NOTE: *To make your own coarse breadcrumbs: Heat the oven to 250ºF (121ºC). Cut 1 day-old baguette into ½-inch-thick (1.2-centimeter-thick) slices. Arrange the slices on a baking sheet in a single layer and bake until lightly golden and dried out, about 1 hour. Let cool completely on a wire rack, then transfer to a food processor; pulse to form coarse crumbs. Transfer the crumbs to a medium-mesh sieve to sift out the fine bread-crumbs and powder. Discard the fine breadcrumbs and powder. Store the coarse crumbs in an airtight container at cool room temperature until ready to use (stored properly, the breadcrumbs will keep well for several weeks). One standard baguette yields about 1½ cups (80 grams) of coarse breadcrumbs.*

PRIMI

Making pasta is a daily practice in Italy.
It has come to universally define the country's cuisine and represents
the heart and soul of any Italian restaurant. Prepared in every
part of Italy, the breadth of pasta shapes and preparations reflects
the dynamic diversity of its regional kitchens.

Throughout Italy, pasta, risotto, and gnocchi take center stage
in the primo, or first, course. Whether delicate or rustic,
these dishes should evoke a sense of satisfying nourishment
akin to what Americans might describe as comfort food. Providing
this type of comfort in a dish while meeting the expectations
of a fine-dining restaurant in Manhattan has been a tireless
pursuit and well worth the effort.

The pasta department is the heart of the Del Posto kitchen. It is given
no shortage of resources, and everything is handmade. Three separate
divisions, each with their own cooks, prepare the primi at the
restaurant every day. One team makes the fillings for stuffed pasta
and the sauces; another team makes the dough, forming and
stuffing it into a variety of shapes; finally, the chefs execute the
dishes during service.

Influenced by age-old Italian practices, these recipes feature
techniques and ingredients found in many different regions.
Refined over many years, they are the fruits of a true labor of love.

SPAGHETTI WITH DUNGENESS CRAB

and Jalapeños

This spaghetti dish appeared on Del Posto's first menu, capturing the spirit of seafood pasta recipes in Italy while incorporating distinctly American ingredients. Dungeness crab from the Pacific Northwest, jalapeño peppers, and fresh olive oil from southern Italy create a piquant and briny sauce for hard-wheat pasta.

This is the only pasta recipe at the restaurant that makes use of packaged pasta. The southern regions of Abruzzo and Campania are known for producing handmade dried pasta—the Neapolitans are nicknamed the *mangiamaccheroni*, "pasta eaters." Extruded through bronze dies, artisanal dried pasta is toothsome, with a rough surface that grips the sauce and releases a good amount of starch into the cooking water. For this recipe, use handmade, hard-wheat (*grano duro*) spaghetti from Abruzzo or Gragnano (in Campania). The quality of the pasta makes all the difference.

Serves 4 to 6

CRAB

1 Dungeness crab (about 2 pounds or 906 grams)

1 medium fennel bulb (150 grams), cut into ¼-inch (6-millimeter) slices

CRAB STOCK

2 tablespoons (30 milliliters) extra-virgin olive oil

1 medium fennel bulb (150 grams), cut into ¼-inch (6-millimeter) slices

1 small yellow onion (125 grams), cut into ¼-inch (6-millimeter) slices

1 cup (236 milliliters) dry white wine

TO SERVE

Kosher salt

½ cup plus 1½ tablespoons (total 140 milliliters) very good extra-virgin olive oil, preferably intense Sicilian (see Larder, page xxix)

6 garlic cloves (24 grams), gently smashed and peeled

3 tablespoons (20 grams) Aleppo pepper

About 3 medium jalapeño peppers (118 grams), seeded and thinly sliced

About 8 medium scallions (95 grams), whites thinly sliced and greens thinly sliced on a long bias (keep whites and greens separated)

1 (1-pound or 450- to 500-gram) package spaghetti, preferably grano duro from Gragnano or Abruzzo

3 tablespoons (45 milliliters) fresh lemon juice

For the crab: Chill the crab in the freezer for 15 minutes to slow its metabolism and partially desensitize its nervous system. Place the chilled crab on a cutting board upside down, with its legs facing up and its head facing away from you. Kill the crab by placing the point of a chef's knife over the bottom of the body and thrusting the knife into the rear nerve center (located under the triangle-shaped "apron"); then quickly remove the knife and, within a few seconds, thrust it into the front nerve center (located between the eyes and where you would imagine the underside of the mouth to be).

Using kitchen shears, separate the claws from the body. Cut away and discard the feathery gills. Turn the body top side up. Separate the head (the top shell) from the body by lifting up firmly and pulling it away from the bottom shell. Then turn the head upside down to keep the brains and all the bits inside.

Set aside the body and claws. Place the head, with the brain and bits facing up, into a shallow skillet with a lid. Add water to come about halfway up the head. Bring the water to a gentle simmer, then cover and steam until the brains are set, about 10 minutes. Remove from the heat, transfer the head to a plate, and refrigerate, uncovered, until completely cooled.

Meanwhile, in a 4- to 5-quart (3.7- to 4.7-liter) wide heavy pot, combine 3 quarts (2.8 liters) water and the fennel. Bring the water to a boil and simmer for 15 minutes to create a light fennel broth.

Add the crab body and claws to the boiling fennel broth. Cook the body for 4 minutes and the claws for 7 minutes, transferring the parts as ready to a plate, then to the refrigerator (uncovered) to cool. Remove the fennel from the broth. Coarsely chop enough to yield ¼ cup (42 grams) and refrigerate until ready to use. Discard the remaining fennel. Strain the broth and reserve.

Cut the cooled crab body lengthwise into thirds. Reserving the shells (of both the body and the claws), carefully pick out the meat from each body section. Using kitchen shears or a mallet, cut or break open the claws and leg knuckles to remove the meat. Refrigerate the crabmeat, covered, until ready to use.

For the crab stock: In a large saucepan, combine the oil, fennel, and onion. Heat over medium heat, stirring occasionally, until the vegetables are tender, 10 to 12 minutes (do not brown). Add the wine, increase the heat to high, and cook until the liquid is reduced by about half, about 3 minutes. Add the reserved crab shells and the reserved fennel broth. Bring to a simmer and cook for 30 minutes, then strain.

Meanwhile, scoop out and transfer the crab brains and bits to a blender. Add the reserved chopped fennel and 3 tablespoons of the crab stock. Purée until creamy and smooth.

To serve: Remove the crabmeat from the refrigerator. Bring a large pot of generously salted water to a boil for the pasta.

Meanwhile, in a 12-inch (30-centimeter) skillet, combine 1½ tablespoons (22 milliliters) of the oil and all of the garlic. Heat over medium heat, stirring occasionally, until the garlic is fragrant and lightly golden, about 1 minute. Remove the pan from the heat, then tilt it to pool the oil to one side. Add the Aleppo pepper to the oil and let it rest for 30 seconds, allowing the pepper flavors to bloom into oil.

Add the jalapeño and the scallion whites to the skillet. Return the pan to medium heat and cook 30 seconds more. Add 1¾ cups (415 milliliters) of the crab stock. Bring the liquid to a simmer and cook for 2 minutes, then remove and discard the garlic. Remove the pan from the heat. Stir in the crab brain purée and set the sauce aside.

Cook the pasta in the boiling water. When the pasta is about 2 minutes from being done according to package directions, gently warm the sauce over medium heat. Drain the cooked pasta, return it to the pot, and immediately add the sauce. Cook over medium-high heat, stirring occasionally, for 1 minute. Then, stirring constantly, drizzle in the remaining ½ cup (118 milliliters) oil. Cook the pasta and sauce just until the sauce returns to a gentle simmer, then stir in the crabmeat and all but a generous pinch of the scallion greens. Remove the pan from the heat and stir in the lemon juice.

Divide the pasta among serving plates. Garnish with the remaining scallion greens. Serve immediately.

❧ WINE PAIRING ❧

The sweet crab and spicy peppers in this spaghetti call out for rosato, a blush wine that bridges the white wine pairings served with the antipasti and the rich red wines paired with the secondo. Each year Del Posto receives a few cases of the Ligurian rosato from Bisson, made from the unique Ciliegiolo grape, which derives its name from the Italian word for "cherry." Bisson's rosato has lush and ripe notes that temper spice and enough minerality to elevate sweet shellfish. If the Bisson is not available, look for a rosato with a bit more density but not too much residual sugar.

ANELLINI DEL PLIN

Del Posto's *anellini,* "little rings," are the restaurent's most stylish finger food. Served in a napkin, these fresh-pasta rings are picked up and dunked into the accompanying black truffle–butter sauce and then dipped into a small bowl of grated Parmigiano-Reggiano. The jewel in these golden rings is a three-meat stuffing from the Langhe area of Piedmont, where *plin* is local dialect for "pinch"—referring to how stuffed pasta is formed.

For the anellini: Heat a large skillet over medium-high heat. Add the oil and heat just until the oil is hot but not smoking. Add the veal, then season with 1 teaspoon (4 grams) salt. Cook, turning once, until the veal is browned on both sides, 2 to 3 minutes. Transfer the veal to a plate.

Add the pancetta to the skillet and cook over medium-high heat until the fat begins to render, 2 to 3 minutes. Add the garlic and cook, turning occasionally, until fragrant and lightly golden, 1 minute more (the pancetta will be golden now, as well). Add the onion, reduce the heat to medium, and continue cooking, stirring occasionally, until the onion begins to soften, 3 to 4 minutes. Add the wine and cook until the liquid is mostly evaporated, then add the veal back to the pan and cook 1 minute more. Add the broth.

Transfer the pan contents to a medium saucepan. Add 1 cup (238 milliliters) water and bring to a simmer. Gently simmer, covered, until the veal is very tender, 1½ to 2 hours.

Stir the prosciutto into the veal mixture, then transfer the pan contents to a metal bowl and chill in an ice bath or in the refrigerator until the meat is cooled to room temperature.

Strain the veal and solids from the liquid, then finely chop the meat and solids with a mezzaluna or pulse in a food processor until just puréed but not pasty. Transfer the filling to a bowl and fold in the cheese. (The filling, which makes double what you need for this recipe, can be made ahead, divided in two, and kept in an airtight container and refrigerated for up to 3 days, or frozen for up to 1 month.)

To form the anellini: Roll out the pasta dough (as instructed on page 103) until you can just see your hand through the pasta sheets, a scant 1 millimeter thick.

Working quickly with one sheet at a time (keeping the remaining sheets covered as instructed on page 103), cut one sheet lengthwise into 2 x 3-inch (5 x 7½-centimeter) rectangles. Place level ½-teaspoon (4-gram) dollops of filling in the center of half of the pasta rectangles.

Using a finger dipped into water or a water-filled spray bottle, lightly dab or mist all of the pasta rectangles to dampen, then, putting the wet sides together, place the unfilled pieces on top of the filled pieces. Using your fingers, gently press out any air; then, using the rounded top side (not the cutting side) of a scant 1-inch (2.25-centimeter) round cutter, gently press to seal the pasta around the filling, forming a slight indentation.

With a pasta wheel cutter, trim the long sides of each rectangle to form a rough eye shape, with the tapered short ends trimmed

ANELLINI

1½ tablespoons (22 milliliters) extra-virgin olive oil

1 pound (453 grams) veal shoulder, chuck, or top round, cut into 1-inch (2.5-centimeter) cubes

Kosher salt

4½ ounces (125 grams) pancetta, cut into 1-inch (2.5-centimeter) pieces

4 garlic cloves (16 grams), gently smashed and peeled

1 medium yellow onion (250 grams), thinly sliced

3 tablespoons (45 milliliters) dry white wine

1 cup (238 milliliters) chicken broth, preferably homemade

⅓ pound (150 grams) prosciutto, cut into small pieces, then finely chopped in a food processor or by hand

3 tablespoons (13 grams) freshly grated Parmigiano-Reggiano cheese (at least 24-month aged; see Larder, page xxiv)

1 batch Fresh Egg Pasta Dough (page 103)

Semolina flour, for dusting

TO SERVE

Kosher salt

5¼ ounces (148 grams) fresh white or black truffles (see Larder, page xxix)

¾ cup (170 grams) unsalted butter, softened

1 cup (64 grams) freshly grated Parmigiano-Reggiano cheese (at least 24-month aged; see Larder, page xxiv)

SPECIAL EQUIPMENT: a pasta or pastry wheel cutter; a scant-1-inch (2.25-centimeter) round cutter

to about ¾ inch (2 centimeters) wide. Wrap the pasta around your index finger to form a ring, then overlap and press the short ends together, misting with water as necessary to seal. Repeat with the remaining pieces, pasta and filling, keeping the pieces covered as you work to keep the pasta from drying before the anellini are formed. Dust the finished anellini with semolina flour as you go.

To serve: Bring a large wide pot of generously salted water to a boil. Meanwhile, using a dampened soft mushroom brush, gently loosen and remove any dirt from the truffles. Use the tip of a paring knife to remove any dirt from the crevices, then brush again. Pat dry the cleaned truffles, then finely grate them into a medium bowl. Add the butter and stir to combine, then transfer to a small saucepan. Heat over very low heat, swirling the butter until melted. Season to taste with salt. Keep warm over very low heat.

Cook the pasta in the boiling water until they float to the surface and puff up, 4 to 5 minutes. Drain the pasta and divide among small cloth-lined serving bowls. Serve immediately, with the truffle butter and cheese each alongside for dipping.

❧ WINE PAIRING ☙

These rich Piedmontese-style anellini taste like autumn, a perfect companion for the region's Nebbiolo grape, named after the early-morning fog that rests on the region's vineyards. From the northern Alpine part of Piedmont to the rolling hills of Barolo in the center of the region, Nebbiolo makes wonderful red wines. One of the smallest regions of Piedmont dedicated to Nebbiolo is Carema, located in the foothills of the Alps on the border of Valle d'Aosta. Ferrando Carema DOC, Ettichetta Bianco (White Label) from this area is elegant with fine tannins, floral aromas with wild berry, and dried forest notes. Its good acidity also keeps the palate bright and clean. If you prefer more robust wines, look south to Barolo producers such as Vietti, Bruno Giacosa, and Cavallotto.

POTATO GNOCCHI
with Piennolo Tomatoes and Thai Basil

My grandma made her gnocchi exactly like these (this is her recipe, in fact), but she often sauced them with an unctuous oxtail ragù or her splendid and poetic pork sparerib sauce. The gnocchi are light as feathers and will change your mind if you have always found them heavy or sticky. Follow the steps carefully, as spuds that are too hot or too cold will radically alter the outcome. —*Mario Batali*

For the gnocchi: Cover the potatoes with 3 inches (8 centimeters) of cold water in a large saucepan. Bring to a boil and cook, uncovered, until the potatoes are fork-tender, 25 to 30 minutes.

Drain the potatoes and, while they are hot, peel them, either by using a paring knife to pull back the papery skins or by rubbing off the skins with your fingers (discard the skins). Cut the potatoes into quarters.

Dust a clean work surface with flour. Working over the flour-dusted work surface, pass the potatoes through the potato ricer or food mill, moving the ricer or mill as you press, to form a thin layer of potatoes over the flour. Let the potatoes stand until cooled to room temperature, 10 to 15 minutes. (Cooling the hot potatoes in a thin layer facilitates moisture evaporation, which helps create light and fluffy gnocchi.)

Dust the top of the potatoes with the ½ cup plus 1½ tablespoons (total 70 grams) flour, then pour the eggs over the top. Using your fingers, very gently mix together the potatoes, eggs, and flour, just until the mixture comes together to form a smooth dough. If the dough is still sticking to your fingers, add a light dusting of flour. (As you work, avoid adding too much flour or overworking the dough; the more gently you mix and form the dough, the softer the gnocchi.)

Cut the gnocchi dough into 6 to 8 pieces. Roll each piece into a ½-inch-thick (1.25-centimeter-thick) rope. Cut each rope crosswise into ¾-inch (2-centimeter) pieces. Gently pressing with your thumb, roll each piece on a gnocchi board (or down the back of a fork) to give it the characteristic ridges, and place on a lightly flour-dusted baking sheet. (The gnocchi can be refrigerated on the baking sheet, uncovered, for up to 2 hours before cooking.)

For the sauce: In a bowl, use your hands to gently crush the tomatoes, then transfer to a large (preferably 12-inch or 30-centimeter) skillet. Heat over medium heat just until warmed through, about 2 minutes, then season with the sugar and salt. Remove from the heat and stir in half of the basil leaves.

To serve: Bring a large wide pot of generously salted water to a boil. Use the bench scraper to quickly but gently transfer the gnocchi to the boiling water. Cook until the gnocchi float and then about 30 seconds more (about 1½ minutes total). Using a slotted spoon, transfer the gnocchi to a colander to drain, then add to the skillet with the tomatoes. Toss to coat with the sauce, then divide among serving plates. Drizzle with oil and garnish with the remaining basil. Serve immediately, with cheese if desired.

Serves 4 to 6

GNOCCHI

Generous 1 pound (500 grams) russet potatoes (about 2 medium)

½ cup plus 1½ tablespoons (total 70 grams) unbleached all-purpose flour, plus more for dusting

2 large eggs, lightly beaten

SAUCE

1 (1-kilogram or 35-ounce) jar piennolo tomatoes (see Larder, page xxix), drained, skins removed and discarded

½ teaspoon (2 grams) sugar

½ teaspoon (2 grams) kosher salt

12 small Thai basil leaves

TO SERVE

Kosher salt

Very good extra-virgin olive oil, preferably intense Sicilian (see Larder, page xxix), for drizzling

Freshly grated Pecorino Fiore Sardo cheese (see Larder, page xxv)

SPECIAL EQUIPMENT: a potato ricer or food mill; a bench scraper; a gnocchi board (optional)

WINTER SQUASH CAPPELLACCI
with Brown Butter

Serves 4 to 6

CAPPELLACCI

1¾ pounds (800 grams) butternut squash, cut in half lengthwise and seeded

1 medium sweet potato (500 grams), cut in half lengthwise

1½ tablespoons (22 milliliters) extra-virgin olive oil

Kosher salt

⅓ cup (75 grams) mascarpone cheese

Generous ½ cup (36 grams) freshly grated Parmigiano-Reggiano cheese (at least 24-month aged; see Larder, page xxiv)

1 tablespoon (12 grams) sugar

½ teaspoon (6 grams) finely grated fresh ginger

½ teaspoon (½ gram) freshly grated nutmeg

1 batch Fresh Egg Pasta Dough (page 103)

Semolina flour, for dusting

SAUCE AND GARNISH

Kosher salt

½ pound (226 grams) unsalted European-style butter (such as Plugrá)

2 fresh sage leaves

¾ cup (50 grams) freshly grated Parmigiano-Reggiano cheese (at least 24-month aged; see Larder, page xxiv)

¼ cup plus 2 tablespoons (total 30 grams) coarsely crushed amaretti cookies (see note)

SPECIAL EQUIPMENT: parchment paper; cheesecloth; a pasta or pastry wheel cutter

Emilia-Romagna takes great pride in its stuffed pastas. Cappellacci di zucca hails from the region's city of Ferrara, where the recipe dates to the 17th-century court cuisine of the Este family. In Ferrara, these large, hat-shaped pastas are filled with nutmeg-spiked barucca squash (a sweet variety from the neighboring Veneto region) and served in a rich meat ragù.

In the nearby town of Mantova, tortelli (large ravioli) are stuffed with pumpkin from the Po River Valley, crumbled amaretti cookies, and mostarda (a spicy-sweet preserve of fruit and mustard seeds). Once served at lavish banquets thrown by the ruling Gonzaga family of Renaissance Mantova, tortelli Mantovani are traditionally dressed with lightly browned butter infused with sage.

Here, we combine elements of these two dishes: Large cappellacci, similar to those found in Ferrara, are stuffed with sweet squash, nutmeg, ginger, sugar, and Parmigiano-Reggiano. They are served gently bathed in browned butter and sage, typical of the tortelli from Mantova.

For the cappellacci: Heat the oven to 350°F (177°C). Arrange the squash and sweet potato, cut sides up, on a parchment-lined rimmed baking sheet. Drizzle with the oil and season with salt. Bake until tender, 45 to 50 minutes.

While warm, peel the squash and sweet potato (discard the skins), place in a large bowl, and mash together with a fork. Place the mixture in the center of a doubled 12-inch (30-centimeter) square of cheesecloth. Gather the cloth around the mixture and gently but thoroughly squeeze to remove excess liquid; keep squeezing until the mixture holds its round shape when removed from the cheesecloth. Discard the liquid.

Return the squash mixture to a dry bowl. Add the mascarpone, Parmigiano, sugar, ginger, nutmeg, and 2 teaspoons (8 grams) salt. Stir to combine well. Adjust the seasoning to taste; the filling should be fairly sweet with a nice presence of ginger and nutmeg.

Roll out the pasta dough (as instructed on page 103) until you can just see your hand through the pasta sheets, a scant 1 millimeter thick. Cut 36 (4-inch or 10-centimeter) squares from the sheets. Dollop 1½ tablespoons (20 grams) of filling into the center of each square. Using a finger dipped into water or a water-filled spray bottle, lightly dab or mist the pasta squares to dampen, then fold in half diagonally to form triangles. Press down firmly but gently around the filling to seal edges and extract any air, then trim at sealed edges with a pasta wheel cutter. Bring the 2 longer arms together, overlapping just slightly at the ends, and press to seal. Dust with semolina flour.

To serve: Bring a large wide pot of generously salted water to a low boil. It's best to

either boil and sauce this pasta in two batches or boil all of the pasta at once and use two large skillets to make the sauce and finish the dish, dividing the butter and sage, and then the cooked pasta, between them.

In a large (preferably 12-inch or 30-centimeter) skillet, melt the butter over medium heat. Whisking constantly, continue cooking until the bubbles subside and the butter is evenly dark brown in color, with a nutty, toasty smell, 5 to 7 minutes.Meanwhile, add the pasta to the gently boiling water and cook until just tender (the pieces will puff a bit when ready), about 5 minutes.

To the brown butter, add the sage, then cook 10 seconds longer. Working quickly, use a large slotted spoon to transfer the pasta to the butter sauce (the sauce will bubble and froth slightly). Remove the pan from the heat and gently toss to coat the pasta with sauce. Spoon the pasta onto warmed serving plates. Sprinkle with the Parmigiano and amaretti crumbs. Serve immediately.

NOTE: *Amaretti are crunchy almond-flavored cookies. They can be purchased at Italian markets and online.*

EGG YOLK GNUDI

with Asparagus, Bird's Nest Style

Gnudi, which means "nudes" in Italian, refers to these dumplings as ravioli fillings naked of their pasta wrappers. Often made with ricotta, flour, chard, and spinach in the central regions of Umbria and Tuscany, they are historically a peasant dish. Elevated from the rustic Italian kitchen, these gnudi were created at Del Posto while developing recipes that incorporate black truffle scraps and early spring asparagus. The dish paints a picture of springtime with fresh ricotta "eggs," lacquered in black-truffle butter and impregnated with runny yolks, resting on a nest of shredded raw asparagus.

For the truffle butter: Using a dampened soft mushroom brush, gently loosen and remove any dirt from the truffles. Use the tip of a paring knife to remove any dirt from the crevices, then brush again. Pat dry the cleaned truffles, then finely grate them into a medium bowl. Add the butter and salt. Stir until well combined. Wrap the butter in a sheet of plastic wrap and chill until firm, at least 1 hour or overnight.

For the gnudi: Line a large fine-mesh sieve with a doubled 12-inch (30-centimeter) square of cheesecloth, then set the sieve over a large bowl. Place the ricotta in the sieve, then fold the cheesecloth over. Place a small plate and a weight (e.g., a can of beans) on top. Let the cheese drain overnight in the refrigerator. Meanwhile, prepare the egg yolks.

In a bowl, whisk together 20 of the egg yolks, then divide evenly among 40 (1.2-inch diameter x .6-inch deep) half-sphere molds. Freeze until solid, at least 5 hours or overnight.

Remove the ricotta from the refrigerator; gently but firmly press to remove excess liquid. Discard the liquid. In a large bowl, using your hands, mix together the ricotta, the remaining egg yolk, the flour, pecorino,

Parmigiano, salt, and nutmeg. Divide the gnudi dough into twenty 2-tablespoon (1-ounce or 28-gram) mounds.

Working quickly, remove 2 frozen egg yolk half spheres from the freezer. Put them together to form a sphere. Hold one mound of dough in the palm of your hand. Create a well in the center with your thumb. Place the egg sphere into the well, then gently form the dough evenly around it to create a smooth round ball. Place the gnudi on a flour-dusted tray, then place in the refrigerator. Repeat to form 20 gnudi. (The gnudi will keep, refrigerated, for up to 1 hour before cooking.)

To serve: Bring a large wide pot of generously salted water to a gentle boil. Meanwhile, trim and then julienne the asparagus. In a bowl, toss together the asparagus, oil, and a generous pinch of salt. Form the asparagus into a loose "nest" on each serving plate.

Cut the chilled truffle butter into small pieces. In a small saucepan, bring 2 tablespoons (30 milliliters) water to a boil. Whisking constantly, add the cold butter one piece at a time to create an emulsified sauce. Remove the sauce from the heat.

Using a slotted spoon, gently but quickly lower 10 gnudi into the gently boiling water.

Serves 8 to 10

TRUFFLE BUTTER

3½ ounces (100 grams) fresh white or black truffles (see Larder, page xxix)

14 tablespoons (200 grams) unsalted butter, softened

1 teaspoon (4 grams) kosher salt

GNUDI

1½ pounds (700 grams) fresh whole-milk ricotta cheese (preferably sheep's milk)

21 large egg yolks (380 grams)

⅓ cup (45 grams) "00" flour, plus more for dusting

Generous ¼ cup (17 grams) freshly grated Pecorino Romano Genuino cheese (see Larder, page xxv)

Generous ¼ cup (17 grams) freshly grated Parmigiano-Reggiano cheese (at least 24-month aged; see Larder, page xxiv)

1½ teaspoons (6 grams) kosher salt

Generous pinch freshly grated nutmeg

TO SERVE

Kosher salt

6 medium stalks green asparagus (150 grams)

6 medium stalks white asparagus (150 grams)

1 tablespoon (15 milliliters) very good extra-virgin olive oil, preferably Tuscan (see Larder, page xxix)

SPECIAL EQUIPMENT: cheesecloth; 2 sheets of silicone half-sphere mini molds (each mold cavity should be 1.2-inch diameter and .6 inch deep and hold .3 ounce), and there should be at least 40 forms (see note)

Cook until the gnudi hold a floating position and then about 2 minutes more, about 5 minutes total. The yolks should be heated enough to be melted and runny but not cooked further. Meanwhile, transfer the sauce to a large skillet and warm over very low heat.

With the slotted spoon, transfer the gnudi to a colander to drain and begin cooking the remaining gnudi. Transfer the cooked gnudi to the skillet with the butter. Gently baste the gnudi with the sauce for 30 seconds, then spoon onto the serving plates. Repeat with the remaining gnudi. Serve immediately.

NOTE: *The (1.2-inch diameter × .6-inch deep) silicone half-sphere mini molds can be purchased online or at specialty cooking supply stores.*

LUNE PIENE
with Truffle Butter

Serves 3 to 6

LUNE PIENE (PASTA MOONS)

3 tablespoons (43 grams) unsalted butter

¼ cup (40 grams) unbleached all-purpose flour

1 cup plus 2½ tablespoons (total 275 milliliters) chilled half-and-half

⅓ pound (142 grams) Castelmagno cheese, rind removed and discarded, cheese chopped into small pieces

1 teaspoon (4 grams) kosher salt

1 batch Fresh Egg Pasta Dough (page 103)

Semolina flour, for dusting

TRUFFLE BUTTER

Kosher salt

7½ tablespoons (105 grams) room-temperature unsalted European-style butter (such as Plugrá)

2¾ ounces (75 grams) black truffle, finely grated (see Larder, page xxix)

SPECIAL EQUIPMENT: parchment paper

The result of a ten-year quest to develop a restrained pasta dish that also expresses a genuine taste of luxury, these *lune piene,* or "full moons," typify the elegance of simplicity. Two delicate rounds of fresh pasta are gently fused together with a scant filling of Castelmagno, a semi-hard cheese from the Piedmont with tangy blue veining, then coated with a silken emulsion of truffle and butter. Prepare two to four lune per person, depending on whether you want to serve this as a small primo or main course. If Castelmagno cheese is not available, Gorgonzola, fontina, taleggio, or robiola can be used instead.

For the lune piene: In a medium saucepan, melt the butter over medium heat. Add the flour and whisk until smooth. Continue cooking, whisking occasionally, to form a light golden sandy-colored roux with a rich, nutty aroma, 3 to 5 minutes.

Whisking, add the half-and-half in a slow and steady stream. Continue cooking, whisking constantly, until the mixture is very smooth and one or two bubbles break the surface, 1 to 2 minutes. Add the cheese, reduce the heat to low, and continue to cook, stirring with a rubber spatula, until the cheese is melted and incorporated into the sauce. Remove the filling from the heat and stir in the salt. (The filling can be used as is, or puréed with an immersion blender, with the addition of 2 teaspoons cold water, to further smooth it or if it appears broken.)

Transfer the filling to an airtight container and chill, covered, until ready to use. (The filling can be made ahead and kept refrigerated, with plastic wrap covering the surface and in a covered container, for up to 5 days, or frozen for up to 3 months. Defrost overnight in the refrigerator and stir vigorously with a wooden spoon to smooth out before using. You will have more filling than you need for this recipe—it is challenging to make it in smaller batches.

Freeze leftover filling for future use, to make more lune, another filled pasta, macaroni and cheese, or fondue.) Roll out the pasta dough to the thinnest setting on your pasta machine (as instructed on page 103). Using a 6-inch (15-centimeter) round cutter or a plate, cut out 24 pasta rounds. (You will have leftover pasta, which can be cut into desired shapes and refrigerated or frozen, following instructions on page 103.)

Dollop 1 tablespoon (10 grams) of filling into the center of half of the pasta rounds. Using an offset spatula or the back of a large spoon, spread the filling over the round, leaving a ½-inch (1.25-centimeter) border. Using a finger dipped into water or a water-filled spray bottle, lightly dab or mist the pasta rounds to dampen, then top with remaining dough rounds. Gently press the rounds together to eliminate any air bubbles. Dust with semolina flour. Layer the finished lune between sheets of semolina-dusted parchment paper.

For the truffle butter (and to serve): Bring a large pot of generously salted water to a low boil.

It's best to work in two batches of 6 lune at a time. If your skillet is smaller than 12 inches (30.5 centimeters), work in three

or four even smaller batches of both pasta and sauce. Have your ingredients organized before proceeding.

Add 6 pasta moons to the gently boiling water and cook for 1 minute. Meanwhile, in a 12-inch (30-centimeter) skillet, melt half of the butter over medium heat, then whisk in 3 tablespoons (45 milli-liters) of the pasta cooking water to emulsify. Whisk in half of the grated truffle and a pinch of salt. Remove from the heat and adjust the seasoning to taste.

Using a large slotted spoon, transfer the lune to the butter sauce and gently swirl the pan over the heat for 30 seconds to coat the moons with sauce. Use the slotted spoon to transfer the lune to serving plates, laying them flat, then drizzle with the remaining sauce from the pan and garnish with the remaining grated truffle. Repeat with the remaining lune and sauce. Serve immediately.

❧ WINE PAIRING ❧

This rich combination of butter, truffles, and fresh egg pasta is a perfect foil for Nebbiolo from the Langhe, which is the southern part of the Piedmont region. The Langhe is home to Barolo and Barbaresco, the king and queen of Nebbiolo. It is also home to truffles. Nebbiolo keeps the palate bright but doesn't interfere with the earthen aroma of the shaved truffle. Produttori del Barbaresco is a wonderful producer, making Barbaresco and Nebbiolo Lagnhe DOC with tradition in mind. Their wines are pure, vibrant in their youth and ethereal as they age.

THREE RISOTTOS

Risotto is ubiquitous throughout northern Italy as an alternative to pasta. More than 40 varieties of rice are grown in Italy, with a large majority flourishing in the fertile Po Valley. The cultivation of Italian rice dates back many centuries, and the Milanese have been making superb risotto dishes for equally as long. Risotto's modern popularity began in the middle of the 19th century, shortly after the unification of Italy, when a newly united public works program dredged the 80-mile-long Canale Cavour through central Piedmont. Connecting the Po and Ticino Rivers, this canal provided a vast network of irrigation channels that transformed northern Italy into one of the world's leading producers of high-quality rice.

Each variety of grain commands distinctly different uses, as they all possess varied textures and flavors that perform differently when cooked. Not all of the best rice for risotto comes from the Piedmont; the vialone nano grain is grown mainly in the wet lowlands of the Veneto region and is the preferred rice for risotto at Del Posto. Vialone nano is shorter and rounder than other varietals such as arborio and carnaroli, and absorbs more liquid during cooking, which means that it will release more starch, providing a creamier base for risotto.

Here, three risotto variations all use the same technique for cooking vialone nano. Stirring, polishing, and resting the rice as it cooks, while carefully monitoring the time, is worth the effort for risotto that is toothsome and creamy with the right *all'onda,* or wave, of liquid.

From left to right:
Vaccha Rossae Risotto (page 79);
Mushroom Risotto (page 80);
and Red Wine Risotto with Carrot
Purée (page 78)

RED WINE RISOTTO WITH CARROT PURÉE

Serves 4 to 6

2¼ cups (533 milliliters) dry red wine, preferably Nebbiolo

1 quart (950 milliliters) chicken broth, preferably homemade

3 tablespoons (45 milliliters) extra-virgin olive oil

3 tablespoons (45 grams) unsalted butter

Generous ⅓ cup (50 grams) finely chopped shallots

2 cups (380 grams) vialone nano rice (see headnote)

Kosher salt

¼ pound (118 grams) Castelmagno cheese (see note), rind removed and discarded, cheese crumbled

1 batch Carrot Purée from orecchiette recipe (page 88)

Freshly grated Parmigiano-Reggiano cheese (at least 24-month aged; see Larder, page xxiv), for serving

In a small saucepan, bring 1¾ cups (415 milliliters) of the wine to a boil and cook until reduced to a scant ½ cup (105 milliliters), about 20 minutes. Remove from the heat and set aside to finish the risotto.

In a medium saucepan, combine the broth and 1¾ cups (415 milliliters) water. Bring just to a simmer, then remove from the heat and cover to keep warm.

In a second medium saucepan, heat 1 tablespoon (15 milliliters) of the oil and 1 tablespoon (15 grams) of the butter over medium to medium-low heat until the butter is melted. Add the shallots and cook, stirring occasionally, until softened, about 3 minutes. Add the rice and ½ teaspoon (2 grams) salt and stir to coat with the oil. Toast the rice, stirring occasionally, just until warm and the edges become translucent, 1 to 2 minutes. Add the remaining (uncooked) ½ cup (118 milliliters) red wine and cook, stirring occasionally, until evaporated.

Add ½ cup (118 milliliters) of the hot broth. Cook, occasionally stirring gently with a large heat-proof rubber spatula, until the liquid has been absorbed. Continue to add hot broth in small batches—just enough to completely moisten the rice—and cook, stirring in the same gentle and occasional manner and into the bottom and sides of the pan, until each successive batch has been absorbed. Adjust the heat as necessary to simmer the rice very gently. Cook the rice in this manner for a total of 10 minutes from the first addition of broth.

Continue to add the broth in the same manner and to cook at a very gentle simmer, but switch to a constant stirring action. As you stir, use the flat side of the spatula to "cream" the rice by polishing it in small batches against the inside wall of the pan. As the creamy starch releases from the rice and accumulates on the sides of the pan, scrape and stir it back into the rice. Cook the rice in this manner until it is creamy and just under al dente, a total of 10 to 14 minutes of stirring and polishing.

Stir in just enough of the remaining broth to completely moisten and barely cover the rice. Remove the pan from the heat, cover with a tight-fitting lid, and let stand until the liquid is absorbed and the rice is al dente, about 5 minutes (keep the remaining broth covered and warm).

Return the pan to medium-low heat. Add just enough of the remaining broth to give the risotto a slightly loose wavy consistency (described as *all'onda*, which literally means "with wave"), about ¾ cup (180 milliliters). Stirring constantly, and allowing each ingredient to incorporate before adding the next, add the remaining 2 tablespoons (30 grams) butter, then the crumbled Castelmagno cheese, then the remaining 2 tablespoons (30 milliliters) oil, and finally the reduced wine. Remove the pan from the heat and adjust the seasoning to taste.

Spoon and spread the carrot purée onto serving plates, then spoon the risotto on top. Serve immediately, sprinkled with Parmigiano, as desired.

NOTE: *If Castelmagno cheese is not available, Gorgonzola, fontina, Taleggio, or robiola can be used instead.*

VACCHE ROSSE RISOTTO

In a medium saucepan, combine the chicken stock and 1¾ cups (415 milliliters) water. Bring just to a simmer, then remove from the heat and cover to keep warm.

In a second medium saucepan, heat 1 tablespoon (15 milliliters) of the oil and 1 tablespoon (15 grams) of the butter over medium to medium-low heat until the butter is melted. Add the shallots and cook, stirring occasionally, until softened, about 3 minutes. Add the rice and ½ teaspoon (2 grams) salt and stir to coat with the oil. Toast the rice, stirring occasionally, just until warm and the edges become translucent, 1 to 2 minutes. Add the wine and cook, stirring occasionally, until evaporated.

Add ½ cup (118 milliliters) of the hot broth. Cook, occasionally stirring gently with a large heat-proof rubber spatula, until the liquid has been absorbed. Continue to add hot broth in small batches—just enough to completely moisten the rice—and cook, stirring in the same gentle and occasional manner and into the bottom and sides of the pan, until each successive batch has been absorbed. Adjust the heat as necessary to simmer the rice very gently. Cook the rice in this manner for a total of 10 minutes from the first addition of broth.

Continue to add the broth in the same manner and to cook at a very gentle simmer, but switch to a constant stirring action. As you stir, use the flat side of the spatula to "cream" the rice by polishing it in small batches against the inside wall of the pan. As the creamy starch releases from the rice and accumulates on the sides of the pan, scrape and stir it back into the rice. Cook the rice in this manner until it is creamy and just under al dente, a total of 10 to 14 minutes of stirring and polishing.

Stir in just enough of the remaining broth to completely moisten and barely cover the rice. Remove the pan from the heat, cover with a tight-fitting lid, and let stand until the liquid is absorbed and the rice is al dente, about 5 minutes (keep the remaining broth covered and warm).

CONTINUED

Serves 4 to 6

1 quart (50 milliliters) chicken stock, preferably homemade

3 tablespoons (45 milliliters) extra-virgin olive oil

3 tablespoons (45 grams) unsalted butter

Generous ⅓ cup (50 grams) finely chopped shallots

2 cups (380 grams) vialone nano rice (see headnote)

Kosher salt

½ cup (118 milliliters) dry white wine

Generous 1½ cups (100 grams) freshly grated Parmigiano-Reggiano Vacche Rosse cheese (at least 24-month aged; see Larder, page xxiv), plus more for serving

25-year aceto balsamico tradizionale (see Larder, page xxvi), for drizzling

---

❧ WINE PAIRING ❧

The Vacche Rosse cheese in this risotto is tangy, rich, and unlike any other hard cheese in Italy. The risotto calls for a wine to fill the background, giving the cheese and creamy rice time to evolve on the palate. Look to the Asti region of Piedmont for the deep red Barbera. A vibrant grape with loads of natural acidity, Barbera cuts through the rich risotto without overriding the flavors of the Vacche Rosse. Giacomo Bologna, Prunotto, and Pio Cesare are three standout producers in Asti—each of them produces a single vineyard Barbera. Giacomo Bologna's Bricco dell'Uccellone is one of the most recognized wines from the region. Prunotto's Costamiol and Pio Cesare's Fides are also wonderful examples of Barbera winemaking at its best.

Return the pan to medium-low heat. Add just enough of the remaining broth to give the risotto a slightly loose wavy consistency (described as *all'onda,* which literally means "the wave"), about ¾ cup (180 milliliters). Stirring constantly, and allowing each ingredient to incorporate before adding the next, add the remaining 2 tablespoons (30 grams) butter, then the Parmigiano, then the remaining 2 table-spoons (30 milliliters) oil. Remove the pan from the heat and adjust the seasoning to taste. Serve immediately, drizzled with the aceto balsamico and sprinkled with extra Parmigiano, as desired.

Serves 4 to 6

2 pounds (906 grams) button mushrooms

Kosher salt

½ pound (225 grams) hen of the woods or other wild mushrooms

7 tablespoons (105 milliliters) extra-virgin olive oil

2 garlic cloves (8 grams), gently smashed and peeled

2 leafy thyme sprigs

3 tablespoons (945 grams) unsalted butter

Generous ⅓ cup (50 grams) finely chopped shallots

2 cups (380 grams) vialone nano rice (see headnote)

½ cup (118 milliliters) dry white wine

Generous 1½ cups (100 grams) freshly grated Parmigiano-Reggiano cheese (at least 24-month aged; see Larder, page xxiv), plus more for serving

MUSHROOM RISOTTO

Clean the button mushrooms and place in a large saucepan. Add 2½ quarts (2.3 liters) water and 1½ teaspoons (6 grams) salt. Bring to a gentle simmer, then cook for 45 minutes. Strain the broth into a large bowl, gently pressing on the mushrooms to extract all of the liquid (discard the mushrooms or save them for another use). Measure the broth, then return it to the saucepan. Add enough water to make a total of 5¾ cups (1.3 liters) of liquid. Bring just to a simmer, then remove the broth from the heat. Adjust the seasoning to taste.

Clean the wild mushrooms and pat well dry with paper towels, then thinly slice. Heat a large skillet over medium-high heat until hot. Add 2 tablespoons (30 milliliters) of the oil and half of the mushrooms and a pinch of salt. Cook (do not stir or season) until the edges are deep golden brown, about 3 minutes. Add 1 garlic clove and 1 thyme sprig, and continue to cook, tossing occasionally, until the mushrooms are just tender, about 2 minutes more. Season with salt to taste, then transfer to a large plate. Wipe the pan clean with a paper towel and repeat with 2 tablespoons (30 milliliters) of the oil and the remaining mushrooms, garlic, and thyme.

Return the broth just to a simmer, then remove from the heat and cover to keep warm.

In a second medium saucepan, heat 1 tablespoon (15 milliliters) of the oil and 1 tablespoon (15 grams) of the butter over medium to medium-low heat until the butter is melted. Add the shallots and cook, stirring occasionally, until softened, about 3 minutes. Add the rice and ½ teaspoon (2 grams) salt and stir to coat with the oil. Toast the rice, stirring occasionally, just until warm and the edges become translucent, 1 to 2 minutes. Add the wine and cook, stirring occasionally, until evaporated.

Add ½ cup (118 milliliters) of the hot broth. Cook, occasionally stirring gently with a large heat-proof rubber spatula, until the liquid has been absorbed. Continue to add hot broth in small batches—just enough to completely moisten the rice—and cook, stirring in the same gentle and occasional manner and into the bottom and sides of the pan, until each successive batch has been absorbed. Adjust the heat as necessary to simmer the rice very gently. Cook the rice in this manner for a total of 10 minutes from the first addition of broth.

Continue to add the broth in the same manner and to cook at a very gentle simmer,

but switch to a constant and vigorous stirring action. As you stir, use the flat side of the spatula to "cream" the rice by polishing it in small batches against the inside wall of the pan. As the creamy starch releases from the rice and accumulates on the sides of the pan, scrape and stir it back into the rice. Cook the rice in this manner until it is creamy and just under al dente, a total of 10 to 14 minutes of stirring and polishing.

Stir in just enough of the remaining broth to completely moisten and barely cover the rice. Remove the pan from the heat, cover with a tight-fitting lid, and let stand until the liquid is absorbed and the rice is al dente, about 5 minutes. (Keep the remaining broth covered and warm.)

Return the pan to medium-low heat. Add just enough of the remaining broth to give the risotto a slightly loose wavy consistency (described as *all'onda*, which literally means "the wave"), about ¾ cup (180 milliliters). Stirring constantly and allowing each ingredient to incorporate before adding the next, add the remaining 2 tablespoons (30 grams) butter, then the Parmigiano, then the remaining 2 table-spoons (30 milliliters) oil.

Remove the pan from the heat. Fold in the mushrooms, then adjust the seasoning to taste. Serve immediately, sprinkled with extra Parmigiano, as desired.

LIDIA'S JOTA

with Smoky Pork and Braised Kale

Serves 6 to 8

WHITE BEAN SOUP

2 cups (390 grams) dried
cannellini beans

1 celery rib (80 grams),
coarsely chopped

½ small yellow onion (75 grams),
coarsely chopped

1 medium carrot (75 grams),
coarsely chopped

1 bay leaf

Kosher salt

½ cup (118 milliliters) extra-virgin olive oil

1 tablespoon plus 1 teaspoon
(total 20 milliliters) white wine vinegar

SMOKED PORK BUTT

3 tablespoons (36 grams) sugar

2 tablespoons (14 grams) coarsely
ground black peppercorns

1 tablespoon (12 grams) kosher salt

1 teaspoon (4 grams) Hungarian paprika

1 pound boneless pork shoulder
or butt roast (not tied)

Cherrywood chips, or your
preferred smoking chips

BRAISED KALE

1 vegetable bouillon cube

1½ tablespoons (22 milliliters)
extra-virgin olive oil

1 garlic clove (4 grams),
gently smashed and peeled

1 cup (90 grams) finely chopped
yellow onion

1 bunch kale (225 grams), center ribs
and stems removed, leaves coarsely
chopped

CONTINUED

In and around the beautiful city of Trieste and throughout Istria, every home and every trattoria has a pot of this hearty soup perking on the stove, especially during the winter months. Most Americans have tried pasta e fagioli or a pasta and bean soup, but Jota's combination of beans and sauerkraut is unique and a perfect example of the Slavic influence on the culinary culture of Trieste. The soup is typically made in big batches and improves after a day or two in the refrigerator. Make sure you do not lose all the acidity from the sauerkraut when you rinse it. *–Lidia Bastianich*

Lidia's Jota recipe is a perfect interpretation of this classic soup from her childhood in Istria. In most versions of this recipe, pork shoulder is braised or stewed with the beans. At Del Posto, smoky flavors are added by slow-smoking a pork butt instead. If you don't have a smoker at home for the pork butt, see the note at the end of the recipe. At the restaurant, the soup base is poured over the pork and sauerkraut mixture at the table.

For the bean soup: In a large saucepan, combine the beans, celery, onion, carrot, bay leaf, and 2½ quarts (2.3 liters) cold water. Soak the beans for 8 hours or overnight.

Place the saucepan with the soaked beans and their liquid and vegetables over medium heat. Bring the liquid to a simmer, then adjust the heat to cook at a gentle simmer, skimming any foam from the surface, until the beans are very tender (some will be broken), 45 to 50 minutes. (Dried beans vary in freshness. Older beans may require longer cooking times. Keep cooking, if necessary, adding water as needed to keep the beans covered by at least 1 inch [2.5 centimeters], until they are very tender.)

Remove and discard the bay leaf. Using a slotted spoon, transfer the vegetables and all but ⅓ cup (60 grams) of the beans to a blender. Add 2½ cups (½ liter) of the bean cooking liquid (reserve the remaining liquid) and 1 tablespoon (12 grams) salt,

then purée until smooth. With the machine running, drizzle in the oil and vinegar. Adjust the seasoning to taste. Cover and refrigerate the soup and the reserved liquid and beans until ready to serve. (The soup can be made ahead and refrigerated for up to 3 days.)

For the smoked pork butt (see note): In a small bowl, mix together the sugar, pepper, salt, and paprika. Rub the mixture all over the pork and inside any cavities. Heat the smoker to 275°F (135°C) and add the chips according to the manufacturer's instructions. Put the pork directly on the smoker rack with the fat side up. Smoke until tender, 2½ to 3 hours, then transfer to a plate and let cool completely.

For the braised kale: In a small bowl, dissolve the vegetable base or bouillon cube in 1 cup (236 milliliters) water. Set aside. In a medium saucepan, combine the oil and

TO SERVE

⅓ pound (150 grams) smoked
slab bacon, cut into ½-inch
(1.25-centimeter) cubes

1½ tablespoons (21 milliliters)
extra-virgin olive oil

1 cup (120 grams) drained sauerkraut

SPECIAL EQUIPMENT: a smoker
(optional; see note)

garlic. Heat over medium-low heat until the garlic is fragrant and lightly golden, about 4 minutes. Add the onion and cook, stirring occasionally, until tender, 3 to 4 minutes more. Add the reserved vegetable base mixture and bring to a simmer, then stir in the kale. Cover and gently simmer, stirring occasionally, until the kale is very tender, about 45 minutes.

To serve: In a large skillet, cook the bacon over medium heat, stirring occasionally, until the fat is rendered and the edges are crispy, 12 to 15 minutes. Meanwhile, in a large saucepan, gently warm the soup, thinning it with the reserved cooking liquid as desired. Pull apart the smoked pork into ½-inch (1.25-centimeter) pieces.

Transfer the bacon to a plate and pour off the fat from the pan (reserve the fat to drizzle over the soup, if you like); wipe the skillet dry with paper towels. Return the bacon to the skillet. Add the smoked pork, braised kale, and the oil and sauerkraut. Heat over medium-high heat, stirring frequently, until the mixture is heated through, about 3 minutes. Divide the pork mixture and reserved beans among shallow serving bowls, then ladle the soup over the top.

NOTE: *If you don't have a smoker, or lack the time to smoke the pork, you can use ¾ pound (340 grams) of smoked pulled pork from your local barbecue restaurant (ask them to leave off the barbecue sauce). Or you can use the spice mixture and pork as indicated here, but bake the pork in a roasting pan, fat side up, at 275°F (135°C) until it is very tender and beginning to fall apart, about 3 hours. The pork can also be omitted altogether.*

PASTA FAGIOLI
with 'Nduja and Tripe Meatballs

Pasta fagioli is one of many Italian dishes with humble beginnings. From region to region, this classic bean soup is interpreted in countless ways. In the North, borlotti beans, pork fat, and grated cheese make for hearty, cool-weather variations. In the central and southern regions, cannellini beans are preferred and sometimes tomato is included. Some recipes are prepared with lard, others with olive oil, and some with broth. The Tuscans are the most boastful of their versions as they have a long-standing tradition of growing heritage beans, giving them the nickname *mangiafagioli,* or "bean eaters."

This variation of the dish breaks from regional traditions and includes tripe meatballs, which were originally developed while creating the recipe for Del Posto's homemade 'nduja, a spicy spreadable sausage from Calabria (see page 54). By experimenting with the recipe for the sausage, which included tripe and pork shoulder, these remarkable—mostly tripe—meatballs were born, almost by accident. Rich and slightly spicy, the meatballs add an unexpected depth and tang to classic pasta fagioli. The soup base is the same as the base for Lidia's Jota (page 82).

For the bean soup: In a large saucepan, combine the beans, celery, onion, carrot, bay leaf, and 2½ quarts (2.3 liters) cold water. Soak the beans for 8 hours or overnight.

Place the saucepan with the soaked beans and their liquid and vegetables over medium heat. Bring the liquid to a simmer, then adjust the heat to cook at a gentle simmer, skimming any foam from the surface, until the beans are very tender (some will be broken), 45 to 50 minutes. (Dried beans vary in freshness. Older beans may require longer cooking times. Keep cooking, if necessary, adding water as needed to keep the beans covered by at least 1 inch [2.5 centimeters], until they are very tender.)

Remove and discard the bay leaf. Using a slotted spoon, transfer the vegetables and all but ⅓ cup (60 grams) of the beans to a blender. Add 2½ cups (½ liter) of the bean cooking liquid (reserve the remaining liquid) and 1 tablespoon (12 grams) salt, then purée until smooth. With the machine running, drizzle in the oil and vinegar. Adjust the seasoning to taste. Cover and refrigerate the soup and the reserved liquid and beans until ready to serve. (The soup can be made ahead and refrigerated for up to 3 days.)

For the meatballs: Trim any solid pieces of fat from the tripe, then rinse thoroughly under cold running water. Place the tripe in a large wide pot. Add 1 tablespoon (15 milliliters) of the vinegar and enough water to cover the tripe by 2 inches (5 centimeters). Bring to a boil, reduce to a simmer, and cook for 30 minutes. Drain and repeat twice.

Serves 6 to 8

BEAN SOUP

2 cups (390 grams) dried cannellini beans

1 celery rib (80 grams), coarsely chopped

½ small yellow onion (75 grams), coarsely chopped

1 medium carrot (75 grams), coarsely chopped

1 bay leaf

Kosher salt

½ cup (118 milliliters) extra-virgin olive oil

1 tablespoon plus 1 teaspoon (total 20 milliliters) white wine vinegar

'NDUJA AND TRIPE MEATBALLS

1 pound (453 grams) honeycomb veal tripe

3 tablespoons (45 milliliters) white wine vinegar

2 celery ribs (180 grams), coarsely chopped

1 small yellow onion (150 grams), coarsely chopped

2 medium carrots (150 grams), coarsely chopped

1 whole vanilla bean

2 bay leaves

1¾ cups (100 grams) panko (Japanese breadcrumbs)

3 tablespoons plus 1 teaspoon (total 50 milliliters) whole milk

Scant ½ cup (100 grams) 'nduja sausage (see note)

1 large egg

CONTINUED

Return the tripe to the pot. Add the celery, onion, carrots, vanilla bean, bay leaves, and water to cover by 2 inches (5 centimeters). Bring to a boil, then reduce to a simmer and cook, adding water if necessary to keep the tripe just covered, until it is tender when pierced with a fork, 2 to 2½ hours. Remove the pot from the heat and let the tripe cool completely in the cooking liquid. (The tripe can be braised ahead and refrigerated, tightly wrapped in plastic, for up to 1 day, or frozen for up to 1 month.)

In a small bowl, stir together the panko and milk; set aside. Remove the tripe from the pot and discard the cooking liquid. Meanwhile, finely chop enough of the tripe to yield ¾ cup (100 grams), then place in a large bowl (save the remaining tripe for another use). Add the 'nduja and mix together until well blended. Stir in the panko mixture and egg to combine. Cover and refrigerate for 10 minutes.

To serve: Heat the oven to 400°F (205°C). Bring a large pot of salted water to a boil. Form the tripe mixture into 16 meatballs (each about 1 inch or 2.5 centimeters in diameter) and place on a baking sheet at least 1 inch (2.5 centimeters) apart. Bake until the meatballs are warmed through and a very light crust forms, about 12 minutes. Meanwhile, cook the pasta in the boiling water until al dente, then drain. In a medium saucepan, gently warm the soup, thinning it with the reserved cooking liquid, if and as desired.

Divide the reserved beans, meatballs, and pasta among shallow serving bowls. Ladle the soup into the bowls. Drizzle with oil and garnish with rice crackers or grilled bread, if desired.

NOTE: *'Nduja is a spicy, spreadable cured Calabrian pork sausage. You can make your own version of 'nduja sausage with the Del Posto's recipe (page 54), or purchase the sausage at Italian markets or online.*

TO SERVE

½ cup (50 grams) small dried pasta shapes, such as ditalini, stelline, or broken pieces of linguine strands

Very good extra-virgin olive oil for drizzling, preferably Tuscan (see Larder, page xxix)

Rice crackers or grilled bread (optional)

WINE PAIRING

A southern Italian rosato frames the combination of earthy, spicy, and gamy flavors in this new take on a classic dish. When pairing wine it is important to consider what recipes come before and after any dish. Rosato from the Calabria, home of 'nduja, offers a nice transition between the whites from the beginning of the meal and the reds to follow for the second and third courses. Calabria produces rosato made from the native grape Gagglioppo, which provides a lively fruit-forward pairing for this dish. Across the Strait of Messina from Calabria, at the foot of Mt. Etna, a tiny region called Faro produces unique rosato. Bonavita Faro Rosato is a plump fruit-forward pairing that balances out spice and complements the savory qualities of the beans and tripe meatballs.

ORECCHIETTE
with Red Lamb Sausage and Carrot Purée

Serves 4 to 6

RED LAMB SAUSAGE

3 tablespoons (45 grams) finely chopped roasted red peppers (roasted at home or from a jar)

1 tablespoon (15 milliliters) dry red wine

1 medium garlic clove (4 grams), coarsely chopped

2 teaspoons (8 grams) kosher salt

1¼ teaspoons (4 grams) sweet paprika

½ teaspoon (1.5 grams) smoked paprika

½ teaspoon (2 grams) freshly ground black pepper

1 pound (453 grams) lamb shoulder, coarsely ground (see notes)

ORECCHIETTE

1 cup (165 grams) durum flour

1 cup (165 grams) semolina flour

¾ cup (110 grams) "00" flour

RYE BREADCRUMBS

5 slices rye bread (⅓ inch or 8 millimeters thick)

CARROT PURÉE

9½ ounces (270 grams) carrots (plus the carrot tops for garnish, if available)

1 cup (236 milliliters) carrot juice

1 teaspoon (5 grams) sugar

Kosher salt

1½ teaspoons (7 milliliters) tangerine oil (see notes)

CONTINUED

Orecchiette, or "little ears," are small cup-shaped pastas that belong to the *pasta corta,* or "short pasta," family. Made from a water-based dough, they are typical of pasta from southern Italy, where less wealthy kitchens couldn't afford the eggs used in northern pastas. Orecchiette come in both fresh and dried variations. They are shaped by pressing and then pulling small pieces of dough off the tip of the thumb, and each cup is carefully turned inside out, producing a rough, striated surface. While they are associated with the region of Puglia, orecchiette are also found in the neighboring Abruzzo, Campania, Molise, and Basilicata regions, where they may be called *orecchie di prete* and *recchietelle.* In Puglia, orecchiette are traditionally served with turnip greens or broccoli rabe—historically, meat was a luxury in the region.

This Del Posto recipe pulls orecchiette from the cucina povera of southern Italy into a decidedly luxurious dish with lamb sausage. Ground lamb shoulder is mixed with paprika and roasted red peppers for a fresh sausage. The sausage is seared until charred on one side before being broken into pieces small enough to fit inside the cups of the cooked orrecchiette. The pasta is finished with an emulsion of the rendered lamb fat, chicken broth, and butter, then dotted with a tangerine-infused carrot purée.

For the sausage: In a blender, combine the roasted red peppers, wine, and garlic and purée until smooth. In a medium bowl, mix together the salt, sweet paprika, smoked paprika, and black pepper. Add the lamb and, using your hands, mix together just until the spices are evenly distributed throughout the meat. Add the purée and mix together to combine. Cover and refrigerate at least 1 hour or overnight.

For the orecchiette: In a large bowl, use your hands to mix together the durum, semolina, and "00" flours, then form a well in the center. Add ¾ cup (177 milliliters) water to the well. Using your hands, mix together until the water is absorbed, then transfer the dough and any flour or bits remaining in the bowl to a clean work surface. With both hands, using your palms primarily, knead the dough until it forms a shaggy but fairly cohesive mass, about 6 minutes. As you work the dough, rip it apart from time to time to expose some of the moisture inside, then push it back together. Once the dough is mostly together, wrap it in plastic and let it rest 10 minutes, then unwrap and knead for 4 to 5 minutes more. You can lightly mist the dough once or twice with water, if needed, but resist the temptation to add more water. This dough is drier than classic

Kosher salt

Scant ½ cup (105 milliliters) chicken broth, preferably homemade

14 tablespoons (200 grams) unsalted butter, cut into small pieces

Scant ½ cup (25 grams) freshly grated Parmigiano-Reggiano cheese (at least 24-month aged; see Larder, page xxiv)

Scant ½ cup (25 grams) freshly grated Pecorino Romano Genuino cheese (see Larder, page xxv)

1½ tablespoons (22 grams) very good extra-virgin olive oil, preferably Ligurian (such as Ceppo Antico, see page xxix)

egg pasta dough, and it produces a deliciously toothsome pasta.

Wrap the dough tightly in plastic wrap and let rest at room temperature at least 15 minutes or up to 1 hour before using. (The dough can be made ahead and kept tightly wrapped and refrigerated for up to 1 day, or formed into orecchiette and frozen for up to 1 month.)

Divide the dough into 6 pieces. Roll one dough piece into a ⅓-inch-diameter (8-millimeter-diameter) rope (keeping the remaining pieces covered with plastic wrap).

Using a table knife, cut the rope crosswise into ½-inch (1.25-centimeter) pieces. With the side of your thumb, gently but firmly press one piece to just flatten it into a coin-like shape, then simultaneously gently but firmly press and drag the coin to create a small lip. Flip the coin over your forefinger to create a small "ear" shape, with the inner surface now on the outside. Transfer the orecchiette to a lightly floured baking sheet and repeat with the remaining pieces and dough.

For the rye breadcrumbs: Heat the oven to 300°F (149°C). Place the bread slices in a single layer on a baking sheet. Bake until the bread is dried out and lightly toasted, 22 to 25 minutes. Let cool completely; then, in a food processor, pulse to form coarse crumbs. Transfer the crumbs to a medium-mesh sieve set over a bowl. Sift out any fine crumbs, which can be discarded or saved for another use. Set aside the coarse crumbs.

For the carrot purée: Trim and peel the carrots. If you have the tops, rinse them well, then pat dry and finely chop about 1 tablespoon to sprinkle over the pasta for garnish. Place in a small bowl, cover with a damp paper towel, and refrigerate until ready to use. Cut enough of the carrots crosswise into ½-inch (1.25-centimeter) rounds to yield 1 cup (150 grams). Cut the remaining carrots into ¼-inch (6-millimeter) dice and set aside.

Combine the carrot rounds, juice, sugar, and 1 teaspoon (2 grams) salt in a small saucepan. Bring the liquid to a boil, then reduce to a gentle simmer and cook until the carrots are very tender, skimming any foam from the surface, about 12 minutes.

Using a slotted spoon, transfer the cooked carrot rounds to a blender (reserving the cooking liquid for the purée and to cook the diced carrots). Add ¼ cup (60 milliliters) of the cooking liquid, then purée until smooth. Transfer the purée to a small bowl.

Add the diced carrots to the pan with the remaining cooking liquid. Add water to just cover, if necessary. Cook at a gentle simmer until the carrots are crisp-tender, about 2 minutes. Drain and rinse the carrots under cold running water (to stop the cooking), then fold them into the purée, along with the tangerine oil. Season with salt to taste.

To serve: Pat the sausage mixture into a 5-inch-diameter (13-centimeter-diameter) patty and place it in the center of a dry 12-inch (30-centimeter) skillet. Place the pan over medium heat and cook the sausage until the bottom is charred and crispy (the top will remain raw), about 35 minutes. When the sausage has about 15 minutes to go, bring a large pot of salted water to a boil.

When you have a charred, crispy bottom on the sausage, remove the pan from the heat and pour off the fat from the pan and discard. Add the broth and, using tongs or a wooden spoon, break up the sausage into

small pieces. Return the pan to medium-low heat. Add the butter and cook, moving the pan back and forth over the heat, until the butter is melted and incorporated into the sauce. Remove from the heat.

Cook the pasta in the boiling water until al dente, about 3 minutes. Drain, then add to the pan with the sauce. Cook over medium heat, tossing occasionally, until the sauce thickens and begins to coat the pasta, 1 to 2 minutes. Remove from the heat. Stirring the pasta, add the Parmigiano and pecorino cheeses. Stir until the sauce is creamy, then drizzle in the oil and toss to combine.

Spoon the pasta onto serving plates. Dollop the carrot purée on top, then sprinkle with the breadcrumbs and a pinch of carrot tops, if using. Serve immediately.

NOTES: *You can ask your butcher to coarsely grind the lamb, or do it yourself: Cut the lamb into 1-inch (2.5-centimeter) cubes and chill in the freezer for 30 minutes. Then, in three or four batches, pulse in a food processor until coarsely ground. Tangerine oil can be purchased in Italian specialty shops or online. Alternatively, you can substitute 1½ teaspoons (7 milliliters) mild, fruity extra-virgin olive oil and 1 teaspoon (1 gram) finely grated orange zest.*

AGNOLOTTI CACIO E PEPE

Golden pasta pockets stuffed with a mixture of ground veal, onions, and pancetta, agnolotti come from the Emilia-Romagna region. This was one of our first recipes at Del Posto; at the time, it seemed very extravagant to purchase ingredients expressly for pasta filling—rather than using the scraps and leftovers.

A regional hybrid, this preparation for agnolotti borrows the classic Roman sauce cheese and pepper, or *cacio e pepe*. There is a lot of talk among traditionalists about the value of using the starchy pasta water as the secret emulsifier for cacio e pepe. Yes, it does work to cream the sauce, and yes, this technique is traditional. But its benefits are often exaggerated. There is more value in quality ingredients and time-tested technique. We use coarsely ground Indian Tellicherry black peppercorns, toasted until fragrant. The sharp and salty sheep's-milk Pecorino Romano Genuino and delicate Sicilian olive oil add intense savory notes that balance out the spicy pepper. The creamy and lactic qualities of a good 24-month-aged Parmigiano-Reggiano cheese and the chilled butter make for a stable emulsion. The final result is a sauce that clings and grabs the pasta while also remaining velvety and fluid.

For the agnolotti: Heat a large skillet over medium-high heat. Add the oil and heat just until it is hot but not smoking. Add the veal, then season with 1 teaspoon (4 grams) salt. Cook, turning once, until the veal is browned on both sides, 2 to 3 minutes. Transfer the veal to a plate.

Add the pancetta to the skillet and cook over medium-high heat until the fat begins to render, 2 to 3 minutes. Add the garlic and cook, turning occasionally, until fragrant and lightly golden, 1 minute more (the pancetta will be golden now, as well). Add the onion, reduce the heat to medium, and continue cooking, stirring occasionally, until the onion begins to soften, 3 to 4 minutes. Add the wine and cook until the liquid is mostly evaporated, then add the veal back to the pan and cook 1 minute more. Add the broth.

Transfer the pan contents to a medium saucepan. Add 1 cup (238 milliliters) water and bring to a simmer. Gently simmer, covered, until the veal is very tender, 1½ to 2 hours.

Stir the prosciutto into the veal mixture, then transfer the pan contents to a metal bowl and chill in an ice bath or in the refrigerator until the meat is cooled to room temperature.

Strain the veal and solids from the liquid, then finely chop with a mezzaluna or pulse in a food processor until just puréed but not pasty. Transfer the filling to a bowl and fold in the cheese. (The filling, which makes double what you need for this recipe, can be made ahead, divided in two, and kept in an airtight container, refrigerated for up to 3 days or frozen for up to 1 month.)

Serves 4 to 6

AGNOLOTTI

1½ tablespoons (22 milliliters) extra-virgin olive oil

1 pound (453 grams) veal shoulder, chuck, or top round, cut into 1-inch (2.5-centimeter) cubes

Kosher salt

4½ ounces (125 grams) pancetta, cut into 1-inch (2.5-centimeter) pieces

3 garlic cloves (16 grams), gently smashed and peeled

1 medium yellow onion (250 grams), thinly sliced

3 tablespoons (45 milliliters) dry white wine

1 cup (238 milliliters) chicken broth, preferably homemade

⅓ pound (150 grams) prosciutto, cut into small pieces, then finely chopped in a food processor or by hand

3 tablespoons (13 grams) freshly grated Parmigiano-Reggiano cheese (at least 24-month aged; see Larder, page xxiv)

½ batch Fresh Egg Pasta Dough (page 103)

Semolina flour, for dusting

CACIO E PEPE

Kosher salt

2 tablespoons (14 grams) coarsely ground black peppercorns, preferably Indian Tellicherry

¼ cup plus 2 teaspoons (total 70 milliliters) extra-virgin olive oil, preferably delicate Sicilian (see Larder, page xxix)

½ pound plus 2 tablespoons (total 256 grams) cold unsalted butter, cut into small pieces

CONTINUED

1 cup (64 grams) freshly grated Parmigiano-Reggiano cheese (at least 24-month aged; see Larder, page xxiv)

1 cup (64 grams) freshly grated Pecorino Romano Genuino cheese (see Larder, page xxv)

SPECIAL EQUIPMENT: a pasta or pastry wheel cutter

To form the agnolotti: Roll out the pasta dough (as instructed on page 103) until you can just see your hand through the pasta sheets, 1 to 2 millimeters thick.

Working quickly with one sheet at a time (keeping the remaining sheets covered as instructed on page 103), cut one sheet lengthwise into long strips that are 2½ inches (6.35 centimeters) wide. Place scant ½-teaspoon (3-gram) dollops of filling down the center of each strip, covering half of the strip and spacing them about 1 inch (2½ centimeters) apart.

Using a finger dipped into water or a water-filled spray bottle, lightly dab or mist the pasta strips to dampen. Fold the top of the pasta down to the bottom and pinch closed, then pinch the pasta between the lumps of filling (upright, not into the table). Using a fluted pasta wheel cutter, trim the long edge of the dough, then cut between the lumps of filling. Dust with semolina flour.

For the cacio e pepe (and to serve): Bring a large wide pot of generously salted water to a low boil. Add the agnolotti and gently boil until the pieces float to the surface and puff up, 4 to 5 minutes. Meanwhile, prepare the sauce.

In a 12-inch (30-centimeter) skillet, gently toast the pepper over medium-low heat until it is aromatic, about 1 minute. Add 2 teaspoons (10 grams) of the oil, then remove the pan from the heat. Add ¼ cup plus 3 tablespoons (100 milliliters) of water to stop the pepper from cooking further. Add the butter and a pinch of salt to the pan and return to low heat, stirring occasionally as the butter melts and the sauce emulsifies.

Drain the pasta, then immediately add it to the skillet with the sauce. Cook over medium-low heat for 30 seconds, then remove the pan from the heat. Stirring constantly with a rubber spatula, quickly sprinkle in the Parmigiano and pecorino cheeses, then drizzle in the remaining ¼ cup (60 milliliters) oil. A splash of water can be used to loosen the sauce, if necessary. Adjust the seasoning to taste. Serve immediately.

BIGOLI WITH DUCK LIVER RAGÙ

Bigoli are hearty string-pasta tubes made from whole-wheat dough extruded through a traditional, hand-cranked pasta machine called a *torchio*. They are a local specialty in northeastern regions of Italy, especially in the Veneto, where they are often paired with different types of waterfowl.

The marshlands and lagoons just north of Venice have long been home to an abundance of aquatic bird life. Starting in the 13th century, the *doge*, the head of the Venetian Republic until the 19th century, organized large-scale hunts on the Marano lagoons. These annual hunting parties chased large red-footed ducks, called *osele selvareghe da i pie rossi* in the local dialect, which the doge gave as gifts to the Venetian nobles at Christmastime. Since then, waterfowl have been recognized as a noble ingredient in the local cuisine.

Extracting the rich and sumptuous flavors from different parts of the duck, this recipe conjures an era of noble dining in the Veneto. Fresh-made bigoli are boiled in homemade duck broth, tossed in duck liver ragù, and then finished with shavings of frozen foie gras.

For the duck broth: Heat the oven to 450°F (232°C) with the rack in the middle. Line a rimmed baking sheet with parchment paper.

Place the duck neck and bones on the prepared baking sheet in a single layer. Roast, rotating the pan halfway through, until the bones are deep golden brown, but never burnt or black, about 45 minutes.

In a 4- to 5-quart (3.7- to 4.7-liter) Dutch oven or a wide heavy pot, heat the oil over medium heat. Add the onion, celery, and carrots and cook, stirring occasionally, until the vegetables are lightly golden and tender, 10 to 12 minutes. Add the roasted duck bones and the bay leaf, then the broth. Gently simmer until the broth is flavorful, about 2 hours. Meanwhile, prepare the bigoli.

For the bigoli: In a large bowl, use your hands to mix together the whole-wheat and "00" flours, then form a well in the center.

Add the milk and eggs to the well. Using a fork, gently break up the yolks and slowly incorporate the flour mixture from the inside rim of the well. Continue until the liquid is absorbed (about half of the flour will be incorporated). With both hands, using your palms primarily, begin kneading the dough until it forms a cohesive mass. Transfer the dough and any flour or bits remaining in the bowl to a clean work surface and continue kneading until the dough is smooth and firm, 7 to 10 minutes.

Wrap the dough tightly in plastic wrap and let rest at room temperature before using, at least 15 minutes or up to 1 hour. (The dough can be made ahead and kept tightly wrapped and refrigerated for up to 1 day or frozen for up to 1 month, either before or after extruding.)

If you have a torchio, fit it with the primary large-hole bigoli die.

Serves 4 to 6

DUCK BROTH

2 pounds (906 grams) duck neck and bones (about 1 carcass), cut into 2-inch (5-centimeter) pieces (see notes)

2 tablespoons (30 milliliters) extra-virgin olive oil

1 medium yellow onion (225 grams), coarsely chopped

2 celery ribs (160 grams), coarsely chopped

2 medium carrots (150 grams), coarsely chopped

1 bay leaf

3 quarts (2.8 liters) chicken broth, preferably homemade

BIGOLI (SEE NOTES)

1¼ cups (172 grams) whole-wheat flour

1 cup (150 grams) "00" flour

⅓ cup (78 milliliters) whole milk

2 large eggs

Semolina flour, for dusting

DUCK LIVER RAGÙ

1 pound (453 grams) duck livers, rinsed under cold running water, then soaked in 1 cup (250 milliliters) whole milk and refrigerated, covered, for at least 8 hours or overnight

1½ tablespoons (22 milliliters) extra-virgin olive oil

Kosher salt and freshly ground black pepper

4 medium sage leaves, finely chopped

TO SERVE

Kosher salt and freshly ground black pepper

CONTINUED

7 tablespoons (100 grams) cold unsalted butter, cut into small pieces

3 tablespoons (10 grams) finely chopped flat-leaf parsley

¾ cup (50 grams) freshly grated Parmigiano-Reggiano cheese (at least 24-month aged; see Larder, page xxiv)

4 ounces (113 grams) foie gras mousse (pâté), mousse removed from packaging (any gelée discarded), wrapped tightly in plastic wrap, and frozen

SPECIAL EQUIPMENT: parchment paper; a torchio or a pasta extruding machine (see notes)

Put the dough through the torchio and cut the pasta strands into 8-inch (20-centimeter) lengths as they emerge. If you don't have a torchio, roll out the dough to ¼ inch (0.63 centimeter) thickness on a well-floured surface. Then cut it into ¼-inch wide (0.63 centimeter), 8 inches (20 centimeters) long. Immediately dust the strands with semolina flour and lay them flat, not touching, on a floured baking sheet. Keep the strands covered with a floured towel until you cook them, for up to 2 hours, or freeze them on the baking sheet, then wrap together in plastic wrap. (Do not thaw frozen pasta before cooking.)

Reserving the solids, strain the broth through a fine-mesh sieve. You should have 2 quarts (1.8 liters) of duck broth. If you have less, add chicken broth or water to make up the difference. Remove and discard the bones and bay leaf. Finely chop enough of the vegetables to make ⅓ cup (100 grams); discard the remaining vegetables.

For the ragù: Drain the milk from the livers and pat dry with paper towels (discard the milk).

In a large (preferably 12-inch or 30-centimeter) skillet, heat the oil over medium-high heat until hot but not smoking. Carefully add the livers (they will splatter a bit) and cook, seasoning generously with salt and pepper and turning once, until golden and cooked to medium-rare in the middle, about 1 minute per side. Transfer to a plate and set aside. Pour off the excess oil from the pan, then add 1 cup (236 milliliters) of the duck broth and cook for 1 minute, scraping up the pan bits. Remove the pan from the heat.

Finely chop the livers, then stir them into the pan along with the chopped vegetables (from the duck broth) and the sage. Set the ragù aside.

To serve: Combine the remaining 7 cups (1.6 liters) duck broth and 2 cups (473 milliliters) water in a wide heavy pot. Bring the liquid to a boil. (You will cook the pasta in this broth and it should taste pleasantly salty. Adjust the seasoning to taste, if necessary.)

Cook the pasta in the boiling broth until al dente. A few minutes before the pasta is ready, bring the ragù just to a simmer over medium-high heat. Add the butter and cook, stirring frequently with a rubber spatula, until the butter is melted and incorporated into the sauce, about 1 minute, then stir in the parsley and a pinch of salt. Remove from the heat and adjust the seasoning to taste.

Drain the pasta, then add it back to the pot. (The broth can be saved for another use.) Add the ragù. Cook over medium heat, stirring occasionally, until the ragù thickens slightly, about 30 seconds. Stir in the cheese; cook 10 seconds more, then remove from the heat.

Divide the pasta among serving plates. Using a sharp vegetable peeler, shave the frozen foie gras mousse over the top of the pasta. Serve immediately.

NOTES: *Duck necks and bones can be purchased from a butcher, or you can buy whole duck and reserve the breasts and legs for other use, such as Apicius duck, p. 135.*

One pound (453 grams) of fresh or dried whole-wheat spaghetti can be used in place of fresh bigoli. If making the bigoli dough, it can be cut into chitarra or tagliatelle if you don't have a torchio to make bigoli. Wrap leftover foie gras mousse in plastic wrap and keep frozen for another use.

100-LAYER LASAGNE
al Ragù Bolognese

Serves 12

RAGÙ BOLOGNESE

2 ounces (56 grams) pancetta, cut into ½-inch (1.25-centimeter) cubes

1 garlic clove (4 grams), finely chopped

1 small yellow onion (200 grams), finely chopped

1½ medium carrots (100 grams), roughly chopped

1½ celery ribs (100 grams), roughly chopped

1½ tablespoons (22 milliliters) extra-virgin olive oil

⅔ pound (283 grams) ground veal

½ pound (226 grams) ground pork

1 tablespoon (12 grams) kosher salt

¼ cup (60 milliliters) dry white wine

1½ tablespoons (32 grams) double concentrated tomato paste

¼ cup (60 milliliters) whole milk

BÉCHAMEL

6 tablespoons (85 grams) unsalted butter

1 cup plus 2 tablespoons (total 85 grams) unbleached all-purpose flour

3 cups (710 milliliters) whole milk

1 teaspoon (4 grams) kosher salt

TO BUILD AND SERVE

Kosher salt

1½ batches Fresh Egg Pasta Dough (page 103)

1 batch Del Posto Tomato Sauce (page 102)

2⅓ cups (150 grams) freshly grated Parmigiano-Reggiano cheese (at least 24-month aged; see Larder, page xxiv)

3 tablespoons (45 milliliters) extra-virgin olive oil

1½ teaspoons (7 grams) unsalted butter

Lasagne alla Bolognese hails from the city of Bologna and is considered part of the *grandi classici,* or "great classics," of the Italian kitchen. Sheets of pasta are layered with Bolognese ragù and creamy béchamel, then baked until the edges are slightly crunchy and the center is warm and oozing.

Our 100-Layer Lasagne is quite different; it was conceived in the early days of the restaurant while trying to create a special pasta for a party Mario and Joe were hosting. Inspired by a recent reading of Hans Christian Andersen's "The Princess and the Pea," we decided to prepare lasagne with 20 sheets of pasta and hide one dried pea in the center as a treat for one lucky guest. This dish has gone through many permutations over the years, and 20 layers grew to 100. But as the layers grew, it became much harder to serve. We built it and baked it, but when sliced it was a mushy mess.

Because all of the elements are cooked before the lasagne is built, we realized it doesn't need to bake in the oven. Now we build it and chill it in the refrigerator, which holds it all together. We simply slice pieces from the cold lasagne and sear them on one side in a pan. This technique warms the lasagne portion, and gives each slice the toasted crispy bits reminiscent of the corner pieces from baked lasagne. This recipe is the fusion of a few labored-upon components and can take awhile to make, especially if using homemade pasta sheets. The good news is that it can be built and refrigerated one day ahead of time. Also, the ragù alla Bolognese is a staple sauce and can be made on its own and tossed with any number of pastas.

For the ragù bolognese: In the bowl of a food processor, combine the pancetta and chopped garlic. Pulse the mixture until it is combined and resembles a paste, then transfer to a bowl. Use a rubber spatula to scrape any remaining bits of paste from the food processor into the bowl with the paste.

Place the carrots and celery in the food processor bowl and pulse until finely chopped. In a large skillet, heat 1 tablespoon (15 milliliters) of the oil over medium-low heat. Add the onion and sauté for 5 minutes. Add the carrot and celery mixture, reduce the heat to low and cook, stirring occasion-ally, until the mixture (the soffritto) is tender and sweet, about 40 minutes (do not brown). Remove from the heat. (The soffritto can be made 1 day ahead and rest overnight in the refrigerator.)

In a 5- to 6-quart (4.7- to 5.6-liter) Dutch oven or heavy pot with lid, combine the pancetta mixture and the remaining ½ tablespoon (7 milliliters) oil. Cook over medium heat, breaking the paste into small bits with a rubber spatula, until the fat is rendered and the bits become crispy on the edges, 5 to 7 minutes. Add the soffritto and cook, stirring to work the two mixtures

CONTINUED

together, for 2 minutes. Add the veal, pork, and salt. Continue cooking, stirring frequently, until the meat is broken into bits and appears cooked through, 10 to 15 minutes.

Make a well in the center of the meat mixture, then add the wine to the well. When the wine comes to a simmer, stir to combine with the meat, then stir in the tomato paste. Reduce the heat to low and gently cook for 1 hour, adding a touch of water if necessary to keep the sauce from drying out. The ragù is done when the meat is tender. Stir in the milk and cook for 10 minutes more. Remove from the heat and let cool to room temperature. (The sauce can be kept, covered and refrigerated, for up to 3 days, or frozen for up to 1 month.)

For the béchamel: In a large saucepan, melt the butter over medium-low heat. Add the flour and cook, stirring frequently with a wooden spoon, until the mixture turns a very light sandy color, 5 to 7 minutes (do not brown). Add about 1 cup (236 millimeters) of the milk, whisking constantly, until the mixture is very smooth. Repeat, fully incorporating the liquid between additions, until all of the milk has been added. Bring to a gentle simmer and cook, stirring frequently and into the edges of the pan, until the sauce is the consistency of a thick cream, about 7 minutes more. Stir in the salt, then transfer the sauce, while hot, to a pastry bag fitted with a ¼-inch (6-millimeter) tip, or to a large resealable freezer bag. Set aside to cool to room temperature.

To build the lasagne: Roll out the pasta dough (as instructed on page 103) until you can just see your hand through the pasta sheets, a scant 1 millimeter thick. Cut the pasta sheets into 30 (6 x 6-inch or 15 x 15-centimeter) squares.

Bring a large wide pot of well-salted water to a boil. Set a bowl of very cold water near the range. Working in batches of 4 or 5 sheets, cook the pasta in the boiling water, about 1 minute per batch, timing immedi-

ately after the pasta is slipped into the water. Using a large sieve or slotted spoon, retrieve the cooked sheets, then immediately plunge them into the bowl of cold water. Let stand about 10 seconds, then lift the sheets one by one from the cold water; let the excess water drip back into the bowl, then hang them over the side of a large empty bowl (overlapping is OK).

If the ragù is cold, gently heat it, stirring occasionally, just to loosen and slightly warm through. The tomato sauce and béchamel can be at room temperature or slightly chilled. If the béchamel is in a freezer bag, cut ¼ inch (6.3 millimeters) off a corner so that you can use it as a piping bag.

Place a generous 2½ cups (510 grams) of the tomato sauce in a bowl. Cover and chill the remaining tomato sauce (you will use it for serving).

In the center of a 9 x 13-inch (23 x 33-centimeter) rimmed baking sheet or baking dish, spread about 1 tablespoon (15 grams) of the tomato sauce. Place 1 pasta sheet over the sauce. Spread about 1 tablespoon (15 grams) sauce on the pasta sheet, then sprinkle with 1 tablespoon (6.5 grams) of the Parmigiano. In a zigzag pattern, pipe the equivalent of about 1 tablespoon (13 grams) of the béchamel over the top, then sprinkle with about 2 tablespoons (30 grams) of the ragù (with the addition of each ingredient, you are "sprinkling," rather than creating a solid layer of each ingredient).

Place a second pasta sheet over the filling. Using your fingers, gently press the top of the sheet from the inside out toward the edges to eliminate any air bubbles, without going so far as to push out the filling. Repeat the layering process with the remaining sauces, cheese, and pasta sheets, following the same order of ingredients for each layer.

Cover the lasagne with plastic wrap and refrigerate at least 6 hours or overnight (this will help set the layers, making them easy to slice before baking).

Line a baking sheet with parchment paper. Using 1 large or 2 small spatulas, transfer the chilled lasagne from the pan to a large cutting board. Using a large knife (ideally one with a long thin blade, such as a carving knife), trim about ⅛ inch (3.4 millimeters) from all four outside edges of the lasagne to create straight edges. Then, using a pressing motion (not sawing), cut the lasagne in half. Gently lift and set one half to the side.

With the knife, mark the top of the remaining lasagne half lengthwise so that when cut, you will have 3 long equal pieces. Cut through the layers (again pressing the knife down rather than sawing), allowing your free hand to catch and gently guide the first slice to fall onto the cutting board with the cut side facing up. Cut the piece in half crosswise. Using a spatula, transfer the cut pieces to the prepared baking sheet (if you need to gently press together the layers, it's fine to do so). Repeat to form 12 total portions, placing the slices as cut in a single layer on the baking sheet. If you are not serving the lasagne within 1 hour, cover the pan tightly with plastic wrap and keep chilled until ready to serve.

Heat the oven to 350°F (177°C). Line a second baking sheet with parchment paper. In a large nonstick or cast-iron skillet, heat 1 tablespoon (15 milliliters) of the oil and ½ teaspoon (2.4 grams) of the butter over medium-high heat until hot but not smoking. Add 2 to 3 lasagne slices (enough to fit in but not crowd the pan) on their sides, or cut side down; reduce the heat to medium and cook (without moving the slices) until the bottom sides are deep golden, 3 to 4 minutes. Using a spatula, transfer the slices to the prepared baking sheet, seared side up. Repeat with the remaining oil, butter, and slices.

Bake the seared slices until just warmed through, 4 to 5 minutes. Meanwhile, in a medium saucepan, gently heat the reserved tomato sauce.

Spoon the warm tomato sauce onto serving plates. Top with the lasagne, seared side up. Serve immediately.

---

4 (28-ounce or 794-gram) cans whole peeled San Marzano tomatoes with their juices

3 tablespoons (45 milliliters) extra-virgin olive oil

10 garlic cloves (40 grams), gently smashed and peeled

1 tablespoon plus 1 teaspoon (total 20 grams) sugar

2½ teaspoons (10 grams) kosher salt

4 basil leaves

DEL POSTO TOMATO SAUCE

In batches, use a food processor, blender, or food mill to purée the tomatoes with their juices until smooth.

In a 6- to 8-quart (5.6- to 7.5-liter) Dutch oven or wide heavy saucepan, heat the oil and garlic over medium heat, stirring occasionally, until the garlic is very lightly golden and fragrant, about 2 minutes. Add the puréed tomatoes, sugar, and salt. Bring to a gentle simmer and cook until reduced by about two-thirds (to 2 quarts or 1.8 liters), about 1½ hours. Stir in the basil, then adjust the seasoning to taste. Remove from the heat and let cool completely. (The sauce can be kept, covered and refrigerated, for up to 3 days, or frozen for up to 1 month.)

PRIMI BASIC RECIPE

FRESH EGG PASTA DOUGH

Fresh pasta dough is made daily at Del Posto, formed and stuffed into many different shapes. Here is the basic fresh pasta dough for the primi recipes in this book. The egg-laden dough is golden in color because it is yolk-fortified, which makes it durable and easy to work with, especially when it's rolled out into thin sheets.

Makes 1¼ pounds (570 grams)

1½ cups (200 grams) "00" flour (see note), plus more for dusting

¾ cup (100 grams) durum flour, plus more for dusting

15 large egg yolks (270 grams)

In a large bowl, use your hands to mix together the "00" and durum flours, then form a well in the center. Add the egg yolks to the well. Using a fork, gently break up the yolks and slowly incorporate the flour mixture from the inside rim of the well. Continue until the liquid is absorbed (about half of the flour will be incorporated). With both hands, using your palms primarily, begin kneading the dough until it forms a mostly cohesive mass. Transfer the dough and any flour or bits remaining in the bowl to a clean work surface and continue kneading and occasionally pulling apart the dough to expose moisture, then pressing it back together, until the dough is smooth and firm, 7 to 10 minutes. (You want a firm dough. If you are having trouble kneading, wrap the dough tightly in plastic wrap and let it rest 10 or 15 minutes, then knead again. An additional yolk can be added if the dough is too dry.)

Wrap the dough tightly in plastic wrap and let rest at room temperature for at least 15 minutes or up to 1 hour before using. (The dough can be made ahead and kept tightly wrapped and refrigerated for up to 1 day, or frozen for up to 1 month; thaw frozen dough in the refrigerator before using.)

To roll out the dough: Unwrap and cut the pasta dough into 4 pieces. Flatten one piece so that it will fit through the rollers of a pasta machine (rewrap the remaining pieces). Set the rollers of the pasta machine to the widest setting, then feed the pasta through the rollers 3 to 4 times, folding and turning the pasta until it is smooth and the width of the machine. Roll the pasta through the machine, decreasing the setting one notch at a time (do not fold or turn the pasta) to the thickness desired per recipe. Cut the sheet in half crosswise, then lightly dust with "00" flour.

Layer the sheets between dry, clean, "00" flour–dusted kitchen towels to keep them from drying out. Repeat with the remaining dough pieces. After cutting the pasta into the desired shape, place on a durum-dusted rimmed baking sheet between sheets of durum-dusted parchment paper. (If you are not using the pasta within 1 hour, wrap the baking sheet tightly in plastic wrap and refrigerate for up to 1 day or freeze for up to 1 week. Do not thaw frozen pasta before cooking.)

NOTE: *There is really no substitute for Italian "00" flour when it comes to making fresh pasta. It is lighter, softer, and more powdery than all-purpose flour. Because it absorbs the liquid smoothly and evenly, the pizzaioli of Naples swear by it for pizza dough, as do the expert pasta makers of Emilia-Romagna. The most readily available "00" flour in the United States is Antico Molino Caputo.*

TIMPANO

The 1996 film Big Night *portrays two Italian* brothers struggling to operate an authentic Italian restaurant on the Jersey Shore in the 1950s. Caught between the business of selling American-Italian-style cuisine and their commitment to making the underappreciated food of their native Italy, they plan a dinner party for the musician Louis Prima, hoping it will save their restaurant from going under. Pulling out all the stops, they prepare timpano, a baked pasta masterpiece from their native Abruzzo. The sensitive and moving montage of scenes depicting the labor-intensive preparation and unveiling of their timpano inspired the development of a timpano for Del Posto.

Timpano means "kettledrum" in Italian. The more common moniker for timpano in Italy is *timballo,* the name of a traditional cylindrical mold, designed to be lined with pasta or pastry and filled with any number of ingredients and baked.

TIMPANO ALLA MANCUSO

Del Posto's chef di cucina, Matt Abdoo, grew up eating his grandmother Valeria Mancuso's timpano at Sunday suppers in Connecticut. Mancuso starts by making meatballs and then adds them to her slow-cooked "Sunday Gravy" of tomato, basil, short ribs, and two types of sausage. Dried pasta is cooked, soppressata and sharp provolone cubed, eggs hard-boiled, and escarole sautéed. Hours later, the sausage, short ribs, and meatballs are removed from the gravy and chopped. She lines the timpano pot with large sheets of homemade pasta, fills it with layers of the cooked dried pasta, gravy, short ribs, sausage, cheese, and eggs. The top of the timpano is wrapped with the pasta sheets and baked. Less than an hour later, it's removed from the oven, rested, and flipped upside down. Finally, the pot is carefully pulled away—revealing a triumph of baked pastas.

Nonna Mancuso is 94 years old now. Her timpano recipe emigrated with her family from Italy to the United States 90 year ago, and Matt has since brought it to the restaurant. Capturing the nostalgic cuisine from his youth and the spirit of celebration depicted in *Big Night,* here is the recipe for Del Posto's Timpano alla Mancuso.

Serves 12

GRANDMA'S MEATBALLS

2½ slices packaged white sandwich bread (such as Pepperidge Farm), crusts removed, bread torn into small pieces

½ cup (120 milliliters) whole milk

½ pound (226 grams) ground beef (80 to 85 percent lean)

½ pound (226 grams) ground pork

5 large eggs

1 garlic clove (4 grams), finely chopped

1½ teaspoons (2.5 grams) finely chopped fresh parsley

1 tablespoon (12 grams) kosher salt

1 teaspoon (4 grams) freshly ground black pepper

¾ cup (50 grams) freshly grated Pecorino Romano Genuino cheese (see Larder, page xxv)

¾ cup (50 grams) freshly grated Parmigiano-Reggiano cheese (at least 24-month aged; see Larder, page xxiv)

GRANDMA'S GRAVY

¾ pound (340 grams) sweet Italian sausages

¾ pound (340 grams) hot Italian sausages

1 pound (453 grams) boneless beef short ribs, cut into 2½-inch (6-centimeter) pieces

Kosher salt and freshly ground black pepper

3 tablespoons (45 milliliters) extra-virgin olive oil

5 garlic cloves (20 grams), gently smashed and peeled

1 medium yellow onion (275 grams), finely chopped

For Grandma's meatballs: Heat the oven to 375ºF (190ºC). In a small bowl, soak the bread in the milk for 2 to 3 minutes, then drain the bread and squeeze out the excess liquid.

Place the beef and pork in a large bowl and form a well in the center. Add the eggs, garlic, parsley, salt, and pepper. Using a fork, beat the eggs to break up the yolks; then, using your hands, mix together the eggs and the meats. Add the drained bread and the cheeses. Stir together just to combine (do not overmix), then let stand for 5 minutes.

Form the mixture into 10 meatballs (each about 2 inches or 5 centimeters in diameter) and place in a 9 x 13-inch (23 x 33-centimeter) baking dish. Bake until the meatballs are mostly cooked through but still pink in the center, about 25 minutes. Meanwhile, prepare the gravy.

For Grandma's gravy: Line a rimmed baking sheet with parchment paper; arrange the sausages on the sheet and bake (with the meatballs) until cooked through and lightly golden, about 25 minutes. Remove the cooked meatballs and sausages from the oven and let cool to room temperature.

Meanwhile, generously season the short ribs with salt and pepper. In a 6- to 8-quart (5.6- to 7.5-liter) wide heavy pot, heat the oil over medium-high heat. Brown the short ribs on all sides, 8 to 10 minutes total, then transfer to a plate. Reduce the heat to medium-low. Add the garlic, then tip the pot at a slight angle to pool the oil. Let the garlic cook in the oil until lightly golden,

1 to 2 minutes. Return the pot flat to the burner. Add the onion and cook, stirring occasionally, until softened, 5 to 7 minutes. Add the tomato paste and continue cooking, stirring constantly, for 2 to 3 minutes. Increase the heat to medium and add the wine. Cook, stirring occasionally, until the mixture thickens back to a paste, about 5 minutes.

In batches, purée the tomatoes (with their juices) in a blender, transferring them to a large bowl as you go. Return the short ribs to the pot, then stir in the puréed tomatoes, 1½ tablespoons (18 grams) salt, and the sugar. Bring to a gentle simmer and cook until the short ribs are very tender and falling apart, about 2 hours.

Add the meatballs and their juices and the sausages to the gravy and simmer 30 minutes more. Stir in the basil, then adjust the seasoning to taste. Remove the gravy from the heat. (The gravy can be made ahead. Once the gravy is cool, remove the meats and separately keep the meats and the sauce, covered and refrigerated, for up to 3 days, or frozen for 1 month.)

For the pasta: Bring a large wide pot of well-salted water to a boil. Set a bowl of very cold water near the range. Line a baking sheet with paper towels.

Divide the pasta dough into 3 equal pieces. Wrap and set aside one piece to save for another use (you should have 13 ounces or 375 grams remaining). Cut each of the remaining 2 pieces in half so that you have 4 equal pieces total. Roll out each piece (as instructed on page 103) until you can just see your hand through the sheet, a scant 1 millimeter thick (do not cut the 4 sheets).

Cook the pasta sheets in the boiling water, about 40 seconds, timing immediately after the pasta is slipped into the water. Using a large sieve or slotted spoon, retrieve the cooked sheets, then immediately plunge them into the bowl of cold water (reserve the pasta cooking water). Let stand about 10 seconds, then lift the sheets one by one from the cold water, letting the excess water drip back into the bowl, then drain on the prepared baking sheet.

Boil the penne in the reserved pasta cooking water until close to but under al dente, about 2–3 minutes less than is stated on the package for al dente, then drain and spread on a baking sheet to cool (the penne will cook further as it both cools and later bakes).

To build the timpano: Heat the oven to 400°F (204°C) with the rack in the middle.

Using a slotted spoon, transfer the short ribs, meatballs, and sausages to a cutting board. (If you prepared the gravy ahead and the meats are chilled or frozen, gently heat to warm through.) Heat the gravy to a simmer, then remove from the heat and cover to keep warm. Shred the short ribs into small pieces. Cut the meatballs into ½-inch (1.25-centimeter) pieces. Cut the sausages into ⅓-inch (8-millimeter) half-moons. Place the meats in a large bowl. Add the cooled penne, the soppressatas, and a scant 1.5 liters (6 cups) of the hot gravy (reserve the remaining gravy for serving). Stir to combine, then stir in the provolone cheeses, the Parmigiano, and the pecorino.

Grease a 5- to 6-quart (4.7- to 5.6-liter) Dutch oven or wide heavy pot with 4 table-spoons (56 grams) of the butter. Line the pot with the pasta sheets, overlapping them as needed to cover the bottom and sides and leaving equal overhang all around.

4½ ounces (127 grams) tomato paste

1 cup (236 milliliters) dry red wine

4 (28-ounce or 794-gram) cans San Marzano tomatoes

2½ tablespoons (30 grams) sugar

10 fresh basil leaves

PASTA

Kosher salt

1 batch Fresh Egg Pasta Dough (page 103)

453 grams (1 pound) dried penne or other short shaped pasta

TO BUILD THE TIMPANO

⅓ pound (150 grams) sweet soppressata, cut into ⅓-inch (8-millimeter) cubes

⅓ pound (150 grams) hot soppressata, cut into ⅓-inch (8-millimeter) cubes

¾ pound (342 grams) mild provolone cheese, cut into ⅓-inch (8-millimeter) cubes

½ pound (226 grams) sharp provolone cheese, cut into ⅓-inch (8-millimeter) cubes

¾ cup (50 grams) freshly grated Parmigiano-Reggiano cheese (at least 24-month aged; see Larder, page xxiv)

¾ cup (50 grams) freshly grated Pecorino Romano Genuino cheese (see Larder, page xxv)

6 tablespoons (85 grams) unsalted butter, softened

6 large hard-boiled eggs, peeled and cut in half lengthwise (optional)

ESCAROLE

¼ cup (60 milliliters) extra-virgin olive oil

2 garlic cloves (8 grams), gently smashed and peeled

CONTINUED

3 pounds (1⅓ kilograms) escarole, leaves separated and coarsely chopped

½ teaspoon (2 grams) kosher salt

TO SERVE

1 large egg (for torching the timpano; optional)

14 ounces (400 grams) fresh whole-milk ricotta cheese

2 tablespoons (30 milliliters) extra-virgin olive oil, plus more for drizzling

Kosher salt and freshly ground black pepper

SPECIAL EQUIPMENT: parchment paper; a butane torch for torching the timpano (optional)

If you are including the boiled eggs, spoon half of the meat and cheese filling into the pot. Spread evenly with a rubber spatula, then arrange the eggs in a circle on top, with the cut sides up and the short ends facing in. Top with the remaining filling, then spread evenly once more. (If you are not including the eggs, spoon all of the filling into the pot, spreading evenly, and proceed.) Fold the pasta over the filling, then spread the remaining 2 tablespoons (28 grams) butter on top. Bake the timpano until the top is golden brown, about 30 minutes. Meanwhile, prepare the escarole.

For the escarole: In a large Dutch oven or wide heavy saucepan with lid, heat the oil and garlic over medium heat until the garlic is fragrant and lightly golden, about 2 minutes. Add the escarole (in batches, if necessary, covering and stirring between batches), salt, and 1 tablespoon (15 milliliters) water. Cook, covered, stirring occasionally, until the escarole is tender, 15 to 20 minutes. Drain any excess liquid from the pot. Cover to keep warm.

To serve: Remove the timpano from the oven and let rest 10 to 15 minutes, then invert onto a cutting board. If you want to torch the timpano, in a small bowl, whisk together the egg and 1 teaspoon (5 milliliters) water, then brush over the top and sides of the timpano. Use a torch to form a crispy golden exterior. Let rest 10 minutes before slicing.

Meanwhile, in a medium bowl, stir together the ricotta, oil, and salt and pepper to taste. In a medium saucepan, gently heat the remaining gravy.

Serve the timpano in one of two ways: Cut the pasta sheet from the top and use a large spoon to scoop portions onto serving plates. Or slice the timpano into 12 wedges and transfer to serving plates. In either case, serve the timpano with gravy spooned over the top, dolloped with the ricotta cheese and the escarole, and drizzled with oil.

❧ WINE PAIRING ❧

The Timpano combines all the classic flavors of the American-Italian kitchen— meatballs, pasta, sharp cheese, spices, and herbs. The Montepulciano D'Abruzzo from Emidio Pepe is an excellent pairing for this bold baked pasta. An icon of Italian winemaking, Pepe is in another league when compared to the conventional Montepulciano D'Abruzzo producers familiar to most Americans. Emidio Pepe is a family operation, producing completely natural wines in Abruzzo from Montepulciano grapes. Their grapes are still crushed by feet, and the wine is fermented with natural yeast in neutral cement tanks (so as not to impart any outside flavors to the wine). The result is a feral, earthy, and dense wine that evolves in the glass as it opens up. It is a pairing that challenges the flavors of the Timpano but acts as that link between the old and the new worlds, as many Italian-American recipes do. The wines are aged in the bottle at the winery until Emido and his family decide they are ready, then they are labeled and released to the market. Because Emidio Pepe is a natural wine, the vintages often can develop unexpectedly in the bottle, and the prices then vary accordingly.

SECONDI: PESCE

Seafood is sacred in Italy, and the five seas
surrounding the Italian peninsula offer an abundant diversity
of fresh fish. Del Posto practices traditional, gentle cooking techniques
for its seafood dishes. Embracing the Italian notion of eating local,
the restaurant works with American seafood, almost exclusively
from the cold North Atlantic waters.

This chapter includes recipes for salmon, whole sea bass, monkfish,
and lobster. The cacciucco is an elegant and complex interpretation
of a rustic shellfish stew from the Tuscan coast, and embraces
the Italian love affair with shellfish and crustaceans. Requiring
multiple steps, building deep layers of flavor from many
different types of seafood, this fisherman's stew is one of the
most complicated but highly rewarding recipes in the book.

ARCTIC CHAR
with Wheat Broth and Grain Salad

Serves 4

WHEAT BROTH AND GRAIN SALAD

¼ cup (45 grams) small brown lentils

½ cup (45 grams) farro, preferably farro piccolo (einkorn)

Kosher salt

Scant ⅓ cup (25 grams) whole-wheat penne or other short pasta

2½ tablespoons (38 milliliters) very good extra-virgin olive oil, preferably intense Sicilian (see Larder, page xxix)

1 tablespoon (15 milliliters) fresh lemon juice

ARCTIC CHAR

About 6⅓ cups (1½ liters) pure olive oil

Kosher salt

4 (6-ounce or 170-gram) center-cut arctic char fillets (skin on)

TO SERVE

8 baby radishes, preferably with tops

4 baby turnips, preferably with tops

Edible flowers and wild baby greens and microgreens for garnish

Maldon sea salt

Very good extra-virgin olive oil, preferably intense Sicilian (see Larder, page xxix), for drizzling

SPECIAL EQUIPMENT: a candy / fry thermometer

Farro, lentils, and whole-wheat pasta create an earthy broth for this olive oil–poached arctic char. The distinctive brodo is made by straining the liquid remaining from overcooked pasta. Combined with cooking liquids from lentils and farro, the broth synthesizes a meatiness that complements the robust salmon notes in arctic char.

For the wheat broth and grain salad: Place the lentils and farro each in a separate medium saucepan. Add 1 quart (946 milliliters) water and a generous pinch of salt to each pan. Over medium heat, bring the water to a gentle simmer. Cook until the lentils and grains are tender but still have a bite, about 15 minutes for the lentils, and 18 to 20 minutes for the farro. As the lentils and grains are done, remove them from the heat and let cool completely in their cooking liquids.

Meanwhile, in a third medium saucepan, combine the pasta, a generous pinch of salt, and 1¼ quarts (1.1 liters) water. Bring the water to a simmer. Cook until the pasta is very soft and the cooking liquid is thick and reduced to about 1½ cups (355 milliliters), about 40 minutes. Strain the pasta cooking liquid into a small saucepan. Discard the pasta.

Reserving their cooking liquids, drain the grains and lentils together through a medium-mesh sieve set over a large bowl. To the pasta liquid, add ¼ cup plus 2 tablespoons (total 90 milliliters) of the grain liquid to make the wheat broth. Discard the remaining grain liquid.

Add the oil and lemon juice to the grain mixture, then toss to combine. Season the grain salad with salt to taste.

For the char: Pour enough of the pure olive oil into a large high-sided skillet to come halfway up the sides of the skillet. Heat over low heat to 110ºF (43ºC). Season the fish on both sides with salt, then slip the pieces into the oil, skin side down. Maintaining the 110ºF (43ºC) temperature, cook the fish just until the skins easily pull away from the flesh, 18 to 20 minutes. Using a spatula, carefully remove the fillets from the oil. Gently lift off and discard the skins.

To serve: Arrange the fish in small shallow serving bowls. Place a small spoonful of the grain salad into the bowls with the fish, then arrange a small spoonful of the remaining grains, and the radishes, turnips, edible flowers, and greens on each of 4 serving plates (save any extra grain salad for another use).

Heat the wheat broth just to a simmer. Season with salt to taste. Spoon about ⅓ cup (79 milliliters) of the warm broth into each of the serving bowls with the fish. Drizzle the salads and the fish with the very good oil. Finish with Maldon sea salt. Serve immediately.

WHOLE BRANZINO

with Fennel and Peperonata

Branzino is a Mediterranean sea bass often farmed off the island of Crete. Good substitutes for this fish on the East Coast include Atlantic striped bass, black bass, or even blackfish—wild fish is best for whole fish preparations. After gently poaching in a delicate tomato and seaweed broth, we keep with traditional Italian ideology and present the fish unadorned, glistening and succulent. Served with a zesty pepper condiment and some charred fennel, this dish is a great example of sophisticated simplicity.

For the dashi poaching liquid: In a medium saucepan, bring the tomato broth and fennel juice to a gentle simmer over medium heat. Skim any foam from the top, then submerge the kombu in the liquid. Cook at a very gentle simmer for 10 minutes, then remove from the heat. Stir in the bonito flakes and a pinch of salt. Let stand 15 minutes, then strain the liquid into a bowl. Discard the solids.

For the peperonata: Pass the tomatoes with their juices through the fine-holed disk of a food mill or purée in a blender, then force through a medium-mesh sieve to extract the seeds. In a medium saucepan, heat 1 tablespoon (15 milliliters) of the oil and the chili flakes over medium heat for 1 minute, then stir in the tomatoes, vinegar, marmalade, salt, and sugar. Bring to a simmer and cook, stirring frequently and into the edges of the pan with a heat-proof rubber spatula, until thickened, about 20 minutes. Remove from the heat and set aside.

Meanwhile, in a medium skillet, heat the remaining 1½ tablespoons (23 grams) of oil and the anchovies over medium heat until the oil begins to bubble, then add the garlic and cook until fragrant, 1 to 2 minutes. Add the fennel and onion. Cook, stirring occasionally, until the vegetables are crisp-tender, 10 to 12 minutes. Stir in the piquillo peppers, then remove from the heat and let cool completely.

In a food processor, pulse the cooled vegetable mixture until finely chopped and combined, then transfer to a bowl and stir in the reserved tomato mixture. Adjust the seasoning to taste.

For the caramelized fennel: Trim and reserve the stems and fronds from the fennel bulbs, then cut the bulbs into 6 wedges each. In a bowl, toss together the fennel wedges, 2 tablespoons (30 milliliters) of the oil, and the sugar and salt. In a large skillet, heat the remaining 1 tablespoon (15 grams) of oil over medium-high heat. Cook the fennel wedges, in batches if necessary, until the cut sides are golden, 3 to 5 minutes per side. Arrange the fennel on a parchment-lined baking sheet. Set aside.

For the branzino: Heat the oven to 350°F (177°C). Rinse the fish under cold running water, then pat dry. Season inside and out with salt and pepper and stuff the cavities with the reserved fennel stems (save the fronds for garnish). Place the fish on a lightly oiled, heatproof platter that will fit in your steamer or in a roasting pan with a rack and lid.

Serves 4 to 6

DASHI POACHING LIQUID

3 cups (709 milliliters) Tomato Broth (see Cool Summertime Minestra, page 24)

2 cups (473 milliliters) fresh fennel juice (from about 1½ pounds fennel bulbs) (see note)

1 ounce (28 grams) kombu seaweed

3 cups (30 grams) bonito flakes

Kosher salt

PEPERONATA

1 (14-ounce or 397-gram) can San Marzano tomatoes

2½ tablespoons (38 milliliters) extra-virgin olive oil

½ teaspoon (1 gram) red chili flakes

¼ cup plus 2 tablespoons (90 milliliters) red wine vinegar

3 tablespoons (60 grams) lemon or orange marmalade

1 teaspoon (3 grams) kosher salt

1 scant teaspoon (3 grams) sugar

2 flat anchovy fillets (7 grams), coarsely chopped

4 large garlic cloves (16 grams), thinly sliced

½ medium fennel bulb (150 grams), cut into ½-inch (1.25-centimeter) cubes

½ medium yellow onion (130 grams), cut into ½-inch (1.25-centimeter) cubes

1½ cups (260 grams) drained and coarsely chopped jarred piquillo peppers

CARAMELIZED FENNEL

2 medium fennel bulbs with stems and fronds (300 grams)

CONTINUED

3 tablespoons (45 milliliters) extra-virgin olive oil

2½ teaspoons (10 grams) sugar

¾ teaspoon (2 grams) kosher salt

BRANZINO

2 (1¼- to 1½-pound or 556- to 680-gram) whole branzino or black bass, scaled and gutted, with head and tail intact

Kosher salt and freshly ground black pepper

SPECIAL EQUIPMENT: a steamer or a roasting pan with a rack and lid

Pour the dashi poaching liquid into the steamer or roasting pan. Add water, if necessary, to bring the liquid just below the rack. Bring to a boil. Reduce to a simmer. Place the platter with the fish on the steaming rack, cover, and steam over low heat for 16 to 20 minutes, depending on the thickness of the fish (plan on 10 minutes for each 1 inch or 2.5 centimeters of thickness at its widest point).

While the fish is cooking, bake the fennel until crisp-tender, 10 to 12 minutes.

Remove from the oven and let stand in a warm place until ready to serve.

When the fish is ready, carefully remove the rack from the steamer or roasting pan, then fillet. Serve with the peperonata and caramelized fennel. Garnish with the fennel fronds.

NOTE: *Fennel juice should be made in a juicer. If you don't have a juicer, it can be purchased at local juice shops.*

LOBSTER WITH ARTICHOKES,
Almonds, Basil, and Tangerine Butter

This recipe brings together Roman-style artichokes, citrus, almonds, and basil for a warm-weather lobster dish. The tails are cooked separately from the claws and knuckles, which are tossed with a tangerine and butter emulsion. The roe from the lobsters is blended with parsley, sage, rosemary, and thyme for a marinade that is brushed onto the split tails before they are quickly broiled. This herbaceous roe turns bright red in the oven, and reinforces the deep-sea flavors of the lobster tails, making good use of what is often discarded.

For the almonds: Heat the oven to 300°F (149°C). Spread the almonds on a rimmed baking sheet. Bake until fragrant and lightly golden, 18 to 20 minutes. Remove from the oven and season with salt while hot. Let cool, then coarsely chop.

For the lobsters: Prepare and cook the lobsters in the same manner as in the Lobster alla Caesar recipe on page 33, with the following changes: Just before cooking the lobsters, remove and reserve the roe. Cook the tails for only 2 minutes (cook the claws as you do in the Caesar recipe). After cooling the tails and claws, slice the underside of the tails lengthwise in their shells to butterfly (leaving the shells on). Remove the meat from the claws and knuckles (discard the shells).

For the lobster roe marinade: In a blender, combine the reserved lobster roe and the oil. Purée until smooth. Transfer to a bowl. Stir in the thyme, rosemary, sage, parsley, and a generous pinch of salt.

For the tangerine butter sauce: In a medium saucepan, bring 1 cup (240 milliliters) of the tangerine juice to a simmer. Cook until reduced to ¼ cup (60 milliliters),

about 15 minutes. Reduce the heat to medium-low and, whisking constantly, add a few tablespoons of the butter. Add the remaining butter a few pieces at a time, whisking constantly, adding more pieces before the previous ones have completely liquefied (the sauce should maintain the consistency of hollandaise) and lifting the pan from the heat occasionally to cool the mixture.

Remove the pan from the heat. In a slow and steady stream, whisk in the oil, then the vinegar, the remaining 1 tablespoon (15 milliliters) of tangerine juice, and salt to taste to form a thin sauce. Keep the sauce off the heat but in a warm place until ready to use.

To finish the lobster tails: Heat the oven to 350°F (177°C). Arrange the lobster tails flesh side up, on a rimmed baking sheet. Drizzle with oil and season with salt. Bake until the meat is just warmed through, 2 to 3 minutes, then remove from the oven. Brush the marinade on the butterflied lobster tail meat and set aside. Heat the oven to broil.

Broil the lobster tails until the roe is bright orange and the tail meat is hot, about 1 minute. Remove from the oven. Using a

Serves 4 to 6

TOASTED ALMONDS

2 heaping tablespoons (22 grams) whole blanched almonds

Kosher salt

LOBSTERS

½ cup (118 milliliters) white wine vinegar

1 large yellow onion (360 grams), coarsely chopped

1 medium carrot (75 grams), coarsely chopped

1 celery rib (80 grams), coarsely chopped

2 tablespoons (18 grams) kosher salt

2 bay leaves

4 (1¼-pound or 566-gram) live lobsters

Extra-virgin olive oil, for drizzling

Kosher salt

LOBSTER ROE MARINADE

3 tablespoons (45 milliliters) extra-virgin olive oil

1 teaspoon (1 gram) finely chopped fresh thyme

1 teaspoon (1 gram) finely chopped fresh rosemary

1 teaspoon (1 gram) finely chopped fresh sage

1 teaspoon (1 gram) finely chopped flat-leaf parsley

Kosher salt

TANGERINE BUTTER SAUCE

1 cup plus 1 tablespoon (total 255 milliliters) fresh tangerine juice (from 4 to 5 tangerines)

10½ tablespoons (150 grams) cold unsalted butter, cut into small pieces

CONTINUED

1½ tablespoons (23 milliliters) very good extra-virgin olive oil, preferably intense Sicilian (see Larder, page xxix)

1 teaspoon (5 milliliters) champagne vinegar

Kosher salt

TO SERVE

1 batch Artichokes alla Romana (page 50), drained and cut into sixths

4 loosely packed cups (48 grams) mixed basil varieties, such as Genoa, purple, Thai, and lemon basil (at least 3 varieties)

2 tablespoons (30 milliliters) fresh tangerine juice

1 tablespoon (15 milliliters) very good extra-virgin olive oil, preferably intense Sicilian (see Larder, page xxix)

Pinch kosher salt

fork, loosen the tail meat in the shells (to make it easy to remove from the shells), then lower the meat back into the shells.

To serve: Place the lobster claw and knuckle meat in the butter sauce. Gently heat over low heat to warm through, then remove from the sauce. Divide the lobster tails, the claw and knuckle meat, and the artichokes among serving plates. Drizzle with the butter sauce. In a large bowl, toss together the toasted almonds, basil leaves, tangerine juice, oil, and salt. Arrange the salad on top of the lobster.

LOBSTER WITH SQUASH,

Shiitake Mushrooms, Brussels Sprouts, and
Balsamic Brown Butter

A cool-weather counterpart to the Lobster with Artichokes (page 119), this recipe showcases robust, earthy flavors with fall and winter ingredients. Lobster is treated as a hearty protein, dressed with balsamic brown butter, and accompanied by Brussels sprouts, squash, and shiitake mushrooms. In order to simplify the cooking process, the vegetables are roasted together on stacked baking sheets.

For the lobsters: Prepare and cook the lobsters in the same manner as in the Lobster alla Caesar recipe on page 33, removing the cooked meat from the shells but leaving the tail pieces whole.

For the walnuts: Heat the oven to 300°F (149°C). Spread the nuts on a rimmed baking sheet. Bake until fragrant and lightly toasted, about 15 minutes. Remove from the oven and season with salt while hot. Set aside.

For the vegetables: Increase the oven temperature to 350°F (177°C). Line two rimmed baking sheets with parchment paper.

Cut the neck of the squash from the base (reserve the base for another use, such as Roots and Fruits antipasto, p. 21). Peel and then cut the neck lengthwise into ⅓-inch-wide (8-millimeter-wide) pieces. Using a 1½-inch (3.8-centimeter) round cutter, cut 12 rounds from the squash pieces.

From the Brussels sprout halves, remove and reserve enough of the outer leaves to yield 1½ loosely packed cups (25 grams). Set aside the leaves. Cut the mushroom stems from the caps.

In a large bowl, toss the squash rounds and Brussels sprout halves with 1½ tablespoons (22 milliliters) of the oil and a pinch each of salt and pepper. Arrange on one of the prepared baking sheets in a single layer,

keeping the squash and the Brussels sprouts separate. Toss the mushrooms in a large bowl with the remaining 1½ tablespoons (22 milliliters) oil. Arrange the mushrooms cap side up on the other prepared baking sheet. Cover with parchment paper. Place the baking sheet of Brussels sprouts and squash on top of the mushrooms in order to weight them down while they cook. Roast the two sheets of vegetables together until they are lightly golden and tender but still toothsome, about 10 minutes for the squash and Brussels sprouts and about 15 minutes for the mushrooms. Transfer the vegetables to a large plate and cool completely.

For the brown butter balsamic vinaigrette: In a medium skillet, heat the butter over medium heat until deep nutty brown (do not burn), whisking constantly, about 3 minutes. Remove the pan from the heat. Whisking constantly, add the vinegar and a scant 2 tablespoons (25 milliliters) cold water to create an emulsified sauce.

Whisking constantly, return the sauce to the heat and bring just to a simmer, then whisk in a generous pinch of salt. Keep the sauce off the heat but in a warm place until ready to use.

For the beurre blanc: In a medium saucepan, bring the wine to a simmer over medium heat and cook until reduced by

Serves 4 to 6

LOBSTERS

½ cup (118 milliliters) white wine vinegar

1 large onion (360 grams), coarsely chopped

1 medium carrot (75 grams), coarsely chopped

1 celery rib (80 grams), coarsely chopped

2 tablespoons (18 grams) kosher salt

2 bay leaves

4 (1¼-pound or 566-gram) live lobsters

TOASTED WALNUTS

1 cup (85 grams) walnut halves

Kosher salt

VEGETABLES

1 medium butternut squash

10 ounces (283 grams) Brussels sprouts, halved lengthwise

¼ pound (133 grams) shiitake mushrooms

3 tablespoons (44 milliliters) extra-virgin olive oil

Kosher salt and freshly ground black pepper

BROWN BUTTER BALSAMIC VINAIGRETTE

4½ tablespoons (64 grams) unsalted butter

1½ tablespoons (23 milliliters) aged balsamic vinegar (see Larder, page xxvi)

Kosher salt

CONTINUED

BEURRE BLANC

3 tablespoons (45 milliliters) dry white wine

1½ tablespoons (23 milliliters) heavy cream

½ pound (226 grams) cold unsalted butter, cut into small pieces

2 tablespoons (30 milliliters) fresh lemon juice

Kosher salt

TO SERVE

1½ tablespoons (23 milliliters) extra-virgin olive oil

Kosher salt

SPECIAL EQUIPMENT: a 1½-inch (3.8-centimeter) round cutter; parchment paper

about half. Add the cream and bring to a simmer. Reduce the heat to medium-low and, whisking constantly, add a few tablespoons of the butter. Add the remaining butter a few pieces at a time, whisking constantly, adding more pieces before the previous ones have completely liquefied (the sauce should maintain the consistency of hollandaise) and lifting the pan from the heat occasionally to cool the mixture. Remove the pan from the heat, then whisk in the lemon juice. Season with salt to taste. Keep the sauce off the heat but in a warm place until ready to use.

To serve: Transfer the beurre blanc to a large skillet. Add the lobster tails, claws, and knuckles. Heat over very low heat to warm the meat through. Meanwhile, in a 12-inch (30-centimeter) skillet, heat the oil over medium-high heat until hot but not smoking. Add the Brussels sprouts, cut sides down, and cook (do not stir) until the cut sides are golden, 1 to 2 minutes. Push the Brussels sprouts to the side of the skillet and season with salt, then add the squash rounds, cut sides down. Season with salt. Let cook 1 minute, then add the mushrooms, walnuts, and another pinch of salt. Cook for 1 minute, add 2 tablespoons (30 milliliters) of the vinaigrette, then toss together the vegetables. Remove the pan from the heat, then add three-quarters of the reserved Brussels sprout leaves and a generous pinch of salt and toss to combine.

Remove the lobster pieces from the beurre blanc, then arrange on serving plates. Distribute the cooked vegetables and nuts and the remaining Brussels sprout leaves evenly among the plates. Spoon the remaining vinaigrette over the top.

❧ WINE PAIRING ❧

The sea, the forest, and the farm are represented in every bite of this dish. The combination of flavors works well with a variety of wines. It can be paired with an oak-aged Carricante, a white wine from the slopes of Mt. Etna in Sicily, which plays off the saline, sweet, herbal, and verdant notes of the lobster and Brussels sprouts. It is a wine with great floral notes and enough vibrant acidity to keep the palate fresh. Red wine can also be paired here by looking to the squash, mushrooms, and balsamic in the recipe. Wines from the far north in Valle d'Aosta, such as Chambave, or the far south in Sicily, such as Etna Rosso, pair well. Both of these wines are light- to medium-bodied with aromas of red fruits, fresh flowers, and earth.

CACCIUCCO WITH GARLIC BREAD SOUP

and Sweet Shrimp alla Busara

Cacciucco is a Tuscan, tomato-stained fish soup that comes from the town of Livorno on the Tyrrhenian Sea. It is one of the many fisherman's stews found around coastal Italy, and it is quite similar to French bouillabaisse. Fish stews such as cacciucco are a staple aboard fishing vessels and in restaurants around working seaports as hearty, warm meals that make use of discarded fish scraps. As a result, the ingredients in a cacciucco always vary, based on what is available and where the soup is made. This recipe has been on our menu since opening day and is the first great example of the restaurant's ability to take an inherently rustic dish and refine it for fine dining, without stripping away its gutsy spirit.

At the restaurant, the prep work and base broth for this recipe are completed early in the day. As we get closer to service, we gently cook soffritto in a saucepot before adding the tomato, the wine, and the base broth. Then the fish is added and poached until tender. Next, we prepare a secondary sauce similar to a creamy garlic bread soup. Last, very small shrimp are quickly sautéed in a sweet paprika, an ingredient from Lidia Bastianich's Istrian heritage. Although these four components of the recipe are kept separate until the dish is served, they come together harmoniously in the bowl. This cacciucco can be simplified slightly by omitting the crab and crab stock and doubling the amount of lobster stock.

For the crab and crab stock: Prepare the crab and crab stock in the same manner as in the Spaghetti with Dungeness Crab recipe on page 59, just until you have picked the crabmeat and prepared the crab stock (omit the steps of reserving the fennel from the crab boil and puréeing the crab brains). Refrigerate the crabmeat and stock separately until ready to use.

For the lobster: Kill the lobsters and prepare a court bouillon in the same manner as in the first two steps of the Lobster alla Caesar recipe on page 33.

Pull out and reserve the roe and tomalley from the lobsters. Separate the claws (with the knuckles attached) and the tails from the bodies. Pull away the top shells from each lobster body, then cut away and discard the gills and brain sacs. Over a bowl, break apart the remaining pieces, reserving the shells, juices, and legs.

Insert a metal skewer or the stem end of a teaspoon between the meat and the top side of each tail shell to keep the tails straight while cooking.

Drop the claws (with knuckles) and the tails into the simmering court bouillon. Cook, partially covered, removing the tails 2 minutes and the claw pieces 9 minutes after the time they enter the water, and immediately transferring to an ice bath

Serves 6 to 8

CRAB

1 Dungeness crab (about 2 pounds or 906 grams)

1 medium fennel bulb (150 grams), cut into ¼-inch (6-millimeter) slices

CRAB STOCK

2 tablespoons (30 milliliters) extra-virgin olive oil

1 medium fennel bulb (150 grams), cut into ¼-inch (6-millimeter) slices

1 small yellow onion (125 grams), cut into ¼-inch (6-millimeter) slices

1 cup (236 milliliters) dry white wine

LOBSTER

½ cup (118 milliliters) white wine vinegar

1 large onion (360 grams), coarsely chopped

1 medium carrot (75 grams), coarsely chopped

1 celery rib (80 grams), coarsely chopped

2 tablespoons (18 grams) kosher salt

2 bay leaves

2 (1¼-pound or 566-gram) live lobsters

RED LOBSTER STOCK

3 tablespoons (45 grams) extra-virgin olive oil

1 large onion (160 grams), coarsely chopped

1 celery rib (80 grams), coarsely chopped

1 medium carrot (75 grams), coarsely chopped

1 (14-ounce or 397-gram) can cherry tomatoes

1 cup (236 milliliters) dry white wine

2 bay leaves

CONTINUED

when done to halt cooking. When completely cool, drain, then crack the shells and remove the meat from the claws and knuckles and tails (reserve the shells). Cut the tail meat crosswise into ⅓-inch (8-millimeter) pieces. Refrigerate the lobster meat, covered, until ready to use.

For the red lobster stock: In a large saucepan, heat the oil over medium-high heat. Add the reserved lobster shells and cook, stirring frequently, until lightly aromatic, about 3 minutes. Remove and set aside the shells. Add the onion, celery, and carrot to the pot. Cook, stirring occasionally, until tender (do not brown), about 8 minutes. Add the tomatoes and their juices and cook, breaking apart the tomatoes with a wooden spoon, 2 to 3 minutes more. Add the wine and cook until reduced by about half. Add the lobster shells, the reserved legs (with all pieces and juices), the roe and tomalley, bay leaves, and 2 quarts (1.8 liters) water. Bring just to a boil, then reduce to a gentle simmer. Cook until the stock is fragrant and flavorful and reduced to about 6⅓ cups (1.5 liters), 45 minutes to 1 hour. Strain the liquid and set aside.

For the cacciucco brodo: Reserving the shells, peel and devein the shrimp. Chill the shrimp, covered, until ready to use. In a 5- to 6-quart (4.7- to 5.6-liter) Dutch oven or wide heavy saucepan with lid, heat the oil over medium heat until hot but not smoking. Add the shrimp shells and cook until they begin to turn red, then add the onion, carrots, and celery. Cook, stirring occasionally, until crisp-tender (do not brown), about 8 minutes. Add the garlic and cook until fragrant and lightly golden, 1 to

2 minutes. Then add the tomatoes and their juices. Cook, breaking apart the tomatoes with a wooden spoon, 2 to 3 minutes more. Add the wine and cook until reduced by about half, then add the mussels and clams. Cover and cook, shaking the pan occasionally, until the shellfish open, 4 to 6 minutes for the mussels and 10 to 14 minutes for the clams. Transfer the shellfish to a bowl as they open. Discard any that do not open.

To the pot, add the lobster stock and 6⅓ cups (1.5 liters) of the crab stock (refrigerate or freeze the remaining crab stock for another use), along with the parsley, thyme, and bay leaf. Bring to a very gentle simmer and cook until the brodo is aromatic, flavorful, and reduced to 2 quarts (1.8 liters), about 1½ hours. Strain and set the cacciucco brodo aside. Meanwhile, remove the mussels and clams from their shells and refrigerate until ready to use (discard the shells).

For the garlic bread "soup": Heat the oven to 350°F (177°C). Cut the baguette crosswise into ½-inch (1.25-centimeter) slices. Arrange on a baking sheet and bake until dry and lightly golden, 12 to 15 minutes. Let cool completely. Meanwhile, combine the oil and garlic in a small saucepan. Heat over low heat, moving the pan off the heat as necessary to keep the garlic from taking on any color, until the garlic is tender, 8 to 10 minutes. Remove from the heat and set aside (you will finish the "soup" just before serving the cacciucco).

For the sweet shrimp alla busara: Increase the oven temperature to 375°F (190°C). Cut the garlic in half lengthwise. Thinly slice one half. Toast the bread crusts in the oven until lightly golden. While still warm, rub the insides of the crusts with the cut side of

CACCIUCCO BRODO

½ pound (225 grams) large or jumbo shrimp

2½ tablespoons (37 milliliters) extra-virgin olive oil

1 large yellow onion (160 grams), coarsely chopped

2 medium carrots (150 grams), coarsely chopped

1½ celery ribs (125 grams), coarsely chopped

4 garlic cloves (16 grams), gently smashed and peeled

1 (14-ounce or 397-gram) can cherry tomatoes

1 cup (236 milliliters) dry white wine

1 pound (453 grams) mussels

15 small littleneck clams

4 large parsley sprigs (30 grams)

3 leafy thyme sprigs

1 bay leaf

GARLIC BREAD "SOUP"

1 (4-inch or 10-centimeter) length of baguette

¼ cup (60 milliliters) extra-virgin olive oil

2 garlic cloves (8 grams), gently smashed and peeled

1 leafy thyme sprig

Scant 1¾ cups (395 milliliters) chicken broth, preferably homemade

Kosher salt

SWEET SHRIMP ALLA BUSARA

1 garlic clove (4 grams)

1 (8-inch or 20-centimeter) filone or baguette, insides removed and discarded, crust torn into 8 equal pieces

1½ tablespoons (23 milliliters) extra-virgin olive oil

CONTINUED

⅔ cup (150 milliliters) white wine

¼ cup (60 grams) cold unsalted butter, cut into small pieces

¼ teaspoon (½ gram) Hungarian sweet paprika

½ pound (230 grams) rock shrimp

Kosher salt

1½ tablespoons (5 grams) coarsely chopped flat-leaf parsley

TOMATO REDUCTION

¾ cup (185 grams) drained canned cherry tomatoes

1½ tablespoons (23 milliliters) extra-virgin olive oil

½ garlic clove (2 grams), thinly sliced

Pinch red chili flakes

2½ tablespoons (16 grams) finely chopped onion

2½ tablespoons (16 grams) finely chopped celery

2½ tablespoons (16 grams) finely chopped carrot

2½ tablespoons (16 grams) finely chopped fennel

⅓ cup plus 1½ tablespoons (total 95 milliliters) dry white wine

TO SERVE

3 ounces (85 grams) large scallops, quartered crosswise

5½ ounces (160 grams) medium squid (bodies and tentacles), bodies cut crosswise into ½-inch-thick (1.25-centimeter-thick) rings, tentacles cut in half if large

Leaves from 1 sprig marjoram

Kosher salt

Red chili flakes

Very good extra-virgin olive oil, preferably Sicilian (such as Olio Verde; see Larder, page xxix), for drizzling

the unsliced garlic. Discard the remaining unsliced garlic.

In a small saucepan, combine the sliced garlic and the oil. Heat over low heat until aromatic, 1 to 2 minutes, then add the wine. Increase the heat to medium-high and cook until the wine is reduced by about half. Reduce the heat to medium-low and add the butter one piece at a time, whisking constantly, to create an emulsified sauce, about 1 minute. Stir in the paprika, then add the shrimp and a pinch of salt. Cook, basting the shrimp with the sauce, just until opaque and cooked through, about 1 minute more. Remove from the heat. Stir in the parsley. Adjust the seasoning to taste.

For the tomato reduction: In a blender or using a food mill, purée the tomatoes until smooth; set aside. In a 5- to 6-quart (4.7- to 5.6-liter) Dutch oven or wide heavy saucepan with lid, heat the oil and garlic over medium heat until aromatic, about 30 seconds. Stir in the chili flakes, then add the onion, celery, carrot, and fennel. Cook, stirring occasionally, until the vegetables are crisp-tender (do not brown), about 2 minutes. Add the puréed tomatoes and cook until the sauce is thickened, about 3 minutes, then add the wine and continue to cook until reduced by half. Remove from the heat and set the tomato reduction aside.

Finish the garlic bread "soup": Add the toasted bread and thyme to the pan with the oil and garlic, then cover with 1 cup (236 milliliters) of the chicken broth and bring to a simmer. Cook until the bread is very soft, 3 to 5 minutes. Remove and discard the thyme. Transfer the pan contents to a blender. Add a generous pinch of salt. Purée until smooth. The "soup" should

be thick but pourable. Reserve and use the remaining chicken broth to thin the soup if necessary.

To serve: Add the cacciucco brodo to the tomato reduction. Bring just to a gentle simmer. Add the reserved raw peeled shrimp. Return to a very gentle simmer. Add the scallops and the reserved lobster, crabmeat, mussels, and clams. Then add the squid and marjoram. Cook just until the squid is tender, about 1 minute more. Remove from the heat. Adjust the salt and chili to taste.

Gently warm the shrimp busara in its sauce over very low heat just to heat through. Meanwhile, using a slotted spoon, transfer the shellfish to wide shallow serving bowls. Heat the cacciucco brodo just to a gentle simmer, then drizzle with the very good olive oil.

Ladle about 1 cup (240 milliliters) of the hot brodo into each bowl, then add a spoonful of the garlic bread soup. Mound the shrimp busara onto the toasted filone and serve on top of or alongside the cacciucco. Drizzle with very good oil. Serve the remaining cacciucco brodo on the side.

This fisherman's stew presents so many beautiful flavors in its layered seafood broth. It is generally best as a dish that transitions the meal into fuller red wines. Traditionally, cacciucco is paired with Sangiovese from the area around Livorno, where the recipe comes from, but there are many directions one can take. One favorite pairing is Stella di Campalto Rosso di Montalcino, which is made with 100 percent Sangiovese from the southern part of Montalcino, southeast of Livorno in the heart of Tuscany. It is light and aromatic, with fine tannins and a bright acidity that plays in concert with the elegance of this complex stew.

MONKFISH PICCATA

Serves 4 to 6

1½ pounds (680 grams) well-trimmed monkfish fillets, cut on the bias into scant ¾-inch-thick (2-centimeter-thick) medallions

Kosher salt and freshly ground black pepper

½ cup (130 grams) Wondra flour, for dredging

3 tablespoons (45 milliliters) vegetable oil

3 tablespoons (45 milliliters) dry white wine

1½ tablespoons (23 milliliters) heavy cream

½ pound (225 grams) cold unsalted butter, cut into small pieces

1½ tablespoons (23 milliliters) fresh lemon juice

⅓ cup (40 grams) salt-packed capers, rinsed and soaked (see Larder, page xxiv)

1½ tablespoons (5 grams) finely chopped flat-leaf parsley

Everyone—yes, everyone—likes lemon and capers. And as players in veal piccata, the flavor profile is an Italian-American standby. When introducing new things to my customers, I often use a recognizable or classic garnish or technique to lessen their trepidation. In 1993, monkfish was still considered adventurous, and I must say that the original version of this dish at Pó became our most popular fish presentation.—*Mario Batali*

At Del Posto, Vignarola (page 150) is served as a *contorno*, or "side dish," for Monkfish Picatta.

Season each piece of fish with salt and pepper, then dredge them in the flour and pat off the excess. In a 10- to 12-inch (25- to 30-centimeter) skillet, heat 2 tablespoons (30 milliliters) of the oil over medium-high heat until just smoking. Working in two batches and adding the remaining oil as needed, cook the fish in the hot oil, on one side only, about 2 minutes, until evenly browned (the fish will finish cooking later in the sauce). Transfer to a large plate lined with paper towels. Remove the skillet from the heat, discard any excess oil, and wipe dry with paper towels.

In the skillet, bring the wine to a boil and cook until reduced by half, then add the cream. Reduce the heat to low. Whisk in the butter, one piece at a time, to create an emulsified sauce, then whisk in the lemon juice. Stir in the capers and parsley.

Transfer the sauce to the skillet, then arrange the fish on top, browned side up. Over very low heat, gently cook the fish in the sauce until just cooked through, about 3 minutes. Transfer to a large platter or serving plates.

SECONDI: CARNE & CONTORNI

The Italians are savvy carnivores, with
long-standing artisanal customs for raising and butchering animals.
The meat course, which comes after the pasta and salads,
is not always the centerpiece of a meal as it can be in America. Meat
preparations for the secondo vary greatly from region to region,
based on local traditions for wild and farmed animals. *Manzo,* or
beef, is part of the regional cuisine of Tuscany and the Alpine
regions of the North, waterfowl are found in the Veneto, and local
heritage-breed pigs are raised in the many different regions in
central and southern Italy. Larger cuts of meat and whole
birds are considered a luxury, rarely found in the cucina povera of
the South, which devised inventive ways to make the most
from inexpensive off-cuts and offal.

At Del Posto, the secondi are informed by regional meat
preparations from both rustic and refined Italian kitchens. In this
chapter, prime cuts create foundations for classic recipes with humble
roots, such as the veal braciole and the abbacchio alla Romana. Our
standing rib roast and veal shank with truffles provide festive and
extravagant experiences for larger parties. Seasonal *contorni,*
side dishes, are paired with specific secondi here but appear as
separate recipes. They are designed to be flexible and can be
matched with any number of protein dishes.

CARNE

APICIUS DUCK WITH SAVOR

De re coquinaria is a fifth-century compendium of Roman recipes (many of which date back to the first century) authored by a small group of unknown gourmands referred to as Apicius. Ancient Roman kitchens from the first century onward celebrated the spices from the Far East and North Africa that became available with the development of Rome's spice trade. This recipe for Long Island duck pays homage to Apicius and ancient Italian recipes with a spiced glaze taken from the pages of *De re coquinaria*. The duck is paired with charred celery and a condiment named Savor, created by our friend Massimo Bottura. We first tasted his Savor in the early 2000s, soon after his restaurant Osteria Francescana received its first Michelin star. This delicious paste is made from quince paste, chestnuts, and apples and rolled in pumpkin seeds. Its lovely combination of sweet and savory elements is the perfect contemporary foil for the antique duck glaze.

For the Savor: Into a medium saucepan, finely grate the zest from the orange and lemon. Juice enough of the orange to yield 3 tablespoons plus 1 teaspoon (total 50 milliliters) juice. Juice enough of the lemon to yield 2 tablespoons plus 1 teaspoon (total 35 milliliters) juice. Add the juices to the pot, along with 1 tablespoon (8 grams) of the pumpkin seeds, then add the pumpkin purée, chestnuts, saba, quince paste, and bay leaf. Gently simmer over medium-low heat, stirring occasionally, until the mixture is thickened to the consistency of thick tomato paste, 12 to 15 minutes.

Remove and discard the bay leaf. Stir in ¼ teaspoon (1 gram) salt. In the bowl of a food processor, purée the mixture until smooth. Transfer to a bowl. Set the Savor aside to cool completely.

In a small skillet, heat the remaining ⅓ cup (40 grams) of pumpkin seeds over medium-low heat, tossing occasionally,

until fragrant and lightly toasted, about 5 minutes. Remove from the heat and season with salt while warm. Transfer to a plate and let cool completely. Meanwhile, stir the pear and apple into the Savor.

For the duck: Heat the oven to 350°F (177°C). Season the duck breasts with salt and pepper, then place, skin side down, in a cold cast-iron or other heavy skillet. Cook over medium heat, pouring off the fat, until golden and just crisp, about 15 minutes. Turn the duck skin side up. Transfer the skillet to the oven and roast until an instant-read thermometer inserted into the center of a breast at the thickest part registers 130°F (54°C) for medium-rare, 8 to 12 minutes.

Meanwhile, roll the Savor into 1-inch (2.5-centimeter) balls. Roll the balls in the reserved pumpkin seeds. Set aside.

Transfer the duck breasts to a carving board and let rest for 10 minutes (reserve

SAVOR

1 orange

1 lemon

⅓ cup plus 1 tablespoon (total 48 grams) raw pumpkin seeds

⅓ cup (85 grams) canned pumpkin purée

About 5 frozen chestnuts (50 grams), thawed and coarsely chopped

2 tablespoons (30 milliliters) saba or vincotto (see notes)

Generous 2 tablespoons (35 grams) quince paste

1 bay leaf

Kosher salt

¼ cup (30 grams) finely diced Anjou pear (or other dense-fleshed pear)

¼ cup (25 grams) finely diced Honeycrisp apple (or other sweet and slightly tart apple)

DUCK

4 (7- to 8-ounce or 200- to 225-gram) Long Island (also called Peking) duck breast halves with skin; excess fat removed and skin scored

Kosher salt and freshly ground black pepper

4 teaspoons (16 grams) La Boîte Mishmish N.33 (see notes)

2 teaspoons (8 grams) La Boîte Cancale N.11 (see notes)

2 tablespoons plus 1 teaspoon (total 47 grams) honey

1 tablespoon (15 grams) lemon or orange marmalade

4 legs duck confit, at room temperature (see notes)

4 celery ribs (with leaves) from the inner heart of the bunch

the skillet). Meanwhile, in a small bowl, stir together the Mishmish N.33 and the Cancale N.11. In a second bowl, stir together 1 teaspoon (4 grams) of the spice mixture and the honey and marmalade to form a glaze. Set aside.

Season the duck confit legs all over with the remaining spice mixture, then place, skin side down, in the skillet. Heat over medium heat until the legs are warmed through with crisp skins, then transfer to a plate. Pour the excess fat from the skillet, then return the skillet to medium heat. Add the celery and cook, turning once, until crisp-tender, about 2 minutes.

Slice the duck breasts crosswise. Brush the breast and leg pieces with the glaze. Arrange on serving plates with the celery and Savor.

NOTES: *Saba is a grape must reduction, similar to vincotto, or cooked wine. Both of these can be purchased at gourmet stores or online. La Boîte is a brand of signature spice blends that can be purchased online. N.33 is a blend of lemon, saffron, and crystalized honey. N.11 is a blend of orange, fennel, and salt. Confit duck legs can be made at home or purchased at gourmet stores or online.*

❧ WINE PAIRING ❧

Duck is always a friend of Pinot Noir, but the Apicius spices give this dish a distinct identity that lends itself to different wines. The spices are a mixture of sweet and savory, evoking notes of big *botti* (large aging barrels found throughout Italy's wineries), and the duck is flat-out rich. The wines of Piedmont, from the northern foothills of the region to the southern towns of Barolo and Barbaresco, will pair well here. Piedmont's native Barbera and Nebbiolo grapes are simply sublime with the duck. Wines from Carema, Lessona, Barolo, Barbaresco, and Gattinara have fine to firm tannins and range from medium-bodied to very full-bodied. Ferrando Carema is a classic Nebbiolo from the far north of Piedmont, and a wonderful pairing.

VEAL BRACIOLE

Thin slices of veal, beef, or pork stuffed with vegetables and rolled up, braciole are usually pan-seared or grilled. The American-Italian kitchen often stews them in a long-cooking braise of tomato and root vegetables. In Italy, braciole are most common in Sicily, where they are generally called *involtini,* meaning "small bundles," and can include some type of cheese in the filling.

This braciole recipe is more delicate than most American-Italian versions. Rather than braised shoulder or leg, tender veal loin is pan-seared and then roasted to medium-rare. The mushroom ragù filling adds depth to the veal, and conjures the earthy flavors and aromas of a slow-cooked cut of meat.

Del Posto's version of Eggplant Parmigiana (page 152) is also inspired by the American-Italian kitchen and is served as contorno for the braciole.

For the porcini ragù: Heat the oven to 450°F (232°C). Rinse the mushrooms under cold running water to remove any grit. Pat well dry with paper towels. On a rimmed baking sheet, toss the mushrooms with 15 milliliters (1 tablespoon) of the oil and season with salt and pepper. Roast until golden, about 15 minutes. Remove from the oven and let cool completely. Coarsely chop the mushrooms.

In a large skillet, heat the remaining 1 tablespoon (15 milliliters) oil over medium heat and add the garlic and shallot. Cook, stirring occasionally, until fragrant (do not brown), about 1 minute, then add the thyme and cook 30 seconds more. Add the mushrooms and cook until the flavors have blended, about 2 minutes, then add the agresto and toss to combine. Transfer the ragù to a plate and let cool completely.

For the veal and sauce: Place the veal on a clean work surface, with one of the short ends of each piece facing you. Season with salt and pepper, then spread the ragù over

the pieces, leaving a ½-inch (1.25-centimeter) border uncovered. Fold the border over the filling, then fold in the side borders to overlap the filling. Roll each piece of veal tightly and secure with kitchen twine. Wrap tightly in plastic wrap and refrigerate at least 1 hour or overnight.

Heat the oven to 350°F (177°C). Remove and discard the plastic wrap from the veal, then season all over with salt and pepper. In a large cast-iron skillet, heat 1½ tablespoons (22 milliliters) of the oil over medium-high heat until hot but not smoking. Beginning with the seam side down, sear the veal until golden brown on all sides, 3 to 4 minutes.

Transfer the skillet to the oven. Roast until an instant-read thermometer inserted into the thickest part of the meat registers 125°F (51°C) for medium-rare, 8 to 10 minutes. Let the veal rest on a carving board for 10 minutes.

Meanwhile, add the remaining 1 tablespoon (15 milliliters) oil to the skillet and heat over medium-high heat. Add the

Serves 4 to 6

PORCINI RAGÙ

7 ounces (200 grams) frozen porcini mushrooms, thawed

2 tablespoons (30 milliliters) extra-virgin olive oil

Kosher salt and freshly ground black pepper

2 garlic cloves (8 grams), finely chopped

1 tablespoon (10 grams) finely chopped shallots

2 sprigs thyme

1 teaspoon (5 milliliters) dry marsala wine

VEAL AND SAUCE

2 veal tenderloins (about 1½ pounds or 680 grams total), butterflied and gently pounded to a ¼-inch (6-millimeter) thickness

Kosher salt and freshly ground black pepper

2½ tablespoons (37 milliliters) extra-virgin olive oil

1 medium carrot (90 grams), cut on the bias into ⅓-inch (8-millimeter) pieces

1 medium celery rib (70 grams), cut on the bias into ⅓-inch (8-millimeter) pieces

4 small cipolline onions, peeled

½ cup (120 milliliters) veal demi-glace (see note)

TO SERVE

Very good extra-virgin olive oil, preferably Tuscan (see Larder, page xxix)

SPECIAL EQUIPMENT: kitchen twine

carrot, celery, and onions. Cook, turning once, until deep golden on both sides, about 2 minutes, then add the demi-glace. Bring the liquid to a simmer and cook, scraping up the pan bits, until reduced by one-quarter, about 3 minutes. Remove from the heat.

Slice the veal crosswise into medallions. Arrange on serving plates with the vegetables. Spoon the pan juices over the top. Drizzle with the very good olive oil.

NOTE: *Veal demi-glace is a slow-cooked, concentrated veal stock, made from veal bones, vegetables, and aromatics. It can be purchased at gourmet stores and online.*

EMILIA-STYLE PORK
with Prosciutto, Parmigiano, and Balsamic

Serves 8

PORK

1 (8-rib) bone-in center-cut rack of pork (5½ to 6½ pounds or 2½ to 3 kilograms), chine bone removed, rib bones frenched, roast tied

Kosher salt and freshly ground black pepper

8 leafy thyme sprigs

8 leafy rosemary sprigs

2 heads garlic, cut in half crosswise

3 tablespoons (45 milliliters) extra-virgin olive oil

TO SERVE

8 very thin slices prosciutto di Parma

25-year balsamic vinegar (see Larder, page xxvi), for drizzling

Very good extra-virgin olive oil, preferably Tuscan (see Larder, page xxix), for drizzling

3 tablespoons (13 grams) freshly grated Parmigiano-Reggiano cheese (at least 24-month aged; see Larder, page xxiv)

The Emilia-Romagna region, known as the breadbasket of Italy, is also home to many iconic culinary delicacies, including Parmigiano-Reggiano, prosciutto di Parma, and traditional balsamic vinegar. Celebrating the region's special products, these center-cut pork chops are crowned with a slice of grilled prosciutto, a sprinkle of Parmigiano, and a drizzle of the best balsamic. They are served with a contorno of smashed and fried sunchokes (page 151).

For the pork: Heat the oven to 500°F (260°C) with the rack in the lower third. Wrap the bone tips with foil to prevent burning.

Generously season the meat all over with salt and pepper, then set, bone side down, in a rack fitted in a roasting pan. Roast for 15 minutes, then reduce the oven temperature to 350°F (177°C). Scatter the herbs and garlic head halves on the rack. Drizzle the meat and the aromatics with the oil.

Continue roasting the meat, rotating the pan one or two times for even browning, until an instant-read thermometer inserted into the pork at the center of the top registers 133°F (56°C) for medium-rare, 45 minutes to 1 hour more. Transfer the roast to a carving board, cover loosely with foil, and let rest for 30 minutes (the internal temperature will rise 5 to 10 degrees).

To serve: Heat a grill or grill pan over medium-high heat. Grill the prosciutto slices, turning once, until crisp and slightly charred. Cut the roast between the bone ribs to form chops. Arrange on serving plates. Drizzle with the vinegar, very good olive oil, and any carving juices. Garnish with the Parmigiano and prosciutto.

❦ WINE PAIRING ❦

Emilia-Romagna's prosciutto and balsamic make the chops a great base for one of Italy's most classic grapes, Sangiovese. Emilia-Romagna may be better known as the home of Lambrusco, but Sangiovese produces noble wines of exciting character throughout the region. Not as subtle as those from nearby Tuscany, Emilia's Sangiovese wines have distinct lush, dark-fruit profiles, making them easier to enjoy in their youth. One of the best producers in Emilia-Romagna, if not the *best*, is San Patrignano. Their 100 percent Sangiovese wine Avi is a perfect example of the region's expression of the grape. Its plump richness, balanced by bright acidity, is a perfect pairing that can be defined by the expression "If it grows together, it goes together."

SLOW-COOKED LAMB ALLA ROMANA

Abbacchio alla Romana is an Easter tradition in Rome and Lazio. Celebrating the resurrection of Jesus, the Lamb of God, this dish is prized by the Romans at springtime. The word *abbacchio* is thought to come from *baccio* in the Roman dialect, referring to a shepherd's stick. Traditionally, abbacchio is a spring lamb that weighs less than 20 pounds (9 kilograms), old enough to graze but still dependent on its mother's milk. There are many recipes for abbacchio alla Romana, but roasting the lamb with a simple mix of herbs and garlic, and sometimes vinegar and anchovy, is standard.

This recipe is portioned for a large group, calling for a whole lamb (to be broken down by a butcher) instead of a smaller spring lamb, which can be hard to find. The recipe can easily be scaled down for fewer people by roasting just the loin chops and racks.

Puntarelle Salad (page 153) is a regionally appropriate contorno for abbacchio alla Romana. Puntarelle is a bittersweet chicory exclusive to Roman cuisine, where it is tossed in a dressing of anchovy, oil, and lemon juice.

Serves 16 to 20

1 (45-pound or 20-kilogram) whole baby lamb, broken down into forelegs, hind legs (with all but a thin layer of fat trimmed), neck, belly flaps, racks (with rib bones frenched), and 6 (1-inch-thick or 2.5-centimeter-thick) loin chops (see note)

1¼ cups (300 milliliters) extra-virgin olive oil

3 large bunches fresh rosemary

3 large bunches fresh thyme

12 fresh bay leaves

Kosher salt and freshly ground black pepper

4 heads garlic, cut in half crosswise

TO SERVE

Very good extra-virgin olive oil, preferably Tuscan (see Larder, page xxix)

Maldon sea salt

SPECIAL EQUIPMENT: 2 (1-gallon or 4-liter) resealable plastic bags; 2 large roasting pans with racks; 18-inch-wide (46-centimeter-wide) heavy-duty foil to cover roasting pans

Place the lamb racks together in a large resealable plastic bag. Repeat with the loin chops. To each bag, add ¼ cup (60 milliliters) of the oil, ½ bunch of each of the herbs, and 2 bay leaves. Press out the air from the bags, then seal. Rub the outside of each bag with your hands to coat the meat with the oil and aromatics. Marinate, refrigerated, at least 4 hours or up to 1 day.

Meanwhile, to roast the forelegs, belly flaps, and neck: Heat the oven to 300°F (149°C). Rub the lamb forelegs, belly flaps, and neck with a total of ¼ cup plus 2 tablespoons (total 90 milliliters) of the oil and season generously with salt and pepper. Arrange in 2 roasting pans fitted with racks. Scatter a total of ½ bunch of each of the herbs, 4 garlic head halves, and 4 of the bay leaves over and around the meat in the pans. Cover the pans with foil, tightly sealing at the edges. Roast until the meat is very tender and pulls away easily from the bones, 3½ to 4 hours.

Remove the pan from the oven. Transfer the meat to a carving board and let it rest, uncovered, for 20 minutes. Remove and discard the herbs and aromatics. Strain the pan drippings through a medium-mesh strainer into a bowl. Chill the drippings in the refrigerator until cold, then scrape off and discard the fat that has formed on top of the pan juices. Cover and return the juices to the refrigerator until ready to serve.

Tear the meat from the bones into chunks. Discard the bones. Keep the meat covered until ready to serve. (The forelegs, neck, and belly flaps can be roasted up to 1 day ahead. If making ahead, keep the meat covered and refrigerated until ready to serve.)

To roast the hind legs: Increase the oven temperature to 500°F (260°C). Rub each of the lamb hind legs with 3 tablespoons (45 milliliters) of the oil and season generously with salt and pepper. Arrange in two roasting pans fitted with racks. Roast for 10 minutes, then reduce the oven temperature to 325°F (163°C). Scatter the remaining herbs, remaining 4 garlic head halves, and remaining 8 bay leaves over and around the meat. Continue roasting until an instant-read thermometer inserted into the thickest part of the meat, not touching the bone, registers 125°F (52°C) for medium-rare, 40 minutes to 1 hour more. Transfer the meat to a carving board and let it rest, uncovered, for 20 minutes (the temperature of the meat will rise to about 130°F or 54°C for medium-rare).

Meanwhile, to reheat the forelegs and neck meat: Reduce the oven temperature to 275°F (135°C). Combine the reserved foreleg and neck meat and the defatted juices in a roasting pan without a rack (save the belly flap meat for another use). Cover and seal the pan tightly with foil. Place in the oven to warm for about 20 minutes (from room temperature) while you grill the racks and chops.

To grill the racks and chops: Prepare or heat a grill to medium-high to high heat. Remove the racks and loin chops from the marinade, letting the excess oil drip off. Season the racks and chops generously with salt and pepper. Sear the racks of lamb over high heat, meaty side down, until well browned, about 6 minutes. Turn the racks so that they are leaning against each other with the bones pointing up and grill until well browned on the bottoms, about 3 minutes. Turn the racks bone side down and continue cooking until an instant-read thermometer inserted into the center of the meat registers 130°F (54°C) for medium-rare, 5 to 8 minutes more. Meanwhile, grill the loin chops, turning once or twice, until an instant-read thermometer inserted into the center of the meat registers 130°F (54°C) for medium-rare, about 14 minutes total.

Transfer the racks and chops to a carving board and let rest for 10 minutes.

To serve: Using a sharp slicing knife, carve the racks between the bones into chops. Thinly slice the meat from each hind leg perpendicular to the bones on each side, then cut the meat from the bones by slicing along the bones. Remove the foreleg and neck meat from the oven. Arrange various cuts of the meat on serving plates. Spoon warm juices over the top. Drizzle with the very good oil and sprinkle with Maldon salt.

NOTE: *Whole baby lamb can be broken down as instructed in the ingredient list by most local butchers.*

STINCO DI VITELLO

Cooking secondary cuts of meat is a great love of mine, and there is nothing better than roasting stinco di vitello, the forefront shanks of a calf. Most people know and have enjoyed the osso buco, which is a cross section of the stinco shank, but roasting the whole shank is wonderful. A traditional dish in the Friuli-Venezia Giulia region of Italy, it takes a while to roast a stinco until all the meat (muscles) around the bone are fork-tender and the cartilage melts into that delicious texture that makes one's fingers stick together. Roasted stinco makes an impressive presentation, as the shank is quite easy to carve in front of guests (and the bones should be left at the table for everyone to pick on). —*Lidia Bastianich*

Large cuts of meat can be served with a variety of contorni, or side dishes, presented family-style or plated with the meat. At Del Posto, the Stinco di Vitello and the Standing Rib Roast is served with a collection of contorni, including Nervetti Salad (page 154), Potato Chip Salad (page 155), and Scafata (page 156).

Place a (2-gallon or 7½-liter) resealable plastic bag into a large bowl. Place the shank in the bag, then fold the top of the bag to form a collar (to help keep the bag open). In a second large bowl, vigorously whisk together 2 quarts (1.8 liters) cold water, 1 cup (192 grams) salt, and the sugar until the salt and sugar are dissolved. Pour into the bag with the shank, then add 2 quarts (1.8 liters) additional cold water. Pressing out the air, tightly seal the bag. Refrigerate for 8 hours or overnight.

Heat the oven to 350ºF (177ºC). Remove the shank from the brine (do not rinse) and generously season with salt and pepper (discard the brine). In a large heavy skillet, heat the oil over medium-high heat. Brown the shank on all sides.

Reserving the skillet and oil, transfer the shank to a large Dutch oven or heavy roasting pan with a lid. Add the celery, carrot, and onion to the skillet; cook over medium-high heat, stirring occasionally, until softened and browned, about 10 minutes. Add the wine and cook until evaporated. Transfer the vegetables to the pan with the shank. Add the broth, mushrooms, herbs, and bay leaf. Bring the liquid to a simmer, then remove from the heat.

Cut a round of parchment paper to fit just inside the Dutch oven. Cover the shank with the parchment. Tightly cover the pan with foil, then with the lid. Braise the shank in the oven until tender, 2 to 2½ hours.

Meanwhile, in a small bowl, stir together the butter and truffle. Transfer to a sheet of plastic wrap. Fold the wrap over, then roll up the butter into a cylinder. Refrigerate until ready to use.

Carefully remove the foil and parchment from the braising pan, then return the pan

Serves 4

1 (4-pound or 1.8-kilogram) bone-in veal shank, fat trimmed

1 cup (192 grams) kosher salt, plus more for seasoning

¼ cup (50 grams) sugar

Freshly ground black pepper

2 tablespoons (30 milliliters) extra-virgin olive oil

2 celery ribs (160 grams), coarsely chopped

1 medium carrot (75 grams), coarsely chopped

1 medium yellow onion (260 grams), coarsely chopped

¼ cup (60 milliliters) dry white wine

1 quart (950 milliliters) chicken broth, preferably homemade

¼ cup (6 grams) dried porcini mushrooms

1 leafy sprig rosemary

1 leafy sprig thyme

1 bay leaf

2 tablespoons (31 grams) unsalted butter, softened

Scant 1 ounce (25 grams) fresh black truffles, finely chopped (see Larder, page xxix)

SPECIAL EQUIPMENT: 1 (2-gallon or 7½-liter) resealable plastic bag; parchment paper; a food mill or medium-mesh sieve

From left to right:
Scafata (page 156);
Potato Chip Salad (page 155);
Standing Rib Roast (page 149);
Nervetti Salad (page 154);
Stinco di Vitello (page 145)

to the oven and cook the shank, uncovered, for 20 minutes (to lightly brown). Transfer the shank to a plate and loosely cover with foil. Drain the vegetables and reserve the cooking liquid. Grind the vegetables through the small holes of a food mill (or force through a medium-mesh sieve) into a medium saucepan. Stir in 1 cup (236 milliliters) of the cooking liquid.

Cut the truffle butter into small pieces. Bring the vegetable sauce to a gentle simmer, then whisk in the truffle butter, one piece at a time. Remove the sauce from the heat. Stand the roast upright, then thinly slice. Serve drizzled with the truffle butter sauce.

❧ WINE PAIRING ❧

Famous in eastern Italy, stinco di vitello illustrates the idea that regional dishes pair well with regional wines. Roasted veal shank is found throughout Friuli, and the wines from the region seem as though they are designed just for this dish. Known mostly for white grapes, Friuli does grow two unique red grapes, Schioppettino and Refosco. Both of these produce medium- to full-bodied red wines with dense dark-fruit notes, distinct herbal qualities, and fine to firm tannins. Ronchi di Cialla's Schioppettino, Scarbolo's Refosco, and a blend from the Bastianich estate called Vespa Rosso are exceptional examples. All three of these wines highlight the richness and density of the stinco but display the classic Italian acidity, which prevents your palate from getting tired.

STANDING RIB ROAST

A large bone-in rib roast highlights the grandeur of Del Posto's hospitality. This opulent prime roast is sliced and served family-style with a variety of contorni, including Nervetti Salad (page 154), Potato Chip Salad (page 155), and Scafata (page 156).

(page 154), Potato Chip Salad (page 155), and Scafata (page 156).

Heat the oven to 500°F (260°C) with the rack in the lower third. Wrap the bone tips with foil to prevent burning.

Generously season the meat all over with salt and pepper, then set it, bone side down, in a roasting pan fitted with a rack. Roast for 15 minutes.

Reduce the oven temperature to 350°F (177°C). Scatter the herbs and garlic halves on the rack, then drizzle the meat and the aromatics with the oil. Roast until an instant-read thermometer inserted into the center of the meat (not touching bone) registers 115°F (46°C), about 1½ to 2 hours more. Transfer the roast to a carving board, cover it loosely with foil, and let it rest for 30 minutes (the temperature of the meat will rise to about 130°F or 54°C for medium-rare).

Slice the meat between the rib bones and serve. Pour any carving juices over the meat.

Serves 8

1 (4-rib) bone-in prime rib roast (9 to 10 pounds or 4 to 4½ kilograms), chine bone removed, rib bones frenched, roast tied

Kosher salt and freshly ground black pepper

8 leafy thyme sprigs

8 leafy rosemary sprigs

2 heads garlic, cut in half crosswise

3 tablespoons (45 milliliters) extra-virgin olive oil

CONTORNI

Contorni, or side dishes, are vegetable-centric preparations served alongside larger secondi. These contorno recipes are portioned for four to six people and can be served family-style or on small side plates. The recipes are pictured with their respective secondi, but they can accompany any number of protein dishes.

VIGNAROLA

This Roman vegetable stew, named for the *vignarole*, the women tasked with weeding and grooming vineyards in early spring around Rome, is served as an antipasto or contorno in springtime. Roman-style artichokes, fava beans, and peas are the base ingredients of most vignarola recipes, but other tender spring vegetables can be included. Vignarola is paired with the Monkfish Piccata recipe on page 130.

Serves 4 to 6

2 medium carrots (150 grams), peeled and cut on a bias into ⅛-inch-thick (3-millimeter-thick) slices

Kosher salt

1 cup (125 grams) shelled fresh fava beans (from 1 pound or 453 grams pods)

1½ tablespoons (22 milliliters) extra-virgin olive oil

1 batch Artichokes alla Romano (page 50), drained and quartered

1 cup (125 grams) shelled fresh or thawed frozen peas

1 celery rib (80 grams), cut on a bias into ⅛-inch-thick (3-millimeter-thick) slices

8 small red pearl onions (80 grams), peeled

1 heaping cup (80 grams) ¾-inch (2-centimeter) Romanesco or regular cauliflower florets

Freshly ground black pepper

Very good extra-virgin olive oil, preferably Ligurian (see Larder, page xxix), for drizzling

Cook the carrots in a small saucepan of generously salted boiling water until crisp-tender, about 2 minutes. Using a slotted spoon, transfer immediately to a medium-mesh sieve and plunge into a bowl of ice water to stop cooking. Let cool 1 to 2 minutes. Lifting the sieve, drain the carrots, then pat dry. (Reserve the cooking water and the ice water.)

Return the water to a boil, add the fava beans, and cook for 1 minute, then drain and plunge into the ice water to stop cooking. Let cool 1 to 2 minutes, then drain and gently peel the beans. Discard the skins.

In a 12-inch (30-centimeter) skillet, heat the oil over medium-high heat until hot but not smoking. Add half of each of the vegetables (the carrots, favas, artichokes, peas, celery, pearl onions, and Romanesco). Cook (do not stir or season) until the edges are just golden, 3 to 4 minutes, then toss and cook 1½ minutes more.

Reduce the heat to medium. Add all the remaining vegetables, 1 tablespoon (15 milliliters) water, and a generous pinch each of salt and pepper. Cook, tossing occasionally, until about half of the vegetables are tender and the rest are crisp-tender, about 3 minutes more. Transfer to a serving plate and drizzle with the very good oil. Serve warm.

SMASHED SUNCHOKES

Sunchokes are Jerusalem artichokes (often called *topinambour* in Italy), tubers that grow on the root systems of the sunchoke flower, a species of sunflower. They have nutty and artichoke flavors and a potato-like texture. Del Posto's roasted, smashed, and fried sunchokes are paired with the Emilia-Style Pork on page 140.

Serves 4 to 6

1½ pounds (680 grams) medium sunchokes, unpeeled

3 tablespoons (45 milliliters) extra-virgin olive oil

Kosher salt and freshly ground black pepper

2½ cups (600 milliliters) vegetable oil, for frying

4 sprigs fresh rosemary

4 bay leaves

SPECIAL EQUIPMENT: a candy / fry thermometer

Heat the oven to 375°F (190°C). On a baking sheet, toss the sunchokes with the olive oil, 1 teaspoon (4 grams) salt, and a generous pinch of pepper. Roast, turning occasionally, until golden and tender, about 1 hour.

Remove the sunchokes from the oven and transfer to a large cutting board. When cool enough to handle, gently press each sunchoke with the heel of your hand to flatten to about ½ inch (1.25 centimeters) thick.

In a large heavy skillet, heat the vegetable oil until a candy / fry thermometer registers 350°F (177°C). In batches of 3 or 4, fry the sunchokes, turning once, until golden with crisp skins, 3 to 3½ minutes per side. Using a slotted spoon, transfer to paper towels to drain. Season with salt while hot.

As you are removing the last batch of sunchokes from the oil, fry the rosemary and bay leaves until aromatic and just crispy, about 30 seconds. Drain on paper towels. Season with salt. Serve the sunchokes immediately with the fried rosemary and bay leaves.

EGGPLANT PARMIGIANA

Serves 4 to 6

5 (11- to 12-inch or 28- to 30-centimeter) Japanese eggplants

1 tablespoon (15 milliliters) extra-virgin olive oil

Kosher salt

4¼ cups (1 liter) vegetable oil, for frying

1 cup (110 grams) rice flour

1⅔ cups (400 milliliters) Del Posto Tomato Sauce (see 100-Layer Lasagne, page 98)

8 ounces (225 grams) burrata cheese, torn into small pieces; or fresh mozzarella, thinly sliced

2 tablespoons (7 grams) Panne Grattato (page 55) or coarse plain breadcrumbs

3 tablespoons (12 grams) grated Parmigiano-Reggiano cheese (at least 24-month aged; see Larder, page xxiv)

3 grams (1 tablespoon) coarsely chopped flat-leaf parsley

SPECIAL EQUIPMENT: parchment paper, a candy / fry thermometer

This classic from the canon of American-Italian recipes is served as a side dish at Del Posto. Baked Japanese eggplant "boats" are stuffed with fried eggplant pieces and tomato sauce, then topped with burrata and breadcrumbs. Portioned for one boat per person, they are paired with the Veal Braciole on page 137.

Heat the oven to 450°F (232°C). Line a rimmed baking sheet with parchment paper.

Halve the eggplants lengthwise. Using a paring knife, carefully cut around the inside edges, then cut out and reserve the flesh, leaving just enough (about ⅛ inch or 3 millimeters) along the interior walls so that the eggplants hold their "boat" shape when baked.

Arrange 8 of the boats flesh side up on the prepared baking sheet. (Discard the remaining 2 boats, but reserve all of the cut-out flesh.) Drizzle with the olive oil and season with salt. Bake until lightly golden, 18 to 20 minutes.

Meanwhile, in a heavy wide saucepan or high-sided skillet, heat the vegetable oil to 375°F (190°C). While the oil is heating, cut the eggplant flesh crosswise into ¾-inch (2-centimeter) pieces. Spread on a large plate and season lightly with salt. Let stand 5 minutes. Dredge the eggplant pieces in the flour, coating them thoroughly and shaking off the excess. In batches, fry until lightly golden and crispy, 1 to 2 minutes per batch. Using a slotted spoon, transfer to paper towels to drain. Season with salt while warm.

Remove the boats from the oven (leave the oven on).

In a bowl, toss together the fried eggplant and tomato sauce. Spoon the mixture into the boats. Top with the burrata. Bake until the eggplant parmigiana are hot and the cheese is melted, 12 to 15 minutes. Remove from the oven. Sprinkle with the panne grattato or breadcrumbs, Parmigiano, and parsley.

PUNTARELLE SALAD

Puntarelle is a unique, bittersweet chicory found in Roman cuisine. The locals have an age-old technique for whittling the puntarelle stalks into thin strips with a paring knife. The strips are then tossed with an anchovy and milk-poached-garlic dressing. The salad is paired with the Slow-Cooked Lamb alla Romana on page 143.

Serves 4 to 6

1 head puntarelle (1½ pounds or 680 grams)

1 cup (240 milliliters) whole milk

4 garlic cloves (16 grams), peeled and halved lengthwise

6 flat anchovy fillets, plus 1 tablespoon (15 milliliters) of their oil

1¼ teaspoons (6 milliliters) fresh lemon juice

Kosher salt

¼ cup (60 milliliters) extra-virgin olive oil

From the puntarelle, trim and discard any bruised or fibrous exterior leaves. Trim the leafy green tops from the remaining leaves, then rinse and drain. Wrap loosely in a barely dampened paper towel, place in a plastic bag, and refrigerate until ready to use. Cut the puntarelle core into individual stalks. Cut the stalks in half lengthwise and whittle them lengthwise into thin slices with a paring knife.

Submerge the slices in a bowl of ice water and soak for 15 to 20 minutes, then drain. Repeat the soaking process twice, using fresh ice water each time (this crisps and curls the puntarelle and removes some of the bitterness, and can be repeated many times).

Meanwhile, combine the milk and garlic in a small saucepan and bring to a gentle simmer over medium heat. Reduce to a bare simmer and cook, stirring occasionally, until the garlic is very tender, 15 to 20 minutes.

In a small skillet, heat the anchovies and anchovy oil over very low heat. Cook, stirring frequently, until the anchovies begin to dissolve, 2 to 3 minutes. Remove from the heat.

Using a slotted spoon, transfer the garlic to a blender. Add 3 tablespoons (45 milliliters) of the milk (discard the remaining milk), the anchovies and their oil, the lemon juice, and a pinch of salt. With the machine running, add the olive oil in a slow and steady stream.

Drain and pat dry the soaked puntarelle, then place in a large bowl with the reserved leafy tops. Toss with the dressing. Adjust the seasoning to taste.

NERVETTI SALAD

Serves 4 to 6

NERVETTI

8 ounces (225 grams) veal
or beef tendon (see note)

1 medium yellow onion
(200 grams), coarsely chopped

1 medium carrot (75 grams),
coarsely chopped

1 celery rib (80 grams),
coarsely chopped

2 leafy sprigs thyme

2 bay leaves

SALAD

1 (15-ounce or 425-gram) can
cannellini beans, rinsed and drained

1 medium carrot (75 grams), peeled
and thinly sliced on the bias

1 celery rib (80 grams), thinly sliced
on the bias

1 large shallot (75 grams), halved
and thinly sliced

¾ cup (12 grams) flat-leaf parsley leaves

3 tablespoons (45 milliliters) very
good extra-virgin olive oil, preferably
Ligurian (see Larder, page xxix),
plus more for drizzling

2½ tablespoons (38 milliliters)
fresh lemon juice

Kosher salt and freshly ground
black pepper

Nervetti are tender pieces of sinew and ligaments from veal and beef.
Seasoned and cooked gently for 3 hours, the nervetti are tossed with
beans, vegetables, and herbs. This salad is served at room temperature
with a small group of other contorni and accompanies the Stinco di Vitello
and Standing Rib Roast on pages 145 and 149.

For the nervetti: In a medium saucepan, combine the tendon, onion, carrot, celery, thyme, and bay leaves. Add water to cover by 3 inches (7.5 centimeters). Bring to a simmer and cook, adding water as necessary to keep the tendon well covered, until the tendon is tender, about 3 hours. Let cool to room temperature in the braising liquid, then refrigerate, covered and in the liquid, at least 4 hours or overnight.

For the salad: Remove the tendon from the braising liquid and carefully cut crosswise into very thin slices. (Discard the liquid and aromatics.) In a large bowl, combine the nervetti, beans, carrot, celery, shallot, parsley, oil, and lemon juice. Toss together to combine. Season with salt and pepper to taste. Serve at room temperature, drizzled with additional oil.

NOTE: *Veal or beef tendon can be purchased from your local butcher.*

POTATO CHIP SALAD

Wild arugula is tossed with lemon juice, Parmigiano, and house-made potato chips for a savory and tangy salad with a distinct crunch. This salad is served with a small group of other contorni and accompanies the Stinco di Vitello and Standing Rib Roast on pages 145 and 149.

For the potato chips: In a heavy medium skillet, heat the vegetable oil until a candy / fry thermometer registers 350°F (177°C). Meanwhile, using a mandoline or other manual slicer, cut the potatoes lengthwise into very thin slices (1 to 2 millimeters thick). Submerge the slices in a bowl of cold water and let stand 5 minutes.

Swish the potato slices in the water (to help release the starch), then drain and blot completely dry in a single layer between layers of paper towels.

Working in batches of 8 to 10 slices, fry the potatoes, turning once or twice, until golden, about 1½ minutes per batch, making sure the oil returns to 350°F (177°C) before adding the next batch. Using a slotted spoon, transfer the fried chips to paper towels to drain. Season with salt while warm.

For the salad: In a large mixing bowl, combine the arugula, Parmigiano, olive oil, lemon juice, and a generous pinch of salt. Toss to combine, then add the tomato raisins and potato chips and toss again. Adjust the seasoning to taste. Serve immediately.

Serves 4 to 6

FINGERLING POTATO CHIPS

2⅓ cups (550 milliliters) vegetable oil, for frying

4 medium fingerling potatoes (170 grams), scrubbed under running water and patted dry

Kosher salt

SALAD

½ pound (226 grams) wild arugula

¾ cup (56 grams) shaved Parmigiano-Reggiano cheese (at least 24-month aged; see Larder, page xxiv)

¼ cup (60 milliliters) extra-virgin olive oil

1½ tablespoons (23 milliliters) fresh lemon juice

Kosher salt

1 batch Tomato Raisins (page 157)

SPECIAL EQUIPMENT: a mandoline or other manual slicer; a candy / fry thermometer

SCAFATA

Serves 4 to 6

3 pounds (1⅓ kilograms) rainbow Swiss chard

1 tablespoon (15 milliliters) extra-virgin olive oil

3 garlic cloves (12 grams), gently smashed and peeled

1 pinch red pepper flakes (about ¼ teaspoon)

1 medium red onion (200 grams), cut into ¼-inch (6-millimeter) dice

Kosher salt

1 (15-ounce or 425-gram) can chickpeas, rinsed and drained

1 batch Tomato Raisins (page 157), cut into halves

Scafata is a traditional recipe for chard and other bitter greens from central Italy that usually includes fresh fava beans. For Del Posto's scafata, the Swiss chard is intentionally overcooked, rendering a unique vegetal flavor, and chickpeas and Del Posto's tomato raisins are used in lieu of favas. Scafata is served with a small group of other contorni and accompanies the Stinco di Vitello and Standing Rib Roast recipes on pages 145 and 149.

Cut the stems and center ribs from the chard, reserving all but any tough portions. Coarsely chop the stems, ribs, and leaves, keeping the leaves separate.

Combine the oil and garlic in a heavy wide saucepan or high-sided skillet. Heat over medium-low heat until the garlic is fragrant, about 2 minutes. Stir in the red pepper flakes, then the onion. Increase the heat to medium and cook, stirring occasionally, until the onion is tender, about 5 minutes.

Add the chard stems and a pinch of salt; continue cooking until the stems are tender, about 5 minutes more. Add the chard leaves, reduce the heat to low, and cover. Cook, stirring occasionally and adding a touch of water as needed to prevent browning, until the stems and leaves are very tender, about 15 minutes. Uncover and cook until the liquid mostly evaporates, about 6 minutes.

Stir in the chickpeas and tomato raisins. Season with salt to taste. Serve warm.

TOMATO RAISINS

These tomato raisins, a great alternative to sun-dried tomatoes, are used in two of the contorno recipes in this chapter: Potato Chip Salad (page 155) and Scafata (page 156). Cherry tomatoes are blanched, peeled, and slow-roasted with thyme at a very low temperature, creating sweet and concentrated flavors.

Makes about 30 tomato raisins

1 pound (453 grams) large cherry tomatoes

1 tablespoon (15 milliliters) extra-virgin olive oil

2½ teaspoons (10 grams) sugar

1 teaspoon (4 grams) kosher salt

2 leafy sprigs fresh thyme

Heat the oven to 200°F (93°C). Line a rimmed baking sheet with parchment paper.

Cut a shallow "X" in the bottom of each tomato. Blanch the tomatoes in boiling water for about 30 seconds, or until the skins start to pull away from the flesh, then plunge them into an ice bath. Let cool for a few minutes, then drain and pat dry. Peel and discard the skins.

In a large bowl, toss together the tomatoes, oil, sugar, and salt, then arrange in a single layer on the prepared baking sheet, at least 1 inch (2.5 centimeters) apart. Scatter the thyme sprigs over the top.

Bake, rotating the pan once halfway through, for 1 hour, then gently turn over the tomatoes. Continue baking until the tomatoes are shriveled and their flavor is concentrated, 1½ to 2 hours more. Remove from the oven and let cool completely.

LE VIRTÙ

As spring arrives in the Abruzzo region, the
restaurants in the small town of Teramo carry out an antique culinary
custom called *Le Virtù*. Prepared around the first of May, or when
the first spring vegetables turn up, Le Virtù celebrates the arrival of
fresh produce and the clearing out of dwindling winter larders
of their final dried and preserved stores.

Le Virtù is an elaborate soup incorporating a large collection of baby
spring vegetables from the region's fertile hills, usually including
peas, fava beans, asparagus, artichokes, beet greens, fennel,
radishes, and multicolored Romanesco—to name just a few. This young
produce is gently cooked, while root vegetables, wild herbs, and the
last of the winter's cured meats—ham bones and trotters—
are stewed separately. Dried farro, lentils, and beans from the pantry
are soaked and boiled (modern versions also include dried
pasta shapes). Virtù requires five different pots cooking
simultaneously, adding one's ingredients to another in a specific
sequence, until it all comes together in one final pot just
before it is served.

LE VIRTÙ

Serves 12

POT 1

1 (3-pound or 1.3-kilogram) pig trotter

2 pig ears (about 8 ounces or
226 grams total)

1 medium yellow onion (300 grams),
roughly chopped

3 celery ribs (240 grams),
roughly chopped

1 large carrot (90 grams),
roughly chopped

2 fresh bay leaves

PERILLA PURÉE

About 2¼ loosely packed cups
(35 grams) fresh mint leaves

60 large leaves (15 grams) fresh
perilla or shiso leaves

¼ cup plus 3 tablespoons (total
105 milliliters) extra-virgin olive oil

1 teaspoon kosher salt

POT 2

3 tablespoons (37 grams)
dried red beans

2 tablespoons (25 grams)
dried cannellini beans

¼ cup (50 grams) dried chickpeas

2½ tablespoons (25 grams)
dried lentils

½ cup (80 grams) farro, preferably
farro piccolo (einkorn)

1 medium leek (180 grams), dark
green top cut in half crosswise (white
and light green parts thinly sliced and
reserved for Pot 5)

1 celery rib (80 grams),
cut crosswise into thirds

1 medium carrot (70 grams),
cut crosswise into thirds

Meaning "The Virtues" in English, the origin tales and folklores surrounding Le Virtù are murky at best, but charming nonetheless. About 150 kilometers northeast of Rome and 30 kilometers from the Adriatic, Teramo sits on one of the many original Roman roads that lead from the sea to the ancient capital. Teramo boasted a number of taverns, where travelers and merchants could get simple meals and a place to stay the night. Offering hearty, inexpensive fare, these ancient public houses certainly contributed rustic soups to the region's culinary heritage. There is a legend in the area that the name Le Virtù comes from a story about seven virtuous maidens who each contributed an ingredient to this special soup. In his wonderful book, *The Food of Italy,* Waverley Root mentions another theory, that only a woman of great virtue would commit to such an endeavor, but he suggests that it probably refers to the fact that the soup includes all "the virtues," or virtuous ingredients, of the spring garden.

Le Virtù is a spectacular culinary tradition that typifies the resourcefulness of ancient cooking and a rewarding undertaking. Making this soup is arguably the best immersion class for anyone wishing to learn how to thoughtfully build and render flavors. Le Virtù is rarely found outside Abruzzo, probably because it's so labor-intensive, calling for upward of 50 ingredients. Years ago, Del Posto took on the project of making Le Virtù in the springtime. Documenting the process has been no small task. Our recipe is lengthy and thorough, and organized pot by pot, which makes it much easier to follow throughout the process.

For Pot 1: In a 9-quart (8.5-liter) Dutch oven or large wide heavy pot with lid, combine the trotter, ears, onion, celery, carrot, and bay leaves. Add 4½ quarts (4.25 liters) cold water, then bring to a simmer over medium-high heat. Reduce to a gentle simmer, cover, and cook until the meat is tender and falls easily from the bones, about 3 hours.

Remove the pot from the heat. Let the meat cool completely in its broth. Strain the cooled broth through a sieve into a large bowl. Transfer the broth to airtight containers and refrigerate until ready to use. (You will have 3 to 4 quarts or 2.8 to 3.8 liters.) Remove and discard the vegetables and bay leaves. Place the ears in an airtight container and refrigerate until chilled and set, at least 3 hours. Meanwhile, pull the meat from the trotter, discarding the skin, tendon, and bones. Shred the meat into bite-sized pieces, then cover and refrigerate until ready to use. Once the ears are chilled and set, thinly slice and return to the refrigerator, covered, until ready to use. (The braise can be prepared up to 2 days ahead.) While the meat is braising, prepare the perilla purée.

For the perilla purée: Bring a small saucepan of water to a boil. Fill a small bowl with ice and cold water. Blanch the mint and perilla in the boiling water for 30 seconds, then drain and immediately plunge into the ice bath. Let the herbs cool 1 to 2 minutes, then drain. Gently but thoroughly squeeze the herbs to remove excess liquid.

In a blender, combine the herbs, oil, salt, 2 small ice cubes, and 1 tablespoon plus 1 teaspoon (total 20 milliliters) cold water. Purée until smooth, then transfer to a small stainless steel bowl. Cover the surface of the purée with plastic wrap and refrigerate until ready to use. (The purée keeps for up to 1 day.)

For Pot 2: Sort through, then rinse the red beans, cannellini beans, chickpeas, and lentils, then combine in a medium saucepan. Add the farro and 2 quarts (2 liters) cold water. Bring the water to a simmer over medium-high heat, then reduce to a gentle simmer. Add the leek top, celery, carrot, and scallion. Cook, adding water if necessary to keep the mixture covered, until the beans, legumes, and farro are tender, 45 minutes to 1 hour (older beans and chickpeas may take longer).

Reserving the cooking liquid, drain the cooked beans, lentils, and farro. (You should have at least 3⅓ cups or 800 milliliters of cooking liquid. If not, add water to make up the difference.) Keep the liquid and the bean mixture separate. Let both cool, then cover and refrigerate until ready to use. (The bean mixture and liquid will keep for up to 3 days.)

For Pot 3: In a medium skillet, heat the oil over medium-high heat. Add the pancetta and bacon and cook, stirring occasionally, until rendered and slightly crisp, about 5 minutes. Reduce the heat to medium, add the garlic, and cook for 10 seconds. Add the onion and continue cooking, stirring occasionally, until the onion is tender (do not brown), about 8 minutes. Add the parsley and cook until the mixture is very tender and the flavors are combined, 8 to 10 minutes more. Remove the pan from the heat.

For Pot 4: In a large wide pot, heat the oil over medium heat. Add the castelfranco, tardivo, radicchio, salt, and 1 tablespoon

1 scallion (17 grams),
cut crosswise into thirds

POT 3

1 tablespoon (15 milliliters)
extra-virgin olive oil

3 ounces (86 grams) pancetta, cut
into ½-inch (1.25-centimeter) cubes

3 ounces (86 grams) slab bacon, cut
into ½-inch (1.25-centimeter) cubes

5 medium garlic cloves (20 grams),
thinly sliced

1 medium yellow onion (300 grams),
thinly sliced

2 cups (40 grams) coarsely chopped
flat-leaf parsley leaves and tender stems

POT 4

2 tablespoons (30 milliliters)
extra-virgin olive oil

2 medium heads (450 grams)
castelfranco (see notes), leaves
and core coarsely chopped

1 large head (225 grams) tardivo
di Treviso (see notes), leaves and core
coarsely chopped

1 small head (150 grams) radicchio,
leaves and core coarsely chopped

½ teaspoon (2 grams) kosher salt

MEATBALLS AND SAUSAGES

1 tablespoon (15 milliliters)
extra-virgin olive oil

1 batch uncooked Grandma's Meatballs
(see Timpano, page 108), rolled into 1-inch
(2.5-centimeter) balls

6 ounces (172 grams)
sweet Italian sausages

6 ounces (172 grams)
hot Italian sausages

CONTINUED

POT 5

Kosher salt

1 cup (112 grams) pennette
or other small pasta shape

POT 6

2 tablespoons (30 milliliters)
extra-virgin olive oil

2 cups (200 grams) mix of small
white, purple, orange, and
Romanesco cauliflower florets

6 braised artichoke hearts
(see notes), quartered (240 grams)

⅓ pound (150 grams) fennel,
coarsely chopped

⅓ pound (150 grams) cipollini
onions, peeled and thinly sliced

2 cups (140 grams) shredded
green cabbage

1 cup (130 grams) shelled
English peas

¼ pound (115 grams) small or
baby zucchini, cut into ½-inch
(1.25-centimeter) cubes

¼ pound (115 grams) small or baby
summer squash, cut into ½-inch
(1.25-centimeter) cubes

1 medium baby bok choy (100 grams),
core and leaves coarsely chopped

1 small Belgium endive (90 grams),
leaves and core coarsely chopped

3 baby turnips (85 grams),
cut into sixths

1 celery rib (80 grams), cut on
the bias into ½-inch (1.25-centimeter)
lengths

6 to 8 small radishes (80 grams),
trimmed and cut into sixths

1 small carrot with tops (70 grams),
carrot cut on the bias into ½-inch
(1.25-centimeter) lengths, tops
coarsely chopped

2 medium stalks green asparagus
(65 grams), trimmed and cut on the
bias into ¾-inch (2-centimeter) lengths

2 medium stalks white asparagus
(65 grams), trimmed and cut on the
bias into ¾-inch (2-centimeter) lengths

8 sugar snap peas (25 grams), strings
removed, peas cut crosswise on the
bias into thirds

8 green beans (20 grams), cut into
1-inch (2.5-centimeter) lengths

8 yellow beans (20 grams), cut into
1-inch (2.5-centimeter) lengths

2 cups (40 grams) coarsely
chopped flat-leaf parsley leaves

8 cherry tomatoes (145 grams)

1 teaspoon (4 grams) kosher salt

TO SERVE

Kosher salt

Very good extra-virgin olive oil,
preferably Tuscan (see Larder,
page xxix), plus more for drizzling

(15 milliliters) water. Cook, stirring
occasionally, until the leaves are wilted
and tender, about 8 minutes. Add ¼ cup
(60 milliliters) of the pork broth from
Pot 1. Cook 1 minute more, then remove
from the heat.

For the meatballs and sausages: Heat the
oven to 325ºF (163ºC). In a large heatproof
skillet, heat the oil over medium-high heat.
Add the meatballs and cook, turning once,
until browned on two sides but not cooked
through, about 4 minutes total. Transfer
to a plate. Brown the sausages in the skillet,
then transfer the skillet to the oven. Bake
until the sausages are cooked through,
8 to 10 minutes. Meanwhile, in Pot 5, make
the pasta.

For Pot 5: Cook the pasta in a medium
saucepan of salted water until just under
al dente, then drain and set aside.

For Pot 6: In a 9-quart (8.5-liter) Dutch
oven or large wide heavy pot, heat the oil
over medium-high heat. Add all of the
vegetables (including the reserved sliced
leek) except for the parsley and tomatoes.
Cook, stirring frequently, until crisp-tender,
6 to 8 minutes. Stir in half of the parsley and
the salt, then remove the pan from the heat.

Add the cooked bean mixture and 3⅓
cups (800 milliliters) of the bean cooking
liquid from Pot 2. Then add the bacon
mixture from Pot 3. Bring to a gentle
simmer over medium heat. Meanwhile, in
a separate pot, combine 3 quarts (2.8 liters)
of the pork broth and the trotter meat and
sliced ears from Pot 1; bring to a simmer
and add to Pot 6. Add the radicchio mixture
from Pot 4. Holding the tomatoes over the
pot, crush and then add. Slice the sausages,

then add them along with the meatballs and ½ teaspoon (2 grams) salt. Cook the mixture at a very gentle simmer just until the meatballs are cooked through, 2 to 3 minutes. Stir in the pasta and the remaining parsley and remove the pot from the heat.

To serve: Adjust the seasoning to taste, then ladle the soup into serving bowls. Drizzle with the perilla purée and very good oil.

NOTES: *Castelfranco and tardivo di Treviso are members of the radicchio family. Regular radicchio, endive, frisée, or other chicories can be substituted if castelfranco and/or tardivo are not available. For the braised artichoke hearts, you can make your own by preparing 6 medium globe artichokes (1.3 kilograms) as directed in the Artichokes alla Romana recipe (page 50), then quartering them. Or purchase one 14-ounce (400-gram) jar or can of good-quality artichoke hearts or quarters (packed in water) and rinse and drain before use.*

DOLCI

Italian desserts are remarkably varied,
and each region is devoted to its own style of dolce, from
the intensely fragrant lemons that grow around Sorrento
to the rich Tuscan chestnuts, high-quality fresh fruits, and nuts
that are abundant on the Italian peninsula and the
cornerstones for the country's sweets. The pastry department at
Del Posto draws inspiration from Lidia Bastianich's love
of off-sweet desserts and a seemingly endless supply of regional
recipes from Italian grandmothers. Translating these
regional desserts into fine dining is not always easy, since most
Italian dolci have roots in rustic home kitchens. But the thoughtful
inclusion of savory elements and seasonal ingredients is the
unifying characteristic of all Italian sweets and has come
to define the restaurant's approach to desserts.

Each of our dessert recipes strikes a balance between savory,
sweet, and tart. Pecorino cheese, polenta, basil, pistachios,
black pepper, and eggplant are just a few of the savory components
found in these dishes. These familiar Italian ingredients come
together with honey, chocolate, ripe fruits, and other sweet elements
for soulful, approachable recipes. The Del Posto attitude toward dolce
is less about rigid structure and innovative textures on the plate, but
rather focuses on comforting, recognizable flavors brought together in
distinctive ways.

In the dining room, the dessert at Del Posto is broken into two
final acts: the larger plated dishes, followed by a selection of
cookies and candies, which complement dessert wine, digestive,
and coffee. Many of our dolci include gelato, and over the
years we have developed a wide variety of styles and unexpected
flavors—from cashew to olive oil. The gelati recipes in this
chapter are designed to be part of specific dishes, but they are
also easy to make and wonderful on their own.

The following two cakes represent Lidia Bastianich's influence on the pastry program at Del Posto. Her palate for off-sweet desserts informs these two seasonal, yeast-based cakes. Both the warm-weather pea cake and the cool-weather chestnut cake feature slightly fermented flavors and spongy texture. Torn into small pieces, they work in concert with their seasonal accompaniments, soaking up sweet fresh strawberry sauce or wine-soaked plums.

STRAWBERRY SAUCE

1 pound (450 grams) Tristar or other high-quality fresh strawberries, hulled

½ cup (100 grams) sugar

½ teaspoon (2½ milliliters) fresh lemon juice

⅛ teaspoon (½ gram) kosher salt

PEA CAKES

¼ cup (60 milliliters) whole milk

1¼ teaspoons (5 grams) active dry yeast

¾ cup plus ¼ teaspoon (total 151 grams) sugar

1½ cups (217 grams) frozen peas, thawed

3 large eggs, yolks and whites separated

Nonstick cooking spray

¼ cup (24 grams) fine plain breadcrumbs

TO SERVE

Very good extra-virgin olive oil, preferably delicate Sicilian (see Larder, page xxix), for drizzling

Strawberry Gelato (page 205)

Confectioners' sugar, for dusting

SPECIAL EQUIPMENT: a standard 12-cup muffin tin

LIDIA'S PEA CAKES
with Strawberry Sauce and Gelato

For the strawberry sauce: Set aside 4 of the best strawberries, then cut the rest in half, or quarters if large. In a blender, purée the cut berries until smooth.

In a heavy medium saucepan, stir together the sugar and ¼ cup (60 milliliters) water so that all of the sugar is damp and none of it is coating the sides of the pan. Bring to a boil over high heat, then continue to cook, gently swirling the pan occasionally, until the mixture turns a light amber color, about 5 minutes. Remove the caramel from the heat, then add the purée. Return the pan to high heat and, whisking constantly, boil the sauce until the sugar is dissolved. Remove from the heat and let cool completely, then whisk in the lemon juice and salt. Thinly slice the reserved berries and gently fold into the sauce. Adjust the seasoning to taste.

For the cakes: Heat the oven to 350°F (177°C). In a small microwave-safe bowl, heat the milk until just warm to the touch, about 10 seconds. In a second bowl, mix together the yeast and ¼ teaspoon (1 gram) of the sugar. Add the yeast mixture to the warm milk. Stir once to combine, then let stand for 10 minutes to allow the yeast to activate.

Meanwhile, in a blender, purée the peas until smooth, then transfer to a medium bowl. In the bowl of an electric mixer fitted with the whisk, beat together the egg yolks and ¼ cup (50 grams) of the sugar on medium-high speed until pale and thickened, 3 to 5 minutes.

Add the yeast mixture to the pea purée. Mix together to combine, then fold in the yolk mixture until no streaks are visible.

Clean and dry the bowl for the electric mixer, then add the egg whites. Using the whisk attachment, beat the whites on high until they reach medium-stiff peaks. Reduce the speed to medium and, in a slow and steady stream, add the remaining ½ cup (100 grams) sugar. Beat until the whites are glossy, about 1 minute more. In three additions, gently fold the whites into the pea mixture to combine.

Lightly coat the 12 cups of the muffin tin with nonstick cooking spray, then sprinkle the bottoms and sides with the breadcrumbs. Fill each cup to just below the top with the batter (discard any leftover batter). Bake until the edges of the cakes are golden and pull away from the edges of the cups, about 16 minutes. (The cakes will have risen and then will fall as they come out of the oven and cool.) Transfer the pan to a wire rack

and let cool 5 minutes, then run a butter knife around the edge of each cup. Invert the cakes onto the rack and let cool completely.

To serve: Cut the 4 reserved strawberries in half. Tear the pea cakes into rough 3-inch (7.5-centimeter) pieces and arrange on individual serving plates with strawberry pieces. Drizzle with the strawberry sauce and the oil. Top with a scoop of the gelato. Dust with confectioners' sugar.

LIDIA'S CHESTNUT CAKES

with Red Wine Plums, Roasted Chestnuts, and Yogurt Sorbetto

Serves 12

CHESTNUT CAKES

⅔ pound (302 grams) peeled frozen chestnuts (about 2 cups), thawed

4½ tablespoons (67 milliliters) extra-virgin olive oil

Finely grated zest from ⅓ of an orange

⅛ teaspoon (½ gram) kosher salt

¼ cup (60 milliliters) whole milk

1¼ teaspoons (5 grams) active dry yeast

¾ cup plus ¼ teaspoon (total 151 grams) sugar

3 large eggs, yolks and whites separated

Nonstick cooking spray

¼ cup (24 grams) fine plain breadcrumbs

ROASTED CHESTNUTS

½ pound (226 grams) peeled frozen chestnuts (about 1⅓ cups), thawed

3 tablespoons (45 milliliters) extra-virgin olive oil

Kosher salt

Finely grated zest of ½ of an orange

Pinch freshly ground black pepper

RED WINE PLUMS

½ cup (100 grams) sugar

1½ cups plus 2½ tablespoons (total 400 milliliters) dry red wine

Finely grated zest of ¼ of an orange

About 1 cup (175 grams) dried plums, cut in half or thirds if large

TO SERVE

Yogurt Sorbetto (page 212)

Very good extra-virgin olive oil, preferably Ligurian (see Larder, page xxix), for drizzling

Finely grated orange zest, for garnish

Confectioners' sugar, for dusting

SPECIAL EQUIPMENT: a standard 12-cup muffin tin

For the cakes: Heat the oven to 350°F (177°C). In a bowl, toss together the chestnuts, 2 tablespoons (30 milliliters) of the oil, the zest, and salt. Spread the chestnuts on a rimmed baking sheet and roast until fragrant and lightly golden, about 18 minutes (leave the oven on for the cakes). Transfer the pan to a wire rack and let the chestnuts cool completely, then transfer to the bowl of a food processor. With the machine running, add the remaining 2½ tablespoons (37 milliliters) oil and 2 tablespoons (30 milliliters) water. Purée until thick and fairly smooth. Transfer to a medium bowl and set aside.

In a small microwave-safe bowl, heat the milk in the microwave until just warm to the touch, about 10 seconds. In a second bowl, mix together the yeast and ¼ teaspoon (1 gram) of the sugar. Add the mixture to the warm milk. Stir once to combine, then let stand 10 minutes to allow the yeast to activate.

Meanwhile, in the bowl of an electric mixer fitted with the whisk, beat together the egg yolks and ¼ cup (50 grams) sugar on medium-high speed until pale and thickened, 3 to 5 minutes.

Add the yeast mixture to the chestnut purée. Mix together to combine, then fold in the yolk mixture until no streaks are visible.

Clean and dry the bowl for the electric mixer, then add the egg whites. Using the whisk attachment, beat the whites on high until they reach medium-stiff peaks. Reduce the speed to medium and, in a slow and steady stream, add the remaining ½ cup (100 grams) sugar. Beat until the whites are glossy, about 1 minute more. In three additions, gently fold the whites into the chestnut mixture to combine.

Lightly coat the 12 cups of the muffin tin with nonstick cooking spray, then sprinkle the bottoms and sides with the breadcrumbs. Fill each cup to just below the top with the batter (discard any leftover batter). Bake until the edges of the cakes are golden and pull away from the edges of the cups, about 16 minutes. (The cakes will have risen and then will fall as they come out of the oven and cool.) Transfer the pan to a wire rack and let cool 5 minutes (leave the oven on for the chestnuts). Run a butter knife around the edge of each cup and invert the cakes onto the rack and let cool completely. Meanwhile, roast the chestnuts and prepare the red wine plums.

For the roasted chestnuts: In a bowl, toss together the chestnuts, 1½ tablespoons (22 milliliters) of the oil, and ⅛ teaspoon (½ gram) salt. Spread the chestnuts on a rimmed baking sheet and roast until fragrant and lightly golden, about 18 minutes. Transfer the pan to a wire rack and let the chestnuts cool completely, then transfer to a bowl. Break the chestnuts in half. Add the remaining 1½ tablespoons (22 milliliters) oil, ⅛ teaspoon (½ gram) salt, the zest, and pepper. Toss to combine.

For the red wine plums: In a heavy medium saucepan, stir together the sugar and 30 milliliters (2 tablespoons) water so that all of the sugar is damp and none of it is coating the sides of the pan. Bring to a boil over high heat, then continue to cook, gently swirling the pan occasionally, until the mixture turns a light amber color, 5 to 6 minutes. Remove from the heat, then add the wine and zest (the mixture will bubble and the sugar will seize up) and whisk to combine. Return the pan to medium heat, bring the liquid to a simmer, and cook, whisking occasionally, until the sugar is completely dissolved and the liquid is slightly reduced, about 5 minutes. Add the plums, return to a simmer, and cook until the fruit is plump, about 5 minutes more. Remove from the heat and let cool completely. (The plums keep, covered and refrigerated, for up to 1 week. Let come to room temperature before serving.)

To serve: Tear the chestnut cakes into rough 3-inch (7.5-centimeter) pieces and arrange on individual serving plates. Spoon the plums and a bit of their syrup onto the plates. Top with a scoop of the sorbetto and the roasted chestnut pieces. Drizzle with the oil, then garnish with zest and dust with confectioners' sugar.

AMOR POLENTA

with Corn Gelato, Blueberry Compote, and Tarragon Sauce

Summer in the Northeast brings sweet corn and ripe blueberries to the table. This late-summer dessert combines these fresh American ingredients with northern Italian tradition. Amor polenta is a simple cake from the Lombardy region and the city of Varese, where it is made with fine-ground polenta and almonds and dusted with powdered sugar. Here, the amor polenta is infused with almond extract, baked, and then grilled—giving it crispy edges, similar to an American-style cornbread.

For the cake: Heat the oven to 350°F (177°C). Lightly coat a 9 x 13-inch (23 x 33-centimeter) baking dish with nonstick cooking spray. Line the bottom with parchment paper and lightly coat the paper with nonstick cooking spray.

In a bowl, whisk together the flour, cornmeal, baking powder, and salt; set aside. In the bowl of an electric mixer fitted with the paddle attachment, combine the butter, granulated sugar, and honey. Beat on medium-high until light and fluffy, about 5 minutes. Using a rubber spatula, scrape down the sides of the bowl. With the machine running on medium-high speed, add the whole eggs and egg yolks, one at a time, waiting until each is incorporated before adding the next (the batter will look grainy). Add the almond extract and the dry ingredients, then mix on medium speed, just to combine.

Scrape the batter into the prepared pan, then dust the top with granulated sugar and confectioners' sugar. Bake until a wooden pick inserted into the center of the cake comes out clean, 20 to 25 minutes. While the cake is baking, prepare the compote and sauce.

For the blueberry compote: Place ¾ cup (100 grams) of the blueberries in a heatproof medium bowl and set aside. In a small saucepan, combine the remaining 1¾ cups (250 grams) of the blueberries and the sugar. Cook over medium heat, stirring occasionally, until the berries are very tender and a thick sauce has formed, about 8 minutes. Pour the hot berry mixture over the reserved berries. Add the lemon juice and salt and gently stir to combine. Let stand until cooled to room temperature. (The compote keeps, in an airtight container and refrigerated, for up to 3 days. Let come to room temperature before serving.)

For the tarragon sauce: Bring a medium saucepan of water to a boil. Add the tarragon and cook for 30 seconds, then drain. Submerge the tarragon in a bowl of ice water for 1 minute, then drain. Gently but thoroughly squeeze the herbs to remove excess liquid.

Place the tarragon in a deep mixing bowl. Add the corn syrup and simple syrup. Using an immersion blender, purée the mixture until smooth. (Due to the small quantity of ingredients, an immersion blender is the best tool to achieve a smooth purée, but you can also use a high-powered blender or mini food processor.) Strain the sauce through a fine-mesh sieve into a small bowl. (The sauce keeps, in an airtight container and refrigerated, for up to 3 days. Let come to room temperature before serving.)

Serves 10 to 12

CAKE

Nonstick cooking spray

¾ cup (95 grams) unbleached all-purpose flour

½ cup (90 grams) fine cornmeal

1 tablespoon plus ½ teaspoon (total 17.5 grams) baking powder

¾ teaspoon (3 grams) kosher salt

14 tablespoons (200 grams) unsalted butter, softened

¾ cup (150 grams) granulated sugar, plus more for dusting

1 tablespoon plus ¾ teaspoon (total 25 grams) honey

3 large eggs

5 large egg yolks (90 grams)

½ teaspoon (2½ milliliters) almond extract

Confectioners' sugar, for dusting

BLUEBERRY COMPOTE

2½ cups (350 grams) blueberries

¼ cup plus 2 tablespoons (total 75 grams) sugar

2 teaspoons (10 milliliters) fresh lemon juice

Pinch kosher salt

TARRAGON SAUCE

3 loosely packed cups (30 grams) fresh tarragon leaves, plus more for garnish

⅓ cup plus 1 tablespoon (total 94 milliliters) light corn syrup

¼ cup plus 1½ tablespoons (total 82 milliliters) simple syrup (see note)

CONTINUED

To serve: Heat a grill or grill pan to medium-high heat. In a bowl, toss together the corn with a drizzle of the extra-virgin olive oil and a pinch of salt, and set aside. Cut the cake into individual slices and lightly brush with the extra-virgin olive oil. Grill until charred and warm, about 2 minutes per side. Drizzle the serving plates with the tarragon sauce and the very good oil. Arrange the cake on top. Spoon a small mound of sbrisolona crumbs alongside, and place a scoopful of the gelato on top. Garnish with the compote, corn, and fresh tarragon leaves.

NOTE: *Simple syrup can be purchased or made at home. Combine sugar and water in a small saucepan and bring to a boil over medium-high heat, stirring to dissolve sugar, about 3 minutes. Remove from heat, let cool, and refrigerate in a tightly sealed jar until ready to use (syrup keeps covered and chilled for 3 months).*

TO SERVE

¾ cup (150 grams) corn kernels cut from 1 ear of shucked and freshly boiled corn

Extra-virgin olive oil, for grilling the corn and cake

Kosher salt

Very good extra-virgin olive oil, preferably delicate Sicilian (see Larder, page xxix), for drizzling

1½ cups (180 grams) Sbrisolona Crumbs (page 200)

Corn Gelato (page 210)

SPECIAL EQUIPMENT: parchment paper

RICOTTA–CHOCOLATE TORTINO

Makes 12 servings

CHOCOLATE–OLIVE OIL CAKES

Nonstick cooking spray

¾ cup (62 grams) unsweetened cocoa powder

1 cup (236 milliliters) well-shaken low-fat buttermilk

¾ cup plus 1 tablespoon (total 200 milliliters) extra-virgin olive oil

2 large eggs

½ teaspoon (2.5 milliliters) pure vanilla extract

2¼ cups plus 2 tablespoons (total 300 grams) unbleached all-purpose flour

2¼ cups (450 grams) sugar

2 teaspoons (10 grams) baking soda

2 teaspoons (8 grams) kosher salt

RICOTTA FILLING

1 stick (114 grams) unsalted butter, softened

3 tablespoons (30 grams) confectioners' sugar

1⅓ cups (340 grams) good-quality fresh whole-milk ricotta cheese, such as Calabro

Pinch kosher salt

GLAZE AND NUTS

2 sticks (227 grams) unsalted butter

⅔ pound (302 grams) coarsely chopped good-quality 66 percent cacao dark chocolate (scant 2 cups)

1 tablespoon plus 1 teaspoon (total 20 milliliters) light corn syrup

1 tablespoon plus 1 teaspoon (total 20 milliliters) good-quality dark rum

Generous ¾ cup (120 grams) Sicilian pistachios, finely chopped

CONTINUED

This tortino indulges serious chocolate cravings without being overly dense or sweet. The chocolate cake is extraordinarily moist because it is made with olive oil and buttermilk. Stuffed with ricotta and glazed with more chocolate, it is then decorated with crunchy pistachios and served with gelato and cake crumbs made from the leftover cake scraps. The olive oil cake recipe can be used on its own for all future chocolate cakes, whether glazed or frosted.

For the cakes: Heat the oven to 350°F (177°C). Lightly coat a 17¾ x 12¾-inch (45 x 32-centimeter) rimmed baking sheet with nonstick cooking spray.

In a small saucepan, whisk together the cocoa powder and 1 cup plus 1 tablespoon (total 250 milliliters) water. Whisking frequently and into the edge of the pan to break up any clumps and prevent scorching, bring the mixture just to a boil over medium-high heat, then remove from the heat. Transfer to a heatproof bowl and set aside to cool.

In a medium bowl, whisk together the buttermilk, oil, eggs, and vanilla.

In the bowl of an electric mixer fitted with the whisk attachment, combine the flour, sugar, baking soda, and salt. Beat the mixture on low for 10 seconds, then increase the speed to medium-low and, in a slow, steady stream, add the buttermilk mixture to the dry ingredients, scraping down the sides of the bowl with a rubber spatula as needed, until the batter is smooth and thick, about 1 minute. In a slow, steady stream, add the cocoa mixture, scraping down the sides of the bowl as needed, just until the cooled cocoa mixture is fully incorporated.

Pour the batter onto the prepared baking sheet. Bake until the center of the cake springs back to a light touch and a

wooden pick inserted into the center comes out clean, 25 to 28 minutes.

Transfer the pan to a wire rack and let the cake cool completely. Wrap the cooled cake (still in the pan) in plastic wrap and refrigerate until firm to the touch, at least 3 hours or up to 3 days.

For the ricotta filling: In the bowl of an electric mixer fitted with the paddle attachment, combine the butter and sugar. Beat on high speed, stopping the mixer twice to scrape down the sides of the bowl, until the mixture is combined and smooth, about 2 minutes. Add the cheese and salt, and continue to beat until well combined, about 1 minute more. Refrigerate, covered, until ready to use. (The filling keeps, in an airtight container and refrigerated, for up to 3 days.)

To assemble the cakes: Using a 2 x 1¾-inch (5 x 4.5-centimeter) cake ring, cut out 24 cake rounds, cutting the rounds as close to one another as possible and rinsing and drying the ring every two or three rounds. Reserve the remaining cake for another use. (The cake will keep, in airtight containers and refrigerated, for up to 3 days or frozen for up to 1 month.)

Heat the oven to 275°F (135°C). Using your hands, crumble the cake scraps. On

Olive Oil Gelato (page 204)

Very good extra-virgin olive oil, preferably Sicilian (such as Olio Verde, see page xxix), for drizzling

SPECIAL EQUIPMENT: 12 (2 x 1¾-inch or 5 x 4.5-centimeter) cake rings; 1 (17¾ x 12¾-inch or 45 x 32-centimeter) rimmed baking sheet

a clean baking sheet, spread the crumbled cake in an even layer. Bake until completely dried out, 45 to 50 minutes. Transfer the pan to a wire rack and let the scraps cool completely.

While the scraps are baking, wash and dry the cake ring that you used to cut out the rounds. Place all 12 rings on a clean baking sheet or large flat platter or plate. Press one cake round into each ring. Divide the ricotta filling among the rings (3 tablespoons or about 40 grams per ring), then place a second cake round on top. Gently but firmly press the top cake round down into the ring to press all 3 layers together. Cover the assembled cakes (in their rings and on the baking sheet) tightly with plastic wrap. Refrigerate for at least 4 hours or overnight.

In the bowl of a food processor, pulse the cooled dried cake scraps to form fine crumbs. Transfer the crumbs to an airtight container and keep covered until ready to use. (The baked crumbs keep at room temperature for up to 2 weeks, or frozen for up to 1 month.)

For the glaze and nuts: Combine the butter and chocolate in a large microwave-safe bowl. Microwave in 10-second intervals, stirring well between intervals, until the chocolate is completely melted. (If you do not have a microwave, melt the butter and chocolate in a double boiler.) Add the corn syrup and rum and whisk to combine. Let stand just until cooled to room temperature, 15 to 20 minutes. (The glaze keeps, in an airtight container at room temperature, for up to 3 days. If you are not using it immediately after it has cooled to room temperature, very gently warm it in the microwave or in a double boiler until it is fluid, then let it cool to room temperature before using.)

Line a rimmed baking sheet with plastic wrap. Place a wire cooling rack on top. Remove the cakes from the refrigerator. Use your hands to warm the outside of each ring for 10 to 15 seconds, then push the cakes out from the molds and place on the glazing rack, spacing them at least 1 inch (2.5 centimeters) apart.

Quickly and evenly pour the chocolate glaze over each cake, letting it run over the sides (the excess that runs into the pan can be scraped up and used again). Give the rack a gentle tap to smooth out the glaze. Reserve the leftover glaze.

Working quickly (before the glaze sets completely), and beginning with the first cake that was glazed, use an offset spatula to transfer one cake from the rack to the palm of your hand. Gently but firmly run the edge of your free thumb around the side of and about three-fourths of the way up the cake, to create a slightly rough textured surface to stick the nuts onto (if you make a hole in your glaze, patch it with the leftover glaze). Coat the textured portion with the chopped pistachios. Repeat with the remaining cakes. (The finished cakes will keep, in an airtight container and refrigerated, for up to 1 day.)

To serve: Arrange one cake on each serving plate. Spoon a small mound of cake crumbs alongside. Place a scoopful of the gelato on top of the crumbs. Drizzle the gelato with very good olive oil.

PECORINO CAKE

with Honey-Vinegar and Caramelized Pears,
Honey Gelato, and Preserved Walnuts

Pears, pecorino, and walnuts are a classic combination for savory salads, pastas, and risottos in northern Italy. But this trio of ingredients can also be sweetened with honey for dessert. Regional honeys are celebrated throughout Italy, especially the artisanal ones made from a single type of flower in a single location. It is worth seeking out Italian honey made from sunflowers or eucalyptus for this recipe, or try experimenting with other mono-varietal honeys.

For the pecorino cake: Heat the oven to 350°F (177°C) with the rack in the middle. Lightly coat the bottom and sides of a 9 x 13-inch (23 x 33-centimeter) baking dish with nonstick cooking spray and line the bottom with parchment paper, then lightly coat the parchment paper with nonstick cooking spray.

In a large bowl, whisk together the flour, pecorino cheese, baking powder, and salt. Set aside.

In the bowl of an electric mixer fitted with the paddle attachment, beat together the sugar, butter, and cream cheese on medium speed until light and fluffy, about 5 minutes. Turn off the mixer. Using a rubber spatula, scrape down the sides of the bowl. Restart the mixer at medium speed. With the machine running, add the eggs, one at a time, waiting until each is incorporated before adding the next. Continue mixing until the batter is smooth, then add the dry ingredients and mix on low speed until just combined. In a slow and steady stream, add the cream, mixing until just combined.

Scrape the batter into the prepared pan. Bake in the center of the oven until the sides of the cake are pulling away from the edges and the center springs back to a light touch, 25 to 30 minutes. Transfer the pan to a rack and let the cake cool completely.

For the pecorino frico: Heat the oven to 375°F (190°C). Spread the cheese on a rimmed baking sheet to a 10-inch (25.5-centimeter) round. Bake until melted and light golden, 5 to 6 minutes, checking occasionally to avoid overbrowning. Transfer the baking sheet to a wire rack and let cool completely. Break the cooled frico into small pieces for garnish. It can be stored in an airtight container for up to 2 days.

For the black pepper honey: In a small saucepan, gently heat the honey on low heat, just until warm and fluid. Remove from the heat and whisk in the pepper. Keep warm until ready to serve.

For the honey-vinegar pears: In a medium bowl, whisk together the honey and vinegar until well combined. Submerge the pear slices in the liquid. Let stand until lightly pickled, 5 to 7 minutes, then drain and discard the liquid. While the pears are pickling, prepare the caramelized pears.

For the caramelized pears: In a medium skillet, heat the oil over medium-high heat until very hot but not smoking. Add the pear cubes, arranging them in a single layer. Cook, without stirring, until lightly golden on the bottom, about 3 minutes. Sprinkle with the sugar and continue to cook, tossing

Serves 12

PECORINO CAKE

Nonstick cooking spray

1 cup plus 2 tablespoons (total 140 grams) unbleached all-purpose flour

1⅓ cups (85 grams) freshly grated Pecorino Romano Genuino cheese (see Larder, page xxv)

1 teaspoon (5 grams) baking powder

½ teaspoon (2 grams) kosher salt

1 cup (200 grams) sugar

1 stick (114 grams) unsalted butter, softened

2 ounces (58 grams) cream cheese

3 large eggs

1 cup (240 milliliters) heavy cream

PECORINO FRICO

½ cup (32 grams) freshly grated Pecorino Romano Genuino cheese (see Larder, page xxv)

BLACK PEPPER HONEY

¼ cup (84 grams) high-quality honey, preferably sunflower or eucalyptus

Pinch freshly ground black pepper

HONEY-VINEGAR PEARS

3 tablespoons (63 grams) high-quality honey, preferably sunflower or eucalyptus

3 tablespoons (45 milliliters) white wine vinegar

1 firm-ripe pear (225 grams), peeled, cored, and very thinly sliced lengthwise

CONTINUED

occasionally, until lightly caramelized, about 2 minutes. Add the butter and salt and toss just until the butter is melted. Remove from the heat.

To serve: Using a serrated knife, thinly slice the walnuts. Using a 2¾-inch (7-centimeter) round cutter, cut out one round from any outside edge of the cake and discard or save; then, using the imprint as a starting point, use the cutter to cut out 12 quarter moons from the cake. (Save the remaining cake for another use; the cake keeps, in an airtight container and refrigerated, for up to 3 days, or frozen for up to 1 month.)

Arrange the cakes on individual serving plates. Arrange the walnuts, honey vinegar pear slices, caramelized pear cubes, and frico around the cakes. Spoon a small mound of sbrisolona crumbs alongside and place a scoopful of the gelato on top. Drizzle the plates with the pepper honey, then dust with confectioners' sugar.

NOTE: *Preserved walnuts can be purchased at gourmet stores or online. They are usually packaged in 18.9-ounce (536-gram) jars. If preserved walnuts are not available, use candied walnuts or lightly toasted walnuts instead.*

❦ WINE PAIRING ❧

Cheesecake at its best, this pecorino dessert is light and lively with a salty tang. Maculan's Dindarello from northern Veneto is made from late-harvest Moscato grapes. Its sweet peach and apricot notes and bright acidity act as a compote or honey complement to the pecorino in the cake.

CARAMELIZED PEARS

1¾ teaspoons (8 milliliters) extra-virgin olive oil

1 firm-ripe pear (225 grams), peeled, cored, and cut into ½-inch (1.25-centimeter) cubes

½ teaspoon (2 grams) sugar

1 teaspoon (5 grams) cold unsalted butter

Pinch kosher salt

TO SERVE

6 preserved walnuts (see note)

1½ cups (180 grams) Sbrisolona Crumbs (page 200)

Honey Gelato (page 204)

Confectioners' sugar, for dusting

SPECIAL EQUIPMENT: parchment paper; a 2¾-inch (7-centimeter) round cutter

SLOW-ROASTED NECTARINES

with Grilled Lemon Pound Cake and Basil Gelato

Serves 8

LEMON POUND CAKE

5 tablespoons plus 1 teaspoon (total 75 grams) unsalted butter, plus more for greasing the pan

¾ cup (83 grams) cake flour

½ teaspoon (2.5 grams) baking powder

½ teaspoon (1 gram) kosher salt

1 cup plus scant 2½ tablespoons (total 230 grams) sugar

⅓ cup plus 2 teaspoons (total 100 grams) almond paste

Finely grated zest of 1 orange

Finely grated zest of 1 lemon

1 teaspoon (4.5 milliliters) pure vanilla extract

4 large eggs

CITRUS GLAZE

½ cup (100 grams) sugar

¼ cup (60 millimeters) fresh orange juice

2 tablespoons (30 millimeters) fresh lemon juice

SLOW-ROASTED NECTARINES

½ cup (168 grams) honey

½ cup (118 milliliters) fresh lemon juice

⅛ teaspoon (½ gram) kosher salt

Pinch freshly ground black pepper

4 firm-ripe nectarines, halved and pitted

3 basil leaves, torn into small pieces, plus more for garnish

CONTINUED

This is a great example of the Italian approach to cooking with fruit. Because the fruit in Italy is so pristine and flavorful, simple recipes go a long way. This dessert enhances the inherent sweetness of nectarines, while also drawing out their savory notes with a pinch of black pepper, citrusy cake, and basil gelato.

For the cake: Heat the oven to 350°F (177°C) with the rack in the middle. Grease a 9 x 5 x 3-inch (23 x 13 x 7.5-centimeter) loaf pan with butter, then line the bottom with parchment paper. Grease the paper with butter.

In a bowl, whisk together the flour, baking powder, and salt; set aside. In the bowl of an electric mixer fitted with the paddle attachment, combine the sugar, almond paste, and orange and lemon zests. Beat on medium speed until well combined, about 5 minutes. Add the butter and vanilla; increase the speed to medium-high and beat until light and fluffy, about 5 minutes. Turn off the mixer. Using a rubber spatula, scrape down the sides of the bowl. Restart the mixer at medium-high speed. With the machine running, add the eggs, one at a time, waiting until each is incorporated before adding the next.

Remove the bowl from the mixer and add the flour mixture. Fold the batter gently with a spatula to fully incorporate the dry ingredients. Scrape the batter into the prepared pan. Bake in the center of the oven for 40 minutes (do not open the oven door during this time). Test the cake with a wooden pick: If it comes out dry, the cake is done. If not, return the cake to the oven, rotating the pan, and continue baking until a wooden pick inserted into the center comes out clean, 5 to 10 minutes more. While the cake is baking, prepare the glaze.

For the glaze: In a small microwave-proof bowl, combine the sugar, orange juice, and lemon juice. Microwave in 10-second intervals, stirring between intervals, to warm the glaze just enough so that the sugar dissolves, about 20 seconds total (do not heat the glaze more than barely warm or it will alter the citrus flavor). Stir together well, then set aside to cool.

When the cake is done, transfer the pan to a wire rack. Run a knife around the inside edges of the pan, then invert the cake onto the rack. Invert the cake again to face up. Let the cake cool for 10 minutes; then, using a wooden pick, poke holes all over the top. Set the rack over a rimmed baking sheet, then pour the glaze over the top of the cake. Let the cake cool completely, at least 1 hour. Meanwhile, prepare the nectarines and citrus sugar.

For the slow-roasted nectarines: Heat the oven to 250°F (121°C). In a large bowl, whisk together the honey, lemon juice, salt, and pepper. Add the nectarines and basil. Stir to coat the fruit with the honey mixture.

Arrange the nectarines in a baking dish, cut side down. Drizzle the honey mixture on top. Roast for 20 minutes. Turn the fruit cut side up and continue roasting for 20 minutes more. Flip cut side down and continue roasting until the fruit just gives to the touch, 10 to 20 minutes more. Remove from the oven. (The nectarines and their

THE DEL POSTO COOKBOOK

CITRUS SUGAR

¼ cup (55 grams) sugar

Finely grated zest of 1 orange

Finely grated zest of 1 lemon

TO SERVE

Extra-virgin olive oil, for grilling

1 cup (120 grams) Sbrisolona Crumbs (page 200)

Basil Gelato (page 208)

Very good extra-virgin olive oil, preferably Sicilian (such as Olio Verde; see page xxix), for drizzling

juices keep, in an airtight container and refrigerated, up to 3 days. If making ahead, let the fruit cool completely in its juices at room temperature, then warm the fruit in its juices in a low-temperature oven just before serving.) When the nectarines are close to done, prepare the citrus sugar and heat a grill to medium-high.

For the citrus sugar: In a bowl, combine the sugar with the orange and lemon zests. Rub together the mixture with your fingers until the sugar is dampened and the mixture is well combined.

To serve: Slice the cake into eight ½-inch-thick (1.25-centimeter-thick) pieces. Brush the cut sides with oil, then grill until deep golden on both sides. Arrange the warm cake on serving plates. Top with the nectarines and sprinkle a pinch of the citrus sugar over the top. Spoon a small mound of sbrisolona crumbs alongside the cakes. Top with a scoop of the gelato. Drizzle with the nectarine juices and the very good oil. Garnish with basil.

BUTTERSCOTCH-MASCARPONE SEMIFREDDO

with Dulce "Milk Jam" and Fresh Fruit

Made in a mixer rather than an ice cream machine, semifreddo is an excellent, fluffier alternative to gelato. Rolled in crunchy cornmeal sbrisolona crumbs for texture, Del Posto's off-sweet butterscotch semifreddo includes mascarpone and a pinch of salt. The dish is sweetened with a few smears of dulce de leche, which we call "Milk Jam" at the restaurant, made by simply slow-cooking condensed milk in its can. If blood oranges and tangerines are not available, serve with other seasonal fruits. In the summer, peaches, plums, and cherries are a great substitute for the winter citrus.

For the semifreddo: In the bowl of an electric mixer fitted with the whisk, beat together the cream and mascarpone on medium-high speed until stiff peaks form, about 20 seconds. Transfer the mixture to another bowl and refrigerate until ready to use. Wash and dry the mixer bowl.

Place the yolks in the clean, dry mixer bowl and, using the whisk attachment, beat on medium-high speed until pale and thickened, about 4 minutes. Meanwhile, in a medium saucepan, melt the butter over low heat; continue to cook, swirling the pan occasionally, until the butter has a nutty aroma and is a rich brown color, 6 to 8 minutes. Add the sugar, rum, vanilla seeds, and salt. Increase the heat to high and bring to a boil. Cook, stirring occasionally, until a thick butterscotch forms, about 4 minutes. Continue cooking until the mixture smells slightly burnt, then remove it from the heat and let it cool slightly, 1 to 2 minutes.

With the mixer running on medium speed, add the butterscotch mixture to the yolks in a slow, steady stream, pouring along the inside of the bowl. Increase the speed to high and beat until the mixture is cool, about 7 minutes.

Transfer the yolk mixture to a large bowl. Using a rubber spatula, and in two additions, fold the mascarpone mixture into the yolk mixture. Pour the mixture into a 6-cup (1.4-liter) freezer-safe loaf pan or other container. Tap the container on the counter a couple of times to eliminate air bubbles. Cover the surface of the semifreddo with plastic wrap, then wrap the pan in plastic wrap. Freeze until firm, at least 3 hours or up to 5 days.

For the dulce "milk jam": Place the can of condensed milk on its side in a wide heavy pot. Cover with water by at least 2 inches or 5 centimeters (the more water, the better). Over high heat, bring the water to a simmer. Reduce the heat to maintain a simmer and cook, checking the pot every 30 minutes to ensure that the water level remains at least 2 inches (5 centimeters) above the can and adding boiling water as necessary to top it off. Cook for 2½ hours for a medium caramel, or up to 3 hours for a darker caramel.

Using tongs, remove the can from the water and set it on a wire rack to let it cool completely, about 2 hours. (Do not open the can while still hot; the pressurized hot caramel may spray.)

When completely cool, open the can and

Serves 8 to 10

SEMIFREDDO

1½ cups (355 milliliters) heavy cream

Scant ½ cup (125 grams) mascarpone cheese

8 large egg yolks (144 grams)

2½ tablespoons (36 grams) unsalted butter

½ cup plus 2 tablespoons (total 141 grams) packed dark brown sugar

2 tablespoons (30 milliliters) dark rum

½ vanilla bean, split in half lengthwise, seeds scraped out, bean saved for another use

⅛ teaspoon (½ gram) kosher salt

DULCE "MILK JAM"

1 (14-ounce or 414-milliliter) can sweetened condensed milk, label removed

TO SERVE

4 blood oranges

3 tangerines

2½ cups (300 grams) Sbrisolona Crumbs (page 200)

scoop out the dulce milk jam. Reheat in a double boiler to desired spreadable or pourable consistency. (Dulce milk jam keeps, covered and refrigerated, for up to 3 weeks.)

To serve: Using a paring knife, cut the peel and white pith from the oranges and tangerines, then cut between the membranes to section the fruit. Dollop and smear about ½ tablespoon (15 grams) of the dulce milk jam onto each serving plate. Arrange the citrus on the plates.

Spread the sbrisolona crumbs on a separate plate. Scoop a portion of semifreddo, then roll it in the sbrisolona and arrange on a serving plate. Repeat with the remaining portions.

✤ WINE PAIRING ✤

Rich and concentrated but still light on its feet, this semifreddo calls for one of Italy's most renowned dessert wines, Passito di Pantelleria. Made on Pantelleria, a small rock of an island south of Sicily and just off the coast of Tunisia, this sweet wine is unique. The hot and windy island is great for drying the local Zibibbo grapes before they are pressed into the Passito. Donnafugata's Ben Ryé, Passito di Pantelleria is one of the most classic and delicious examples. Golden, caramelized, and rich, the wine accents the butterscotch but is fresh enough to prevent the pairing from becoming too sweet.

GRAPPA PANNA COTTA
with Sour Raisins and Green Grapes

Semisweet, smooth, and creamy, this delicate panna cotta blends grappa into the cream. It is topped with sugared grapes, from which grappa is made, crunchy croutons, and golden raisins that have been rehydrated with tart and tangy verjus.

Serves 8

SOUR RAISINS

½ cup (118 milliliters) verjus (see note)

½ cup (90 grams) golden raisins

½ cup (118 milliliters) grade A maple syrup

PANNA COTTA

2⅔ sheets (5⅓ grams) gelatin

1½ cups plus 2½ tablespoons (total 392 milliliters) heavy cream

¾ cup (178 milliliters) whole milk

½ cup (100 grams) sugar

Nonstick cooking spray (optional)

2 tablespoons (30 milliliters) high-quality grappa

CROUTONS

3 loosely packed cups (80 grams) filone or rustic Italian bread, crusts trimmed and discarded, bread torn into irregular bite-sized pieces

Scant 2½ tablespoons (30 grams) sugar

1 tablespoon plus 2 teaspoons (total 25 milliliters) extra-virgin olive oil

½ teaspoon (2 grams) kosher salt

GREEN GRAPES

24 muscat grapes (93 grams), halved

Scant ½ tablespoon (5 grams) sugar

½ teaspoon (2½ milliliters) fresh lime juice

TO SERVE

Torn mint leaves

Very good extra-virgin olive oil, preferably delicate Sicilian (see Larder, page xxix), for drizzling

SPECIAL EQUIPMENT: eight 5- to 10-ounce ramekins or eight plastic 1-quart containers

For the sour raisins: In a small bowl, pour the verjus over the raisins to cover. Cover and let stand at room temperature for 3 days.

In a small saucepan, combine the raisins and maple syrup. Bring just to a simmer over low heat, then remove from the heat and let stand until cooled to room temperature. (The raisins in their syrup can be kept, in an airtight container at room temperature, for up to 2 weeks. Add more syrup, if necessary, to keep the raisins fully covered.)

For the panna cotta: Fill a small bowl with ice and cold water. Submerge the gelatin in the ice water. Set aside. In a medium saucepan, bring the cream, milk, and sugar just to a bare simmer, whisking frequently to dissolve the sugar, then remove the pan from the heat. Drain the gelatin, then squeeze out the excess liquid. Add the gelatin to the hot cream mixture and stir to dissolve. Let stand until cooled to room temperature.

Lightly coat eight ramekins or other containers with nonstick cooking spray. (We use the lids from plastic quart containers because we like a wide shallow mold, but you can use anything you like. If you prefer to serve the panna cotta in the mold, you do not need to coat with cooking spray.) Add the grappa to the panna cotta base and whisk to combine, then divide the mixture among the prepared ramekins. Refrigerate until set, about 3 hours. (Once set, the panna cotta can be kept, loosely covered with plastic wrap and refrigerated, for up to 3 days.)

For the croutons: Heat the oven to 350°F (177°C). In a bowl, toss together the bread, sugar, oil, and salt. Spread the bread on a rimmed baking sheet and bake, stirring once halfway through, until golden and dried out, 10 to 15 minutes. Transfer the baking sheet to a wire rack and let the croutons cool completely.

For the green grapes: Heat the oven to broil. In a bowl, toss together the grapes, sugar, and lime juice. Arrange the grapes on a baking sheet, cut sides up. Broil until the sugar melts and the grapes are just warm to the touch, 2 to 3 minutes. Transfer the pan to a wire rack and let the grapes cool to room temperature.

To serve: Unmold the panna cottas onto individual serving plates. Sprinkle with the sour raisins (drained from the syrup), croutons, and grapes. Garnish with the mint and a drizzle of oil.

NOTE: *Verjus is a tart juice pressed from unripened grapes and can be purchased at gourmet markets and online.*

CRESPELLE D'AUTTUNO

Serves 10

CRESPELLE

6½ tablespoons (92 grams) unsalted butter

¼ cup (28 grams) cornstarch

½ cup (60 grams) buckwheat flour

1 tablespoon plus 1 teaspoon (total 10 grams) unbleached all-purpose flour

2 tablespoons (25 grams) sugar

1 teaspoon (4 grams) kosher salt

3 large eggs, lightly beaten

1 cup (236 milliliters) whole milk

Nonstick cooking spray

ROASTED SQUASH

1 kabocha or acorn squash (about 1¾ pounds or 800 grams), seeded and cut into ¾-inch (2-centimeter) cubes

3 tablespoons plus 1 teaspoon (total 50 milliliters) extra-virgin olive oil

1 tablespoon sugar

1¼ teaspoons (5 grams) kosher salt

CHAMPAGNE CARAMEL

½ cup (100 grams) sugar

¼ cup (60 milliliters) champagne vinegar

2 sticks (227 grams) unsalted butter, cut into small pieces

¼ teaspoon (1¼ milliliters) fresh lemon juice

Pinch kosher salt

TO SERVE

1¼ cups (150 grams) Sbrisolona Crumbs (page 200)

Ricotta Gelato (page 206)

Confectioners' sugar

These egg and buckwheat flour crepes can be accompanied by a variety of different ingredients, given the season. The autumnal crepes include roasted squash and a tangy caramel, but any number of summer fruits can be substituted during warmer months. The champagne caramel—sweet, sour, and salty—is wonderful drizzled over a scoop of gelato.

For the crespelle batter: Melt the butter in a small heavy saucepan over medium-low heat, then cook over low heat, swirling the pan occasionally, until the butter has a nutty aroma and is a rich brown color, 8 to 10 minutes. Pour the brown butter into a large bowl (including the browned milk solids on the bottom of the pan). Let cool to room temperature.

To the bowl with the butter, add the cornstarch, buckwheat flour, all-purpose flour, sugar, salt, eggs, and milk. Purée the ingredients using an immersion blender, or vigorously whisk by hand to combine. Refrigerate, covered, for 1 hour. Meanwhile, roast the squash and prepare the champagne caramel.

For the roasted squash: Heat the oven to 350°F (177°C). On a rimmed baking sheet, toss the squash with the oil, sugar, and salt. Roast, stirring once halfway through, until the squash is tender, about 15 minutes, then broil until lightly golden, 2 to 3 minutes. Transfer the pan to a wire rack and set aside.

For the champagne caramel: In a heavy medium saucepan, stir together the sugar and 2 tablespoons (30 milliliters) water so that all of the sugar is damp and none of it is coating the sides of the pan. Bring to a boil over high heat, then continue to cook, gently swirling the pan occasionally, until

the mixture turns a light amber color, 5 to 6 minutes. Remove from the heat, then add the vinegar (the mixture will bubble) and whisk to combine. Return the pan to medium-low heat and cook, whisking occasionally, until the sugar is dissolved. Whisk in the butter, lemon juice, and salt to combine. Remove the sauce from the heat and let stand while you make the crespelle. (The cooled caramel can be kept, in an airtight container and refrigerated, for up to 1 week. Let come to room temperature before serving.)

Heat the oven to 250°F (121°C). Line two baking sheets with parchment paper.

To cook the crespelle: Remove the batter from the refrigerator. Whisk well to combine. Heat an 8-inch (20-centimeter) nonstick skillet over medium heat. Lightly coat the skillet with nonstick cooking spray and add about 2 tablespoons batter, swirling to cover the bottom of the skillet. Cook, undisturbed, until the edges turn golden and the center begins to puff, about 2 minutes. Using a heatproof rubber spatula, loosen the edges and then, using your fingers, flip the crespelle and cook until the bottom is dry and set, about 30 seconds longer. Transfer the crespelle to the prepared baking sheet. Repeat with the remaining batter, whisking the batter between crespelle and coating the skillet with nonstick spray between every

four or five crespelle, or as necessary. As the crespelle cool, you can stack them on the baking sheets. (The completely cooled crespelle can be stacked on a plate, wrapped tightly with plastic wrap, and refrigerated for up to 3 days.)

To serve: Warm the crespelle and the roasted squash in a low oven just until warmed through, then arrange on serving plates. Spoon a small mound of sbrisolona crumbs alongside and top with a scoopful of the gelato. Drizzle with the champagne caramel and dust with confectioners' sugar.

PINEAPPLE CROSTATAS
with Pistachio Butter and Candied Pistachios

The area around Bronte, in northeastern Sicily, produces bright green, intensely flavored pistachios. Del Posto candies these coveted Sicilian pistachios and uses their buttery cream as a complement to sweet pineapple crostatas. Grilling the pineapple before it goes into the crostata pastry mellows the fruit's aggressive sweetness.

For the crostata dough: In the bowl of an electric mixer fitted with the paddle attachment, combine the flour, sugar, polenta, and salt; mix on medium-low speed to combine. Add the butter; mix on medium-low speed for 30 seconds, then increase to medium and continue mixing just until the butter pieces are pea-sized with some large pieces remaining.

With the machine running, pour in ¼ cup plus 1 teaspoon (total 64 milliliters) ice water in a slow, steady stream, mixing just until the dough begins to bind and holds together when squeezed in the palm of your hand, 5 to 10 seconds. If the dough is too dry, add a bit more water, 1 table-spoon (15 milliliters) at a time.

Turn out the dough onto a clean work surface and shape it into a flattened disk. Wrap in plastic wrap and refrigerate at least 30 minutes or overnight. (The dough can be frozen for up to 1 month; thaw it overnight in the refrigerator before using.)

For the filling: Heat a grill to medium-high heat. In a bowl, toss together the pineapple with the oil. Grill, turning once, until golden, 3 to 4 minutes per side. Transfer to a baking sheet and let cool, then cut into ½-inch (1.25-centimeter) pieces, discarding the cores.

In a bowl, toss the grilled pineapple pieces with the sugar and zest. Let stand for at least 15 minutes while you prepare the candied pistachios and roll out the crostata dough.

For the candied pistachios: Heat the oven to 350°F (177°C). In a bowl, toss together the pistachios, egg white, sugar, and salt, mixing well to coat the nuts evenly. Spread the nuts on a baking sheet. Bake, stirring every 3 minutes, until the nuts are just dried out, 8 to 10 minutes total. Transfer the baking sheet to a wire rack and let the nuts cool completely.

To shape, fill, and bake the crostatas: On a piece of parchment paper lightly dusted with flour, roll out the dough to a ⅛-inch (3-millimeter) thickness. Transfer the dough, on the parchment, to a baking sheet. Chill until firm, about 30 minutes.

Line a second baking sheet with parchment paper. Remove the dough from the refrigerator. Using a 5-inch (12.5-centimeter) round cutter, cut out 12 dough rounds, rerolling the scraps once. Working with one round at a time, center the dough in the palm of your hand and begin to make a fist in order to create a cup. Then crimp together the four or five folds that form around the outside of the cup. It should resemble a star with a cup in the center that is about 1½ inches (3.8 centimeters) in diameter and 1 inch (2.5 centimeters) deep. (To shape the crostata dough properly, the dough should be just warm enough to be

CONTINUED

Makes 12 individual crostatas

CROSTATA DOUGH

3 cups (375 grams) unbleached all-purpose flour

¼ cup plus 1¼ teaspoons (total 57 grams) sugar

¼ cup (38 grams) instant polenta

1 tablespoon (12 grams) kosher salt

2 sticks plus 2 tablespoons (total 255 grams) chilled unsalted butter, cut into small pieces

1 large egg, lightly beaten for egg wash

Turbinado sugar, for sprinkling

PINEAPPLE FILLING

1 fresh pineapple (about 4½ pounds or 2 kilograms), peeled and cut crosswise into ½-inch (1.25-centimeter) rounds

1½ teaspoons (7 milliliters) extra-virgin olive oil

¼ cup plus 2 tablespoons (total 75 grams) sugar

Finely grated zest of 1 orange

CANDIED PISTACHIOS

1¾ cups (225 grams) Sicilian pistachios (see notes)

1 tablespoon (15 milliliters) lightly beaten egg white

3 tablespoons (36 grams) sugar

½ teaspoon (2 grams) kosher salt

PISTACHIO BUTTER

¼ cup (70 grams) pistachio cream spread (see notes)

1 teaspoon (5 milliliters) very good extra-virgin olive oil, preferably delicate Sicilian (see Larder, page xxix)

¼ teaspoon (1 gram) kosher salt

malleable without cracking while you fold and pinch. You may need to return the rounds to the refrigerator to maintain the proper temperature as you work.) Transfer the shaped cups to the prepared baking sheet, spacing the cups at least 1 inch apart. Chill the shaped dough in the refrigerator until firm, about 15 minutes.

Heat the oven to 375ºF (190ºC).

Drain the pineapple mixture and discard the liquid. Using a small spoon, divide the pineapple among the crostata crusts, making sure to first tuck pieces into the corners of each crust, so that each is filled completely, before mounding the filling to the top.

Brush the outsides of the crusts with egg wash, then sprinkle with the turbinado sugar. Bake, rotating the baking sheet once halfway through, until the crusts are deep golden on the bottom and sides, 20 to 25 minutes. Using a spatula, transfer the crostatas to a wire rack and let cool 5 minutes before serving. (The crostatas keep, first cooled completely, then placed in an airtight container and kept at cool room temperature, for up to 8 hours. If making ahead, gently warm in a 350ºF [177ºC] oven for 3 to 5 minutes before serving.) While the crostatas are baking, prepare the pistachio butter.

For the pistachio butter: In a bowl, stir together the pistachio cream spread, oil, and salt until well combined and fluid.

To serve: Drizzle the pistachio butter on each serving plate. Top with the crostatas. Sprinkle with candied pistachios. Serve with the pistachio gelato.

NOTES: *Sicilian pistachios, especially those from Bronte, are considered some of the best in the world and are known for their intense flavor. Sicilian pistachios and Sicilian pistachio cream can be purchased at gourmet markets or ordered online. Marco Colzani pistachio cream spread is one of the best available.*

TO SERVE

Pistachio Gelato (page 209)

SPECIAL EQUIPMENT: a 5-inch (12.5-centimeter) round cutter; parchment paper

---

❦ WINE PAIRING ❦

Known as the international sign of hospitality, pineapple is welcomed into the Italian kitchen for these crostatas. The combination of caramelized roasted fruit and comforting crostata pastry seeks a concentrated wine with some savory elements and acidity. Enter Marsala. This is not your grandmother's cooking wine, used for Chicken Marsala, but a wine of history, depth, and beauty. Marco De Bartoli's five-year-old Vigna La Miccia Marsala is a perfect introduction to a wine that in the 1700s ruled the world's wine trade. Savory, sweet, rich, and bright, this wine refreshes the palate after each sip.

EGGPLANT AND CHOCOLATE CROSTATA

CREAM CHEESE DOUGH

4 ounces (114 grams) cream cheese, softened

6 tablespoons (86 grams) unsalted butter, softened

1 large egg yolk (18 grams)

1½ cups (188 grams) unbleached all-purpose flour

½ teaspoon (2 grams) kosher salt

EGGPLANT

4 pounds (1.8 kilograms) Fairy Tale or Japanese eggplant

½ cup plus 2 tablespoons (total 150 milliliters) extra-virgin olive oil

Nonstick cooking spray

ALMOND SPREAD

1 stick (125 grams) unsalted butter, softened

½ cup plus 3 tablespoons (total 136 grams) sugar

1¼ cups (125 grams) almond flour

3 large eggs

Finely grated zest of 1 lemon

CHOCOLATE SAUCE

½ cup (2¾ ounces or 80 grams) coarsely chopped best-quality dark chocolate

2 tablespoons (30 milliliters) extra-virgin olive oil

⅛ teaspoon (½ gram) kosher salt

CONTINUED

Eggplant and chocolate is a summer dessert combination found in and around the city of Naples. Served toward the end of summer, when eggplant is abundant, it's often a rustic, chilled dessert built from layers of fried or roasted eggplant and semisweet dark chocolate. Generally associated with the cucina povera, Del Posto refines the combination as an eggplant crostata, drizzled with olive oil–infused chocolate sauce.

For the cream cheese dough: In the bowl of an electric mixer fitted with the paddle attachment, beat the cream cheese and butter on medium speed until combined, about 1 minute. Scrape down the sides of the bowl, then add the egg yolk and beat until just incorporated. Add the all-purpose flour and salt, then beat until just combined.

Turn out the dough onto a clean work surface. Divide it in half, shape into 5-inch (13-centimer) disks, and wrap separately in plastic wrap. Refrigerate for at least 1 hour or overnight. (You need only one disk for this recipe. The dough can be double-wrapped and frozen for up to 1 month. Thaw one disk overnight in the refrigerator before using.)

For the eggplant: Line a baking sheet with parchment paper. Trim and peel half of the eggplant. Beginning at the stem end, cut one of the peeled eggplants crosswise into ³⁄₁₆-inch-thick (5-millimeter-thick) slices, stopping when you see seeds (a couple of seeds in 1 or 2 slices from each eggplant are OK, but not more), then repeat with the next eggplant. You want a total of 1 pound (453 grams) of the slices; continue peeling and slicing the eggplant until you have enough (save the pieces with seeds and any remaining unpeeled eggplant for another use).

Place the eggplant slices in a large bowl. Drizzle with the oil and toss to coat. Lightly coat a panini press with nonstick cooking spray. In batches, arrange the eggplant slices in a single layer on a hot panini press, then press and cook the eggplant until golden and tender, 2½ to 3 minutes per batch. Transfer the finished slices to the prepared baking sheet and let stand until completely cool.

For the almond spread: In the bowl of an electric mixer fitted with the paddle attachment, beat together the butter and sugar on medium speed, stopping the mixer to scrape down the sides of the bowl once or twice, until the mixture is very smooth, about 3 minutes. Add the almond flour and beat on medium speed until well combined. With the machine running on medium speed, add the eggs, one at a time, waiting until each is incorporated before adding the next (the spread will appear loose and slightly grainy; this is OK). Add the zest and beat just to combine. (The almond spread makes a scant 2½ cups or 512 grams, which is enough for 5 crostatas. It is very similar to an almond cream called frangipane and can be used in classic pastries such as almond croissanta. It is also a good filling for thumbprint cookies or stuffed French toast. It keeps, in an airtight container and

TO BAKE THE CROSTATA

1¼ teaspoons (6 grams) cold unsalted butter, cut into small pieces

2½ teaspoons (10 grams) sugar

2¼ teaspoons (16 grams) honey

2¼ teaspoons (11 milliliters) white wine vinegar

Pinch kosher salt

TO SERVE

Ricotta Stracciatella (page 206)

Confectioners' sugar, for dusting

SPECIAL EQUIPMENT: parchment paper; a panini press

refrigerated, for up to 3 days, or frozen for up to 1 month. It should be portioned into smaller containers before freezing unless using it all at once.)

For the chocolate sauce: In a microwave-safe bowl, heat the chocolate in 10-second intervals, stirring between each interval, until the chocolate is completely melted. Stir in the oil and salt. Let cool completely, then set aside, covered, until ready to use.

To bake the crostata: Heat the oven to 350º (177ºC). Between two sheets of parchment paper, roll out one disk of the dough to a ⅛-inch (3-millimeter) thickness. Transfer to a rimmed baking sheet, then remove and discard the top sheet of parchment paper. Spread a scant ½ cup (102 grams) of the almond spread over the dough (reserve the remaining almond spread for future crostatas). Arrange overlapping eggplant slices on top. Dot with the butter and sprinkle with the sugar. Cover the baking sheet with foil, sealing the foil tightly at the edges. Bake for 30 minutes, rotating the pan once halfway through (do not lift the foil), then remove the foil and continue to bake until the crust is evenly golden underneath, about 8 minutes more. Meanwhile, in a small bowl, whisk together the honey, vinegar, and salt.

Transfer the baking sheet to a wire rack. Brush the top of the warm crostata with the honey mixture.

To serve: Remove the crostata from the baking sheet, slice, and serve warm with a scoop of ricotta stracciatella, a drizzle of the chocolate sauce, and a dusting of confectioners' sugar. (The crostata can be cooled completely and kept at room temperature, uncovered, for up to 12 hours before serving. Heat in a low oven, uncovered, to warm just before serving.)

❧ WINE PAIRING ❧

This crostata transcends any notions that vegetables cannot star in the last dish of the night. Earthy eggplant combined with melted dark chocolate provides an exciting opportunity to drink Italy's red sweet wines. Throughout Italy, producers experiment with drying their grapes, concentrating their natural sugars, before pressing them into wine. The most famous of these is the Recioto della Valpolicella (the precursor to Amarone), a dense, rich, and very sweet wine from the Veneto region that complements dark chocolate. Or turn to Sicily and one of the island's most famous grapes, Nero d'Avola. Known more for its dry red wines, Nero d'Avola is pushed to the limit by winemaker Arianna Occhipinti. Old vine, and late harvest, Occhipinti's Passo Nero, 2011, has earthy spice notes mixed with dark blue and black berries that work with both the eggplant and the chocolate.

ZABAGLIONE CLASSICO

Any collection of dolce recipes wouldn't be complete without zabaglione, the frothy custard infused with dry marsala wine from Sicily. The origins of this classic recipe can be traced to the 16th-century recipes of Scappi, and probably even earlier. It can be made without sugar for savory dishes, and the marsala wine is often substituted with other dessert wines such as sherry and Moscato. At Del Posto, it is made Mario-style, fluffy and loose, or Lidia-style, which is more custardy and dense. Both are nice options, differentiated by how much whisking is needed and how long the custard is cooked. This recipe calls for using a balloon whisk with less time over heat, creating Mario-style zabaglione.

Serves 4 to 6

12 large egg yolks (216 grams)

½ cup (120 milliliters) dry marsala

½ cup (100 grams) sugar

1 teaspoon salt

Put the egg yolks, marsala, and then the sugar and salt into a medium heatproof bowl. Set the bowl over a medium saucepan filled with 1 inch of gently simmering water (the bowl should be over but not touching the water, creating the effect of a double boiler). Cook, constantly whisking the egg yolk mixture and making sure to whisk into both the center and the sides of the bowl, until the mixture is thick and holds a ribbon when the whisk is lifted, 5 to 8 minutes. Don't cook the zabaglione for too long or it will curdle. Using a balloon whisk can be helpful in adding air to the mixture, keeping it fluffy.

Spoon the zabaglione into serving cups or bowls. Serve warm or slightly cooled, with fresh berries, if desired.

SBRISOLONA CRUMBS

Makes 4¾ cups (570 grams)

1¾ cups plus 2 tablespoons (total 233 grams) unbleached all-purpose flour

Scant 1½ cups (233 grams) instant polenta

¾ cup (150 grams) sugar

2 teaspoons (8 grams) kosher salt

1¾ teaspoons (8 grams) baking powder

Finely grated zest of ½ lemon

Finely grated zest of ½ orange

1 large egg

½ vanilla bean, split lengthwise, seeds scraped out and reserved, bean saved for another use

2 sticks (233 grams) cold unsalted butter, cut into small pieces

SPECIAL EQUIPMENT: parchment paper

Many of the dishes in this chapter call for a crunchy garnish of *sbrisolona* crumbs. Polenta cake from the town of Montova in western Lombardy, sbrisolona is traditionally made with almonds (or almond flour) and yellow polenta. At Del Posto, the polenta batter is infused with citrus zest instead of almonds to make tangy-sweet cake crumbs.

Heat the oven to 350°F (177°C). Line a baking sheet with parchment paper.

In a medium bowl, whisk together the flour, polenta, sugar, salt, baking powder, and zests just to combine. Add the egg and vanilla bean seeds. Stir together the mixture by hand, rubbing between your hands to evenly disperse the egg and vanilla.

Transfer the mixture to a food processor. Add the cold butter. Pulse just until the butter is pea-size; do not overmix. (In lieu of a food processor, a pastry cutter or two butter knives can be used to cut in the butter.)

Spread the mixture evenly onto the prepared baking sheet. Bake, stirring then respreading evenly and breaking up clumps as needed every 5 minutes until the sbrisolona is lightly golden, about 20 minutes total. Transfer the pan to a wire rack and let cool completely. (Sbrisolona crumbs keep, in an airtight container at room temperature, for up to 2 weeks.)

GELATI & SORBETTI

For many Americans, gelato is Italy's greatest culinary achievement next to pasta. Mastering the art of gelato is no small feat, and pastry chef Brooks Headley crafted an expansive roster of magnificent gelati and sorbetti using unexpected savory and herbaceous ingredients—from corn to basil. Almost all of the dessert recipes in this chapter call for one of these gelati.

2 cups plus 2 tablespoons
(total 500 milliliters) whole milk

6 large egg yolks (108 grams)

¼ cup plus 2 tablespoons
(total 90 milliliters) extra-virgin olive oil

¼ cup plus 2 tablespoons
(total 72 grams) sugar

⅓ cup (79 milliliters) heavy cream

¼ cup (60 milliliters) sweetened
condensed milk

¼ cup (25 grams) nonfat
dry milk powder

2 tablespoons (25 grams) dextrose
powder (see note)

1 tablespoon (20 grams) honey

½ teaspoon (2 grams) kosher salt

OLIVE OIL GELATO

In a large bowl, combine the milk, egg yolks, oil, sugar, cream, condensed milk, milk powder, dextrose powder, honey, and salt. Purée the ingredients using an immersion blender, or vigorously whisk by hand to combine. Refrigerate, covered, until well chilled, at least 4 hours or overnight. Freeze the gelato base in an ice cream machine according to the manufacturer's instructions. Transfer the gelato to an airtight container and place plastic wrap directly over the surface to prevent ice crystals from forming. Cover the container and freeze until firm, about 2 hours. (The gelato will keep for up to 5 days.)

NOTE: *Dextrose powder is a natural grape sugar that is less sweet than cane sugar and helps keep gelato elastic and smooth. It can be purchased online.*

Makes 1 quart

2 cups plus 2 tablespoons
(total 500 milliliters) whole milk

6 large egg yolks (108 grams)

⅓ cup (79 milliliters) heavy cream

¼ cup (60 milliliters) sweetened
condensed milk

¼ cup (25 grams) nonfat
dry milk powder

2½ tablespoons (25 grams)
dextrose powder (see note)

½ cup (168 grams) honey, preferably
sunflower or eucalyptus

¾ teaspoon (3 grams) kosher salt

HONEY GELATO

In a large bowl, combine the milk, egg yolks, cream, condensed milk, milk powder, dextrose powder, about ⅓ cup (105 grams) of the honey, and the salt. Purée the ingredients using an immersion blender, or vigorously whisk by hand to combine. Refrigerate, covered, until well chilled, at least 4 hours or overnight. Freeze the gelato base in an ice cream machine according to the manufacturer's instructions. Transfer about one-third of the gelato to an airtight container, then swirl in a little bit of the remaining 3 tablespoons (63 grams) honey. Repeat with the remaining gelato and honey. Place plastic wrap directly over the surface to prevent ice crystals from forming. Cover the container and freeze until firm, about 2 hours. (The gelato will keep for up to 5 days.)

NOTE: *Dextrose powder is a natural grape sugar that is less sweet than cane sugar and helps keep gelato elastic and smooth. It can be purchased online.*

STRAWBERRY GELATO

In a large stainless steel bowl, gently stir together the strawberries, 2 tablespoons (24 grams) of the sugar, and the lemon juice and salt. Let stand at room temperature for 1 hour, or refrigerate, covered, overnight.

Transfer the strawberry mixture to a blender. Purée until smooth, then strain through a medium-mesh strainer into a large bowl. Add 2 tablespoons (40 grams) of the seeds and pulp (from the strainer) to the strained purée. Discard the remaining seeds and pulp. To the bowl with the purée, add the remaining ¼ cup plus 2 tablespoons (total 72 grams) sugar and the milk, egg yolks, cream, condensed milk, milk powder, dextrose powder, and honey. Purée the ingredients using an immersion blender, or vigorously whisk by hand to combine. Refrigerate, covered, until well chilled, at least 4 hours or overnight.

Freeze the gelato base in an ice cream machine according to the manufacturer's instructions. Transfer the gelato to an airtight container and place plastic wrap directly over the surface to prevent ice crystals from forming. Cover the container and freeze until firm, about 2 hours. (The gelato will keep for up to 5 days.)

NOTE: *Dextrose powder is a natural grape sugar that is less sweet than cane sugar and helps keep gelato elastic and smooth. It can be purchased online.*

Makes 1½ quarts

1 pound (450 grams) strawberries, hulled, then cut into halves or quarters if large

½ cup (96 grams) sugar

1½ tablespoons (23 milliliters) lemon juice

⅛ teaspoon (½ gram) kosher salt

2 cups plus 2 tablespoons (total 500 milliliters) whole milk

6 large egg yolks (108 grams)

⅓ cup (71 milliliters) heavy cream

¼ cup (60 milliliters) sweetened condensed milk

¼ cup (25 grams) nonfat dry milk powder

2 tablespoons (25 grams) dextrose powder (see note)

1 tablespoon (20 grams) honey

RICOTTA GELATO AND RICOTTA STRACCIATELLA

Makes 1½ quarts

RICOTTA GELATO

3 cups (750 grams) good-quality fresh whole-milk ricotta cheese, such as Calabro

1¾ cups (414 milliliters) simple syrup (see note)

½ cup (170 grams) honey

Scant ½ teaspoon (1.5 grams) kosher salt

RICOTTA STRACCIATELLA (OPTIONAL)

¾ cup (117 grams) best-quality coarsely chopped bittersweet chocolate

Stracciatella means "shred" in Italian, and when it comes to gelato, it is a cream-based gelato studded with shards of chocolate. Here is the recipe for ricotta gelato, which is wonderful on its own and called for in our Crespelle d'Auttuno recipe (page 190), and instructions for making it into our version of stracciatella.

In a large bowl, combine the ricotta, simple syrup, honey, and salt. Purée the ingredients using an immersion blender, or vigorously whisk by hand to combine. Refrigerate, covered, until well chilled, at least 4 hours or overnight.

Freeze the gelato base in an ice cream machine according to the manufacturer's instructions. Transfer the gelato to an airtight container and place plastic wrap directly over the surface to prevent ice crystals from forming. Cover the container and freeze until firm, about 2 hours. (The gelato will keep for up to 5 days.)

If you'd like to make ricotta stracciatella: While the ricotta gelato is freezing in your ice cream maker, freeze a large stainless steel bowl. Place the chocolate in a microwave-safe bowl and heat in 10-second intervals, stirring well between intervals, until the chocolate is just completely melted. (If you don't have a microwave, use a double boiler to melt the chocolate.) Set aside.

Transfer the just-frozen ricotta gelato from the ice cream maker to the frozen bowl. Working quickly, in four additions, drizzle the cooled melted chocolate over the gelato in thin zigzag lines. Using a large rubber spatula, quickly and forcefully fold the chocolate into the gelato (you want the chocolate to break into shards) until well combined. When all of the chocolate has been folded into the gelato, transfer the gelato to an airtight container and place plastic wrap directly over the surface to prevent ice crystals from forming. Cover the container and freeze until firm, about 2 hours.

NOTE: *Simple syrup can be purchased or made at home. Combine sugar and water in a small saucepan and bring to a boil over medium-high heat, stirring to dissolve the sugar, about 3 minutes. Remove from heat, let cool and refrigerate in a tightly sealed jar until ready to use (syrup keeps covered and chilled for 3 months).*

BASIL GELATO

Makes 1½ quarts

6½ loosely packed cups
(100 grams) basil leaves

2 cups plus 2 tablespoons
(total 500 milliliters) whole milk

6 large egg yolks (108 grams)

¼ cup plus 2 tablespoons
(total 72 grams) sugar

⅓ cup (71 milliliters) heavy cream

¼ cup (60 milliliters) sweetened
condensed milk

¼ cup (25 grams) nonfat
dry milk powder

2 tablespoons (25 grams)
dextrose powder (see note)

1 tablespoon (20 grams) honey

⅛ teaspoon (½ gram) salt

This same recipe can be used to make parsley or mint gelato: Simply substitute the same amount of flat-leaf parsley leaves for the basil, or 5½ loosely packed cups (80 grams) coarsely chopped mint.

Bring a large saucepan of water to a boil. Fill a large bowl with ice and cold water. Blanch the basil in the boiling water for 30 seconds, then drain and immediately plunge into the ice bath. Let the basil cool completely, then drain. Gently but thoroughly squeeze the herbs to remove excess liquid.

In a blender, purée the basil and 1 cup (237 milliliters) of the milk to combine. Strain the mixture through a medium-mesh strainer into a large bowl. Discard the solids. To the basil milk, add the remaining 1 cup plus 2 tablespoons (total 263 milliliters) milk and the egg yolks, sugar, cream, condensed milk, milk powder, dextrose powder, honey, and salt. Purée the ingredients using an immersion blender or vigorously whisk by hand to combine. Refrigerate, covered, until well chilled, at least 4 hours or overnight.

Freeze the gelato base in an ice cream machine according to the manufacturer's instructions. Transfer the gelato to an airtight container and place plastic wrap directly over the surface to prevent ice crystals from forming. Cover the container and freeze until firm, about 2 hours. (The gelato will keep for up to 5 days.)

NOTE: *Dextrose powder is a natural grape sugar that is less sweet than cane sugar and helps keep gelato elastic and smooth. It can be purchased online.*

PISTACHIO GELATO

Heat the oven to 350°F (177°C). Spread the nuts on a baking sheet and bake until just warm to the touch, 7 to 8 minutes. Transfer the baking sheet to a wire rack and let the nuts cool completely.

Place the cooled nuts in a food processor and pulse three or four times to coarsely chop (or coarsely chop by hand). Set aside 1 cup (133 grams) of the nuts. Place the remaining nuts in a medium saucepan and add the milk. Bring the mixture just to a boil over medium heat. Remove from the heat and let cool to room temperature. Transfer to an airtight container and refrigerate for at least 12 hours or up to 1 day.

Strain the mixture through a medium-mesh strainer into a large bowl. Discard the solids. To the infused milk, add the egg yolks, cream, sugar, condensed milk, milk powder, dextrose powder, honey, and salt. Purée the ingredients using an immersion blender or vigorously whisk by hand to combine. Refrigerate, covered, until well chilled, at least 4 hours or overnight.

Freeze the gelato base in an ice cream machine according to the manufacturer's instructions. Fold in the reserved chopped nuts, then transfer the gelato to an airtight container and place plastic wrap directly over the surface to prevent ice crystals from forming. Cover the container and freeze until firm, about 2 hours. (The gelato will keep for up to 5 days.)

NOTES: *Sicilian pistachios, especially those from Bronte, are considered some of the best in the world and are known for their intense flavor. They can be purchased at gourmet markets or ordered online. Dextrose powder is a natural grape sugar that is less sweet than cane sugar and helps keep gelato elastic and smooth. It can be purchased online.*

Makes 1¼ quarts

4 cups (532 grams) Sicilian pistachios (see notes)

4¼ cups (1 liter) whole milk

6 large egg yolks (108 grams)

⅓ cup (80 milliliters) heavy cream

¼ cup plus 2 tablespoons (total 75 grams) sugar

¼ cup (60 milliliters) sweetened condensed milk

¼ cup (25 grams) nonfat dry milk powder

2 tablespoons (25 grams) dextrose powder (see notes)

1 tablespoon (20 grams) honey

⅛ teaspoon (½ gram) salt

CORN GELATO

Makes about 1½ quarts

2 ears corn, shucked

1 quart (1 scant liter) whole milk

½ cup plus 2½ tablespoons
(total 131 grams) sugar

7 large egg yolks (126 grams)

⅓ cup plus 1 tablespoon
(total 97 milliliters) heavy cream

¼ cup (25 grams) nonfat
dry milk powder

2 tablespoons plus 2½ teaspoons
(total 35 grams) dextrose powder
(see note)

1 tablespoon plus 1 teaspoon
(total 20 milliliters) light corn syrup

⅛ teaspoon (½ gram) salt

Heat a grill or grill pan to high heat. Grill the corn, turning occasionally, until the kernels are charred and cooked through, about 10 minutes total. Transfer to a cutting board. Let stand until cool enough to handle, then cut the cobs in half crosswise. Cut the kernels from the cobs and reserve both the cobs and the kernels.

Place the kernels and the milk in a large bowl and purée using an immersion blender. (If you don't have an immersion blender, use a standard blender to purée about half of the milk with the kernels, then combine with the remaining milk and whisk.)

Transfer the mixture to a large saucepan and add the cobs. Bring just to a simmer over medium heat, then remove from the heat and let cool to room temperature. Transfer to an airtight container and refrigerate at least 12 hours or up to 1 day.

Strain the milk mixture through a fine-mesh sieve into a large bowl, pressing on the solids to extract as much liquid as possible. Discard the solids. To the bowl, add the sugar, egg yolks, cream, milk powder, dextrose powder, corn syrup, and salt. Purée the ingredients using an immersion blender or vigorously whisk by hand to combine. Refrigerate, covered, until well chilled, at least 4 hours or overnight.

Freeze the gelato base in an ice cream machine according to the manufacturer's instructions. Transfer the gelato to an airtight container and place plastic wrap directly over the surface to prevent ice crystals from forming. Cover the container and freeze until firm, about 2 hours. (The gelato will keep for up to 5 days.)

NOTE: *Dextrose powder is a natural grape sugar that is less sweet than cane sugar and helps keep gelato elastic and smooth. It can be purchased online.*

CASHEW GELATO

Heat the oven to 350°F (177°C). Spread the nuts on a baking sheet and bake, stirring occasionally, until very dark and just shy of beginning to burn, 20 to 23 minutes. Transfer the baking sheet to a wire rack and let the nuts cool completely.

Place the cooled nuts in a food processor and pulse three or four times to coarsely chop (or coarsely chop by hand). Set aside 1 cup (145 grams) of the nuts. Place the remaining nuts in a medium saucepan. Add the milk. Bring the mixture just to a boil over medium heat. Remove from the heat and let cool to room temperature. Transfer to an airtight container and refrigerate at least 12 hours or up to 1 day.

Strain the mixture through a medium-mesh strainer into a large bowl. Discard the solids. To the infused milk, add the egg yolks, cream, sugar, condensed milk, milk powder, dextrose powder, honey, and salt. Purée the ingredients using an immersion blender or vigorously whisk by hand to combine. Refrigerate, covered, until well chilled, at least 4 hours or overnight.

Freeze the gelato base in an ice cream machine according to the manufacturer's instructions. Fold in the reserved chopped nuts, then transfer the gelato to an airtight container and place plastic wrap directly over the surface to prevent ice crystals from forming. Cover the container and freeze until firm, about 2 hours. (The gelato will keep for up to 5 days.)

NOTE: *Dextrose powder is a natural grape sugar that is less sweet than cane sugar and helps keep gelato elastic and smooth. It can be purchased online.*

Makes 1 quart

4 cups (580 grams) unsalted raw cashews

4¼ cups (1 liter) whole milk

6 large egg yolks (108 grams)

⅓ cup (80 milliliters) heavy cream

¼ cup plus 2 tablespoons (total 75 grams) sugar

¼ cup (60 milliliters) sweetened condensed milk

¼ cup (25 grams) nonfat dry milk powder

2 tablespoons (25 grams) dextrose powder (see note)

1 tablespoon (20 grams) honey

⅛ teaspoon (½ gram) salt

YOGURT SORBETTO

Makes 1 quart

1⅓ cups (315 milliliters)
simple syrup (see note)

1 pound (450 grams) labneh

⅛ teaspoon (½ gram) kosher salt

This simple sorbetto is made with labneh, which can be purchased at most markets and Middle Eastern grocers. It is a rich and tangy cheese made by draining the watery liquids from yogurt. If labneh is not available, drained Greek yogurt can be substituted: Spoon yogurt into a cheesecloth, suspend it over a bowl, and refrigerate for at least 24 hours. This will allow some of the liquid to drain from the yogurt and intensify its flavor.

In a large bowl, combine the simple syrup, labneh, and salt. Purée using an immersion blender, or vigorously whisk by hand to combine. Refrigerate, covered, until well chilled, at least 4 hours or overnight.

Freeze the sorbetto base in an ice cream machine according to the manufacturer's instructions. Transfer the sorbetto to an airtight container and place plastic wrap directly over the surface to prevent ice crystals from forming. Cover the container and freeze until firm, about 2 hours. (The gelato will keep for up to 5 days.)

NOTE: *Simple syrup can be purchased or made at home. Combine sugar and water in a small saucepan and bring to a boil over medium-high heat, stirring to dissolve the sugar, about 3 minutes. Remove from the heat, let cool, and refrigerate in a tightly sealed jar until ready to use (syrup keeps covered and chilled for 3 months).*

SOUR APRICOT SORBETTO

For the sour apricot purée: Place the apricots in a large bowl and cover with the verjus. Cover and let stand at room temperature for at least 48 hours or up to 3 days. (The apricots must be submerged in the liquid while they soak; add more verjus, if necessary, to keep them covered.) Meanwhile, prepare the sorbet syrup.

For the sorbet syrup: In a large bowl, prepare an ice bath. In a medium saucepan, bring 2 cups (475 milliliters) water to a full, rolling boil. Whisk in the sugar and dextrose powder. Return the mixture to a boil, then remove from the heat. Transfer the sorbet syrup to a heatproof bowl. Chill in the ice bath until cold. Transfer the sorbet syrup to an airtight container and refrigerate until ready to use. (The sorbet syrup keeps, in an airtight container and refrigerated, for up to 3 weeks.)

To finish the purée: Drain the apricots (discard the verjus), then transfer to a blender or food processor. With the machine running, add 1 cup (236 milliliters) water in a slow and steady stream. Purée the mixture well, stopping the machine from time to time and scraping down the bowl as necessary, until it is very smooth. Using a rubber spatula, force the purée through a medium-mesh strainer into a bowl (work

it well to be sure to extract as much of the silky smooth purée as possible). Discard the fibrous bits left behind.

Measure the purée (you should have about 2¼ cups [532 milliliters]), then transfer to a medium bowl. Add half the amount (by volume) of the sorbet syrup: For example, for 2¼ cups (532 milliliters) of the purée, add 1⅛ cups (266 milliliters) of the sorbet syrup (save the remaining sorbet syrup to make additional batches of the sorbet). Whisk together to combine, then whisk in the lemon juice and salt. Transfer the sorbetto base to an airtight container and refrigerate until well chilled, at least 4 hours or overnight.

Freeze the sorbetto base in an ice cream machine according to the manufacturer's instructions. Transfer the sorbetto to an airtight container and place plastic wrap directly over the surface to prevent ice crystals from forming. Cover the container and freeze until firm, about 2 hours. (The sorbetto will keep for up to 5 days.)

NOTES: *Verjus is a tart juice pressed from unripened grapes and can be purchased at gourmet markets and online. Dextrose powder is a natural grape sugar that is less sweet than cane sugar and helps keep gelato elastic and smooth. It can be purchased online.*

Makes about 1 quart

SOUR APRICOT PURÉE

2 cups (300 grams) dried apricots

1¾ cups (414 milliliters) verjus (see notes)

1 teaspoon (5 milliliters) fresh lemon juice

⅛ teaspoon (½ gram) kosher salt

SORBET SYRUP

2¼ cups (450 grams) sugar

¾ cup (120 grams) dextrose powder (see notes)

INTERMEZZO

Cashew Gelato (page 211)

Sour Apricot Sorbetto (page 213)

Very good extra-virgin olive oil, preferably intense Sicilian (see Larder, page xxix), for drizzling

Finely grated orange zest

Malden sea salt

This small palate cleanser has become a staple at Del Posto, served between the last savory course and the first sweet course. It combines the Cashew Gelato and the Sour Apricot Sorbetto and should be made in modest portions.

For each serving, spoon a small scoop or spoonful of the gelato, then a small scoop or spoonful of the sorbetto, into a small (2-ounce or 60-milliliter) cup or glass. Drizzle with the oil, then sprinkle with the zest and salt.

BISCOTTI & CARAMELLE

Cookies and candies are the final act at
Del Posto, served with coffees, dessert wines, and liqueurs. Italian
cookies and candies have a distinct balance of sweet and savory, and
these are no different. Each one of these small confections has an
unusual detail, such as a hit of salt or citrus. From chocolate popsicles
filled with olive oil gelato, to amaro-glazed doughnuts, to simple
buckwheat sugar cookies, here is an eclectic group of seven final
indulgences.

From left to right, top to bottom:
*Bastoncini with Olive Oil Gelato
(page 225);
Buckwheat Zuccherini (page 223);
Sour Melon Candy (page 224);
Amaro-Glazed Bomboloni
(page 222);
Candied Grapefruit (page 224);
Brutti ma Buoni (page 220);
and Polenta–Polenta Mini Crostatas
(page 221)*

BRUTTI MA BUONI COOKIES

Brutti ma buoni means "ugly but good" in Italian. These traditional meringue-style cookies usually feature whole almonds and almond filling or batter. Del Posto's version mixes blanched hazelnuts, which are roasted and powdered, into the meringue batter instead.

Makes about 28 cookies

½ pound (226 grams) blanched hazelnuts (see note)

3½ large egg whites (105 grams)

1¼ cups (250 grams) sugar

1 teaspoon (4 grams) kosher salt

¼ teaspoon (scant ¾ gram) cinnamon

¼ teaspoon (1.25 milliliters) pure vanilla extract

SPECIAL EQUIPMENT: parchment paper or 2 silicone baking liners (such as Silpat)

Heat the oven to 325°F (163°C) with racks in the middle and upper third. Line two baking sheets with parchment paper or silicone baking liners.

Spread the hazelnuts on a rimmed baking sheet. Toast in the oven on the middle rack, stirring twice, until golden, 18 to 20 minutes. Transfer the pan to a wire rack and let the nuts cool completely.

Reduce the oven temperature to 300°F (149°C).

In the bowl of a food processor, pulse the cooled nuts to a fine powder (make sure the nuts are completely dry and do not overmix; otherwise, the nuts will become pasty). Set aside.

In the bowl of an electric mixer fitted with the whisk attachment, beat the egg whites on medium-low speed until they are frothy and begin to increase in volume, about 3 minutes. With the machine running, slowly add the sugar, then continue beating for 5 minutes. Increase the speed to high and beat until the mixture becomes thicker and shiny, about 10 minutes. Fold in the powdered hazelnuts, salt, cinnamon, and vanilla.

Drop about 2-tablespoon (20-gram) spoonfuls of batter onto the prepared baking sheets, spacing them at least 2 inches (5 centimeters) apart. Bake, rotating the pans once halfway through, until the cookies are lightly golden and set, 35 to 40 minutes. Transfer the baking sheets to wire racks and let the cookies cool completely. The cookies keep, in an airtight container at room temperature, for up to 2 weeks.

NOTE: *If you can't find blanched hazelnuts, you can use the skin-on type: Spread the nuts on a rimmed baking sheet and bake at 325°F (163°C) until they are lightly golden and the skins blister, 15 to 20 minutes. Wrap the warm toasted nuts in a clean kitchen towel and rub to remove the loose skins. Don't worry about skin that does not come off. Let cool completely, then transfer the nuts to the food processor and proceed with the recipe.*

POLENTA–POLENTA MINI CROSTATAS

These diminutive crostatas are made from thin polenta chips dolloped with polenta pudding and topped with our signature sour raisins.

For the polenta chips: Heat the oven to 300ºF (149ºC). Line two baking sheets with silicone liners or parchment paper, then lightly coat with nonstick cooking spray.

In a small saucepan, bring 1½ cups (354 milliliters) water just to a boil. Whisk in the instant polenta and salt. Cook, whisking, just until the polenta thickens, about 1 minute. Remove from the heat, then whisk in ¼ cup plus 2 tablespoons (total 90 milliliters) hot tap water. Using an immersion blender, or in a food processor, purée the polenta until it is pale and smooth, about 3 minutes.

Divide the polenta between the two baking sheets and spread into very thin even layers (the polenta should be almost transparent). Bake until thoroughly dried and crisp, 40 to 50 minutes (the "chips" will be puffed and broken; this is OK). Transfer the baking pans to wire racks and let the chips cool completely. (The chips keep, in an airtight container at room temperature, for up to 1 week.)

For the polenta pudding: In a medium saucepan, whisk together the milk, coarse polenta, sugar, and salt. Cook over medium-low heat for about 2 hours, whisking occasionally, and then more frequently as the liquid reduces and begins sticking to the bottom of the pan. Continue to cook, whisking frequently, until the polenta is very thick and tender, 30 to 35 minutes more. Remove from the heat.

In a bowl, beat together the eggs; then, whisking vigorously, add about 1 tablespoon (12 grams) of the hot polenta to the egg mixture. Repeat four times, then add the egg mixture to the polenta mixture. Return the pan to low heat and, whisking constantly, cook for 2 minutes. Remove from the heat, add the oil and butter, and whisk well to combine. Transfer the pudding to a bowl and cover the surface with plastic wrap. Let stand until cooled to room temperature. (The pudding keeps, refrigerated in an airtight container, for up to 3 days. Let come to room temperature before serving.)

To serve: Break the chips into bite-sized pieces. Spoon the pudding onto the chips, then top with Sour Raisins, if using, and zest. Repeat with the remaining pudding and chips. Serve immediately.

Makes about 7 dozen small crostatas

POLENTA CHIPS

Nonstick cooking spray

½ cup plus 1 tablespoon (total 90 grams) instant polenta

⅛ teaspoon (½ gram) kosher salt

POLENTA PUDDING

5 cups (1.2 liters) whole milk

⅓ cup plus 1 tablespoon (total 55 grams) coarse polenta, preferably Anson Mills

½ cup (100 grams) sugar

1¼ teaspoons (5 grams) kosher salt

2 large eggs, lightly beaten

2 tablespoons (30 milliliters) extra-virgin olive oil

2 tablespoons (28 grams) unsalted butter

TO SERVE

1 batch Sour Raisins (see Grappa Panna Cotta recipe, page 188), optional

Finely grated zest of 1 orange

SPECIAL EQUIPMENT: 2 silicone baking liners (such as Silpat) or parchment paper (the silicone liners are preferable here, for ease)

AMARO-GLAZED BOMBOLONI

Makes 5 dozen doughnut balls

BOMBOLONI

6 tablespoons (85 grams)
unsalted butter, melted

¼ cup (50 grams) sugar

1 teaspoon (4 grams) kosher salt

1 teaspoon (5 grams) active dry yeast

3 cups (382 grams) unbleached
all-purpose flour, plus more
for dusting

1½ cups (220 grams) bread flour

Finely grated zest of ½ orange

½ teaspoon (2.5 milliliters)
pure vanilla extract

Peanut oil, for frying

AMARO GLAZE

1¾ cups plus 2 tablespoons
(total 210 grams) confectioners' sugar,
plus more for dusting

½ cup (120 milliliters) amaro liqueur

⅛ teaspoon (½ gram) kosher salt

SPECIAL EQUIPMENT: a 17¾ x 12¾-inch
(45 x 32-centimeter) rimmed baking
sheet; a candy / fry thermometer; a
1-inch (2.5-centimeter) round cutter

Bomboloni are Italian doughnuts, often filled with pastry cream, then dusted with sugar and cinnamon. But Del Posto's bomboloni are varnished (American-style) with an herbaceous amaro glaze and then sprinkled with confectioners' sugar.

For the bomboloni: In the bowl of an electric mixer fitted with the dough hook, combine 1¼ cups (425 milliliters) warm water with the butter, sugar, and salt. Mix on medium speed just until the mixture comes together. Add the yeast and mix just to combine.

Add the all-purpose flour, bread flour, zest, and vanilla. Mix on medium-low speed for 6 minutes, then increase the speed to medium and continue to mix until the dough is smooth and sticky, about 6 minutes more. Cover the bowl with plastic wrap and let the dough stand at warm room temperature until it has doubled in bulk, about 3 hours.

Generously dust a 17¾ x 12¾-inch (45 x 32-centimeter) rimmed baking sheet with flour. Turn out the dough onto the prepared baking sheet, then press it out in an even layer until it covers the sheet and is about ¼ inch (6 millimeters) thick. Cover the dough loosely with plastic wrap and refrigerate until it is firm enough to cut, about 1 hour. Meanwhile, make the glaze.

For the glaze: In a medium bowl, whisk together the confectioners' sugar, amaro, and salt. Set aside.

Using a floured 1-inch (2.5-centimeter) round cutter, cut out the bomboloni.

In a large high-sided skillet or wide heavy pot, heat 2 inches of oil to 350°F (177°C). Working in batches of 6 to 8, fry the bomboloni, turning them with a slotted spoon, until they are uniformly golden, about 2 minutes per batch. Transfer to paper towels to drain. Dip into the glaze to coat, then transfer to a plate. Let stand 1 to 2 minutes to allow the glaze to set, then dust with confectioners' sugar. Serve warm.

BUCKWHEAT ZUCCHERINI

Zuccherini, or "little sugars" in Italian, are simple sugar cookies. Perfect alongside coffees and after-dinner drinks, these rustic-style zuccherini are made with hearty buckwheat flour and polenta.

In a large bowl, whisk together the all-purpose flour, buckwheat flour, polenta, and salt. In the bowl of an electric mixer fitted with the paddle attachment, beat the butter and sugar on medium speed until light and fluffy, about 3 minutes. Add the flour mixture and beat until just combined.

Place the dough between two sheets of parchment paper and roll out to a ¼-inch (6-millimeter) thickness. Transfer to a baking sheet and refrigerate until firm, about 30 minutes.

Heat the oven to 325ºF (163ºC) with racks in the middle and upper third. Line two baking sheets with parchment paper.

Remove the top sheet of parchment paper. Using a 2-inch (5-centimeter) round cutter (or other cutter of similar size), cut out 5½ dozen cookies, rerolling scraps once. Place the rounds at least ½ inch (1.25 centimeters) apart on the prepared baking sheets. Sprinkle with sugar.

Bake, rotating the sheets halfway through, until the edges of the cookies begin to brown, about 16 minutes. Transfer the baking sheets to a wire rack and let cool completely. The cookies keep, in an airtight container at room temperature, for up to 2 weeks.

Makes about 5½ dozen sugar cookies

1½ cups (190 grams) unbleached all-purpose flour

⅔ cup (80 grams) buckwheat flour

2½ tablespoons (25 grams) instant polenta

1¼ teaspoons (5 grams) kosher salt

2 sticks (240 grams) unsalted butter, softened

⅔ cup (133 grams) sugar, plus more for sprinkling

SPECIAL EQUIPMENT: parchment paper; a 2-inch (5-centimeter) round cutter (or any another available shape cutter of similar size)

CANDIED GRAPEFRUIT

Makes about 30 pieces

DEHYDRATED GRAPEFRUIT

1 fresh pink grapefruit

½ cup (118 milliliters) Aperol liqueur or Campari

TO SERVE

2 tablespoons (60 grams) Dulce "Milk Jam" (see Butterscotch–Mascarpone Semifreddo, page 185)

¼ cup (30 grams) Sbrisolona Crumbs (page 200)

SPECIAL EQUIPMENT: a dehydrator (optional)

For the dehydrated grapefruit: Using a sharp paring knife, cut the peel and white pith from the grapefruit. Cut between the membranes to release the fruit sections. Cut the sections lengthwise into pieces about ¼ inch (6 millimeters) thick; keep the pieces as uniform in thickness as you can to ensure even dehydrating.

Arrange the sections in a single layer in a small heatproof baking dish. In a small saucepan, heat the Aperol over medium-high heat just to a simmer, then pour over the grapefruit. Let stand at room temperature 3 to 4 hours.

Drain the fruit from the Aperol, then arrange in a single layer on a dehydrator tray. Dehydrate at 125ºF (52ºC) according to the manufacturer's instructions. (Alternatively, you can dehydrate the fruit in the oven: Lightly coat a parchment-lined baking sheet with nonstick cooking spray. Arrange the fruit on the parchment and dry for 6 to 12 hours in the oven set at its lowest heat setting with the door propped open.) The dehydrated grapefruit keeps, in an airtight container at room temperature, for up to 1 week.

To serve: Spread a little dulce milk jam on a dehydrated grapefruit piece, then roll the grapefruit lengthwise into a small cone. Dip one end into the sbrisolona crumbs. Repeat with as many pieces of the dehydrated grapefruit as you wish to serve immediately.

SOUR MELON CANDY

Makes about ¼ pound candy

DEHYDRATED CANTALOUPE

¼ pound (113 grams) dried cantaloupe

1 cup (237 milliliters) verjus (see notes)

TO SERVE

½ cup (100 grams) sugar

⅛ teaspoon (scant ¾ gram) malic acid (see notes)

SPECIAL EQUIPMENT: a dehydrator (optional)

For these double-concentrated sour candies, dried cantaloupe is rehydrated in tart verjus and then dehydrated again.

For the dehydrated cantaloupe: In a medium bowl, combine the dried cantaloupe and verjus. Cover and refrigerate for 2 days.

Drain the cantaloupe (the verjus can be saved for another round of the candy, or to use in drinks or for another purpose). Arrange the fruit in a single layer on a dehydrator tray and dehydrate at 125ºF (52ºC) according to the manufacturer's instructions. (Alternatively, you can dehydrate the fruit in the oven: Lightly coat a parchment-lined baking sheet with nonstick cooking spray. Arrange the fruit on the parchment and dry for 6 to 12 hours in the oven at its lowest heat setting with the door propped open.) The dehydrated melon keeps, in an airtight container at room temperature, for up to 1 week.

To serve: In a small bowl, stir together the sugar and malic acid. Toss as much of the dehydrated melon in the sour sugar as you wish and serve immediately.

NOTES: *Verjus is a tart juice pressed from unripened grapes and can be purchased at gourmet markets and online. Malic acid, an organic powdered compound with tart and sour flavors, can be ordered online. It adds tang to the sugar coating the dehydrated cantaloupe.*

BASTONCINI
with Olive Oil Gelato

Filled with silky olive-oil gelato, these small *bastoncini*, or "popsicles," are inspired by the crunchy, oozy chocolate-coated Magnum ice cream bar (the European version of the American Dove bar).

Chill two parchment-lined rimmed 9 x 13-inch (23 x 33-centimeter) baking sheets (or one large baking sheet) in the freezer overnight.

For the chocolate coating: In a microwave-safe bowl, combine the cocoa butter, dark chocolate, and unsweetened chocolate. Microwave in 10-second intervals, stirring between each interval, just until completely melted and combined (be very careful not to burn the mixture). Whisk in the oil to combine. Set aside to let cool to room temperature. Meanwhile, prepare the breadcrumbs.

For the breadcrumbs: Heat the oven to 300ºF (149ºC). Arrange the baguette slices on a baking sheet. Bake until dried out and crunchy, about 10 minutes. Transfer the sheet to a wire rack and let cool completely.

In a food processor, pulse the toasted slices until coarse crumbs form (or crush the slices using a see-saw motion under the weight of a heavy pan). In a medium-mesh strainer, sift the crumb mixture over a bowl. Set aside the small coarse crumbs (Grape-Nuts sized crumbs are perfect) for this recipe. Save the fine crumbs for another use.

In a large skillet, heat the oil over medium-high heat until it begins to smoke. Add the breadcrumbs and cook, stirring frequently, until toasted and golden, about 5 minutes. Using a slotted spoon, transfer to paper towels to drain. Season generously with salt while warm. Let cool completely, then transfer to a small bowl.

To assemble the bastoncini: Working quickly with one baking sheet at a time, use a mini ice cream scoop to scoop the gelato into balls and place on the prepared baking sheet (return the sheet to the freezer from time to time to keep the scoops from melting). Push a lollipop stick into each scoop. Return the baking sheet to the freezer for 30 minutes.

Have your chocolate coating ready, at room temperature and still fluid.

Working quickly and with one baking sheet at a time, dip one gelato ball into the chocolate coating to completely cover. While the chocolate is still setting, dip the ball into the breadcrumbs, then return it to the baking sheet. Repeat with the remaining pops (return the baking sheet to the freezer from time to time, as needed, to keep the bastoncini from melting). Once all of the bastoncini are dipped, return them to the freezer for at least 30 minutes before serving.The bastoncini keep, in an airtight container and frozen, for up to 1 week.

NOTE: *Cocoa butter is nondairy and made from the cold pressed oils of cacao nibs. It is available at gourmet markets and online.*

Makes 4 dozen popsicles

CHOCOLATE COATING

½ cup plus 1½ tablespoons (total 2½ ounces or 75 grams) coarsely chopped raw cocoa butter (see note)

About ½ cup (2 ounces or 62 grams) coarsely chopped 66 percent cacao dark chocolate

About 1½ tablespoons (½ ounce or 12 grams) coarsely chopped unsweetened chocolate

1 teaspoon (5 milliliters) extra-virgin olive oil

BREADCRUMBS

1 day-old baguette, cut into ½-inch (1.25-centimeter) slices

5 tablespoons (75 milliliters) extra-virgin olive oil

Kosher salt

TO ASSEMBLE

3 cups (600 grams) Olive Oil Gelato (page 204)

SPECIAL EQUIPMENT: 48 lollipop sticks (available online and at baking and craft supply stores); 2 rimmed 9 x 13-inch (23 x 33-centimeter) baking sheets (preferable), or 1 large baking sheet; a mini (½-ounce) ice cream scoop

REFLECTION FROM BACK OF HOUSE

MAKING THIS BOOK HAS provided me with the unique opportunity to pause, reflect, and articulate a few things about myself and the restaurant. I have been here at Del Posto for more than a decade. Working only here, full-time. All of the recipes you find in this book come from years of research and development. They are laid out in front of you, tested and tweaked for you to make at home. I want you to feel comfortable making them as complete dishes, but also mine them for their well-tested techniques and separate components, which can be applied to your own cooking. Each process and dish was thoughtfully created. Much of the development of these recipes goes far beyond just making wonderful Italian food, but they are the result of both practical and philosophical considerations.

Many things have changed on our planet since we opened the restaurant in 2005. Our culture has become more food-obsessed. The speed of technology has changed all of our lives in ways we couldn't have imagined. Our ability to access information is nearly instant, and, in turn, has made most of us even more impatient regarding almost everything. As a result, fine dining in the traditional sense has basically been retired because people are uninterested in taking the time to eat that way.

At the same time, America has, at long last, discovered regional cuisines of its own that we can all be truly proud of. In most parts of this country you can now find beautifully prepared food that is both seasonally inspired and affordable. These changes make it very difficult for a large, fancy, expensive restaurant, focusing on old-style European cuisine and service, to remain current. But they have forced us to think long and hard about our choices. How do we deliver a relevant, but also an authentic, old-world dining experience to our speed-obsessed culture?

Answering this question defines the work at Del Posto and, of course, begets many more questions. What do our clients want from us, who do they want us to be, what role do we play in their lives, how do we stay in business for the length of our 25-year lease? How do we excite and nurture our guests? How do we make, and keep, traditional, nourishing fare edgy? We are a huge place with a huge staff charging huge prices. How do we encourage 400 people a day to come to this restaurant? How do we provide a couple celebrating an anniversary an unforgettable evening as they dine next to 12 colleagues conducting a business deal? Certainly not by offering them the same experience. And a customized dining experience is, well, as old-school as it gets.

Yes, the customer *is* always right. We enjoy giving people what they want. We create menus and offer a style of service that encourages people to make choices and have preferences. We enjoy accommodating people's differences. Del Posto is not a sequestered experience. We want you to have what you want. Our food is designed to be deconstructed, with maximum flexibility—letting us switch around

or substitute items when necessary. We enjoy the challenge of offering personalized dining to our guests. And we thrive at making these challenges imperceptible to them. It's what we do. And it takes a village of talented people—50 chefs and 50 people in the front of house for daily service. We have employed over 1,200 people since we opened in 2005.

We focus the majority of our creative efforts on managing and mitigating any and all dietary preferences and desires through a very complex matrix of ingredient deconstruction and substitution. The Del Posto training process for our chefs has come to thrive under these complicated parameters.

Few people are still able to operate large-scale kitchens this way for many reasons, namely a general lack of support, resources, budget, staff, knowledge, interest, and, of course, time. We do what we do because we can and because we should. We are lucky.

Although we free-style from time to time in the kitchen...it's not really our thing. I feel that the best use of our time is to stick with the basics. I stake our reputation on providing reliable, well-practiced service and cuisine. As stewards of regional Italian food, wine, and culture, we *insist* on cooking our food low and slow, the old-fashioned way. On the flicker of a flame, one bubble at a time.

Good menu planning includes preparing for food allergies and dietary restrictions. The kitchen at Del Posto is committed to best practices when it comes to allergens and personal preferences. To make your meal planning easier, here is a guide to potential allergens, including ingredients found inside processed products, for each of the recipes in this book.

ASSAGGI	MEAT	PORK	SHELLFISH	SEAFOOD	GARLIC	ONION	LEGUMES	NUTS	KERNELS	SEEDS	BUTTER	MILK/DAIRY	EGG	CORN	GLUTEN	SOY	TRUFFLES & MUSHROOMS	NIGHTSHADE	NITRITES	MUSTARDS	SULFITES	CHOCOLATE	CITRUS	STONEFRUIT
Suppli di Marchesi						x					x	x	x								x			
Marinara Soup with Caper Salt					x													x			x			
Baccalà Croquettes with Red Pepper Jelly				x							x	x						x		x	x			
Palline di Pane	x	x			x	x					x	x			x		x	x	x		x			
Ceci Farinata							x				x	x						x					x	
Tuna and Truffle Sfere				x								x						x						
Chicken and Egg Salad Tramezzini	x											x		x							x			
Veal Tartar and Potato Chip Clubs	x					x										x	x	x			x		x	
Mini Lobster and Corn Crostatas			x	x							x	x	x	x	x			x						

ANTIPASTI	MEAT	PORK	SHELLFISH	SEAFOOD	GARLIC	ONION	LEGUMES	NUTS	KERNELS	SEEDS	BUTTER	MILK/DAIRY	EGG	CORN	GLUTEN	SOY	TRUFFLES & MUSHROOMS	NIGHTSHADE	NITRITES	MUSTARDS	SULFITES	CHOCOLATE	CITRUS	STONEFRUIT
Snipped Herb and Lettuce Salad with Peach Citronette																					x		x	x
Radicchio and Lettuces with Lemon-Ginger Balsamic Dressing																					x		x	
Insalata Primavera della Terra with Citron Vinaigrette, Italian Ricotta, and Rosemary Crumbs											x	x	x	x	x						x		x	
Roots and Fruits with Robiola Sformato and Quince Vinaigrette								x	x			x	x					x	x			x			
Cool Summertime Minestra with Basil Pesto Tortellini and Burrata				x		x					x	x			x			x			x			
Live Large Scallop Crudo with 'Nduja, Asparagus, Mushrooms, and Grilled Scallions			x	x		x											x	x	x		x		x	
Seared Scallops, Sunchoke Purée, Puntarelle, and Grapefruit with Black Truffle Vinaigrette			x	x		x										x	x	x			x		x	
Lobster alla Caesar with Pickled Onions and Breadcrumbs Oreganata			x	x	x	x				x		x	x		x						x		x	
Lobster Salad with Burrata and Fermented Broccoli Rabe			x	x		x						x			x			x			x		x	
Fried Calamari with Spicy Caper Butter Sauce				x							x	x						x			x		x	
Charred Octopus With Ceci, Celery Hearts, and 25-Year Balsamic Vinegar				x	x	x															x		x	
Vitello Tonnato with Olive Crostone, Fried Capers, Chives, and Lime Cells	x			x	x								x		x						x		x	
Beef and Truffle Carpaccio with Sage Grissini and Artichokes Alla Romana	x				x						x	x			x			x			x		x	
Warm Cotechino with Lentils and Prosecco Zabaglione	x	x			x	x	x					x	x						x	x	x			
Del Posto 'Nduja Sausage	x	x																x	x					
Panne Grattato (Fried Breadcrumbs)															x								x	

PRIMI

	MEAT	PORK	SHELLFISH	SEAFOOD	GARLIC	ONION	LEGUMES	NUTS	KERNELS	SEEDS	BUTTER	MILK/DAIRY	EGG	CORN	GLUTEN	SOY	TRUFFLES & MUSHROOMS	NIGHTSHADE	NITRITES	MUSTARDS	SULFITES	CHOCOLATE	CITRUS	STONEFRUIT
Spaghetti with Dungeness Crab and Jalapeños			x	x	x										x			x			x		x	
Anellini del Plin	x	x			x						x	x	x		x		x		x		x			
Potato Gnocchi with Piennolo Tomatoes and Thai Basil											x	x			x			x						
Winter Squash Cappellacci with Brown Butter								x			x	x	x		x									
Egg Yolk Gnudi with Asparagus, Bird's Nest Style											x	x	x		x		x							
Lune Piene with Truffle Butter											x	x	x		x		x							
Red Wine Risotto with Carrot Purée	x					x															x		x	
Vacche Rosse Risotto	x					x					x	x									x			
Mushroom Risotto				x		x					x	x					x				x			
Lidia's Jota with Smoky Pork and Braised Kale	x	x			x	x	x											x	x		x			
Pasta Fagioli with 'Nduja and Tripe Meatballs	x	x			x	x						x			x			x	x					
Orecchiette with Red Lamb Sausage and Carrot Purée	x				x						x	x			x			x			x		x	
Agnolotti Cacio e Pepe	x	x			x	x					x	x			x					x	x			
Bigoli with Duck Liver Ragù	x					x					x	x	x		x									
100-Layer Lasagne al Ragù Bolognese	x	x			x	x					x	x	x		x			x	x					
Fresh Egg Pasta Dough													x		x									
Timpano alla Mancuso	x	x			x						x	x	x		x			x	x		x			

SECONDI - PESCE

	MEAT	PORK	SHELLFISH	SEAFOOD	GARLIC	ONION	LEGUMES	NUTS	KERNELS	SEEDS	BUTTER	MILK/DAIRY	EGG	CORN	GLUTEN	SOY	TRUFFLES & MUSHROOMS	NIGHTSHADE	NITRITES	MUSTARDS	SULFITES	CHOCOLATE	CITRUS	STONEFRUIT
Arctic Char with Wheat Broth and Grain Salad				x			x								x								x	
Whole Branzino with Fennel and Peperonata				x	x	x												x			x		x	
Lobster with Artichokes, Almonds, Basil, and Tangerine Butter			x	x		x		x			x	x									x		x	
Lobster with Squash, Shiitake Mushrooms, Brussels Sprouts, and Balsamic Brown Butter			x	x		x		x			x	x					x				x		x	
Cacciucco with Garlic Bread Soup and Sweet Shrimp alla Busara			x	x	x	x					x				x			x			x			
Monkfish Piccata				x							x	x			x						x		x	

SECONDI - CARNE

	MEAT	PORK	SHELLFISH	SEAFOOD	GARLIC	ONION	LEGUMES	NUTS	KERNELS	SEEDS	BUTTER	MILK/DAIRY	EGG	CORN	GLUTEN	SOY	TRUFFLES & MUSHROOMS	NIGHTSHADE	NITRITES	MUSTARDS	SULFITES	CHOCOLATE	CITRUS	STONEFRUIT
Apicius Duck with Savor	x							x	x	x											x		x	
Veal Braciole	x				x	x											x	x			x			
Emilia-Style Pork with Prosciutto, Parmigiano, and Balsamic	x	x			x							x							x		x			
Slow-Cooked Lamb alla Romana	x				x																			
Stinco di Vitello	x					x					x						x				x			
Standing Rib Roast	x				x																			
Le Virtù	x	x			x	x	x								x				x	x				

CONTORNI

	MEAT	PORK	SHELLFISH	SEAFOOD	GARLIC	ONION	LEGUMES	NUTS	KERNELS	SEEDS	BUTTER	MILK/DAIRY	EGG	CORN	GLUTEN	SOY	TRUFFLES & MUSHROOMS	NIGHTSHADE	NITRITES	MUSTARDS	SULFITES	CHOCOLATE	CITRUS	STONEFRUIT
Vignarola					x	x	x																	
Smashed Sunchokes																								
Eggplant Parmigiana												x			x			x					x	
Puntarelle Salad				x	x							x											x	
Nervetti Salad	x					x	x																x	
Potato Chip Salad												x						x					x	
Scafata					x	x	x											x						
Tomato Raisins																		x						

DOLCI

	NUTS	KERNELS	SEEDS	BUTTER	MILK/DAIRY	EGG	CORN	GLUTEN	SOY	NIGHTSHADE	SULFITES	CHOCOLATE	CITRUS	STONEFRUIT
Lidia's Pea Cakes with Strawberry Sauce					x	x							x	
Lidia's Chestnut Cakes with Red Wine Plums and Roasted Chestnuts	x				x	x		x			x		x	x
Amor Polenta with Corn Gelato, Blueberry Compote, and Tarragon Sauce				x	x	x	x	x					x	
Ricotta-Chocolate Tortino	x			x	x	x	x	x				x		
Pecorino Cake with Honey-Vinegar and Caramelized Pears and Preserved Walnuts	x			x	x	x	x	x			x		x	
Slow-Roasted Nectarines with Grilled Lemon Pound Cake	x			x	x	x		x					x	x
Butterscotch-Mascarpone Semifreddo with Dulce "Milk Jam" and Fresh Fruit				x	x	x	x						x	
Grappa Panna Cotta with Sour Raisins and Green Grapes		x			x			x			x			
Crespelle d'Auttuno				x	x	x	x	x			x		x	
Pineapple Crostatas with Pistachio Butter and Candied Pistachios	x				x		x	x	x				x	
Eggplant and Chocolate Crostata	x			x	x	x		x		x		x	x	
Zabaglione Classico						x					x			
Sbrisolona Crumbs			x	x			x	x					x	

GELATO & SORBETTI

	NUTS	KERNELS	SEEDS	BUTTER	MILK/DAIRY	EGG	CORN	GLUTEN	SOY	NIGHTSHADE	SULFITES	CHOCOLATE	CITRUS	STONEFRUIT
Olive Oil Gelato					x	x								
Honey Gelato					x	x								
Strawberry Gelato					x	x							x	
Ricotta Gelato and Ricotta Stracciatella					x							x		
Basil Gelato					x	x								
Pistachio Gelato	x				x	x								
Corn Gelato					x	x	x							
Cashew Gelato	x				x	x								
Yogurt Sorbetto					x									
Sour Apricot Sorbetto											x		x	x

BISCOTTI & CARAMELLE

	NUTS	KERNELS	SEEDS	BUTTER	MILK/DAIRY	EGG	CORN	GLUTEN	SOY	NIGHTSHADE	SULFITES	CHOCOLATE	CITRUS	STONEFRUIT
Brutti Ma Buoni Cookies	x		x			x								
Polenta-Polenta Mini Crostatas			x	x	x	x	x						x	
Amaro-Glazed Bomboloni			x	x				x					x	
Buckwheat Zuccherini				x			x	x						
Candied Grapefruit				x	x		x	x					x	
Sour Melon Candy											x		x	
Bastoncini								x				x		

ACKNOWLEDGMENTS

AS MOST CHEFS KNOW, a cook's life can be challenging, comes with many personal sacrifices, and requires a lot of support from those around you.

There would not be a book without the people who have helped me get this far in life. Thank you, Mom, for introducing me to the chickpea. Thank you, Dad, for teaching me about integrity. Thank you to my kids, Riley and Jasper, for keeping my mind fresh and nimble. Thank you, Christine, for being such an amazing parent to them. Thanks, Nastassia, for pushing me to do more, and better.

My journey as a chef has allowed me the opportunity to work with many dedicated, passionate, and thoughtful people. Thanks to all my alma mater Johnson & Wales for starting me off in the right direction. Thank you, Scott Bryan and JGV, for teaching me to think, move, and evaluate with purpose. *Un grande bacione* to Cesare Casella for being a sounding board, my friend, and a reality check.

I would like to thank Mario, Joe, and Lidia for entrusting Del Posto to our team. You taught me that given the proper resources, facility, support, talent, knowledge, and interest, absolutely anything is possible.

I am truly grateful for the vision and emotional intelligence of my partner and compatriot, Jeffrey Katz. Without our relationship, Del Posto could not be.

I owe much to my close confidants and chefs di cucina at Del Posto: Matt Abdoo, who is responsible for the majority of the recipes you'll find here; my dear friend and my favorite nonna, Melissa Rodriguez-Mcmahan, for her old-school style, maturity, and keen guidance; Tony Scotto, for his immense creative talents, and for committing most of his young adult life to our kitchen; Michael Davis, who was a true consigliere to me and was pivotal in helping us to find our way; Kevin Garcia, one of my oldest and closest friends, who gave me the confidence to accept this position at the restaurant; and Joshua Saffer, for his fresh exuberance and ability to recognize our future.

Brooks O. Headley, you are simply the best dessert chef ever! Thanks to Justine MacNeil for her contribution and development of the pastry recipes found here. I look forward to her becoming the next, best dessert chef ever.

Thank you to Jeff Porter for the poignant wine pairings in this book and his ability to share his deep knowledge while resisting wine elitisms. Also, Michael Greeson, Henry Davar, and Morgan Rich for their past and future dedication to our wine collection.

It takes a community of these like-minded people to operate Del Posto every day.

Close to 1,200 young women and men have worked at the restaurant in the last 12 years. I can't possibly name them all individually, but I hope they know that this cookbook and this restaurant could not exist without their tireless support and selfless dedication. And thanks to all the chefs, cooks, and unsung kitchen heroes out there who inspire me in life.

Thank you to all of those who have worked as part of Antipasti, Assaggi, Primi x 3, Meat, Fish, Dessert teams and Prep, Facilities, Banquets, Receiving, Porters, and Dishwashers (especially Jesus). I must thank Andres and the entire Lopez family; and Carlos Rodriguez for his warm sensibility and his poetic touch; as well as our supremely hospitable and hardworking maître d's, coat check guys, phone talkers, hosts, floor managers, captains, sommeliers, bar keepers, front waiters, back waiters, food runners, bread team, baristas, polishers, and, of course, Sabino Robles.

Adam McCloud, thank you for working at Del Posto not once, but twice, and keeping this "machine" well lubricated and citrus-scented. Chloe Brownstein, we really appreciate you giving us your twenties, your infectious enthusiasm, and your unusual combination of skill sets.

Thank you, my friend and hero, Michael Wilson, for curating every last detail found between these two covers, and for finding greater value and purpose in our work than may have been expected.

Michael and I would like to thank Mindy Fox for her laser-focused, persnickety approach to her art and for helping to make Del Posto recipes that actually work at home. Thanks to Paulette Tavormina for her wonderful fine-art food images—we think her art in this book speaks for itself. Thanks to G. Giraldo for his candid and immersive style of behind-the-scenes photography.

Thank you, Josephine Dillon at Richard Ginori, for being the most cooperative collaborator imaginable. Richard Ginori of Florence is the finest pure porcelain in the world since 1735. We'd also like to thank Antonella Rana for the loan of her exquisite Navarini Rame hand-hammered copper, and Alessi for their brilliantly designed vintage wares and collaborative working relationship.

Thank you, Tony Gardner, for five long, hard years of guidance as my agent; and Karen Murgolo and the rest of Grand Central Life & Style, for giving Michael and me an opportunity to make the restaurant cookbook we wanted.

Last, in the words of the great Irish playwright Samuel Beckett:

All of old. Nothing else ever. Ever tried. Ever failed. No matter. Try again. Fail again. Fail better.

INDEX

C

Cacciucco with Garlic Bread Soup and Sweet Shrimp alla Busara, 125

Cacio e Pepe, Agnolotti, 93

Calamari, Fried, with Spicy Caper Butter Sauce, 39

Candied Grapefruit, 224

cannellini beans
    in Lidia's Jota with Smoky Pork and Braised Kale, 82
    in Nervetti Salad, 154

cantaloupe, dehydrated, in Sour Melon Candy, 224

capers
    about, xxiv
    Fried Calamari with Spicy Caper Butter Sauce, 39
    Marinara Soup with Caper Salt, 5
    in Monkfish Piccata, 130
    Vitello Tonnato with Olive Crostone, Fried Capers, Chives, and Lime Cells, 45

Cappellacci with Brown Butter, Winter Squash, 66

carne. *See also* beef; lamb; pork; veal
    about, 133

Carpaccio, Beef and Truffle, with Sage Grissini and Artichokes alla Romana, 49

Carricante, 124

Carrot Purée
    Orecchiette with Red Lamb Sausage and, 88
    Red Wine Risotto with, 78

carrots, in Vignarola, 150

Cashew Gelato, 211
    in Intermezzo, 214

Castelmagno cheese
    in Lune Piene with Truffle Butter, 72
    in Red Wine Risotto with Carrot Purée, 78

Ceci Farinata, 8

Cesanese, 144

Champagne, 34

Champagne Caramel, in Crespelle d'Auttuno, 190

Charred Octopus with Ceci, Celery Hearts, and 25-Year Balsamic Vinegar, 42

Chestnut Cakes with Red Wine Plums, Roasted Chestnuts, and Yogurt Sorbetto, Lidia's, 171

Chicken and Egg Salad Tramezzini, 9

chickpeas
    Ceci Farinata, 8
    in Charred Octopus with Ceci, Celery Hearts, and 25-Year Balsamic Vinegar, 42
    in Scafata, 156

Chocolate and Eggplant Crostata, 196

Chocolate–Olive Oil Cakes, in Ricotta–Chocolate Tortino, 176

cod, Baccalà Croquettes with Red Pepper Jelly, 6

contorni
    about, 150
    Eggplant Parmigiana, 152
    Nervetti Salad, 154
    Potato Chip Salad, 155
    Puntarelle Salad, 153
    Scafata, 156
    Smashed Sunchokes, 151
    Vignarola, 150

cookies
    about, 217
    Brutti Ma Buoni Cookies, 220
    Buckwheat Zuccherini, 223
    Polenta–Polenta Mini Crostatas, 221

Cool Summertime Minestra with Basil Pesto Tortellini and Burrata, 24

Corn Gelato, 210
    Amor Polenta with Corn Gelato, Blueberry Compote, and Tarragon Sauce, 173

Cotechino with Lentils and Prosecco Zabaglione, Warm, 51

crab
    in Cacciucco with Garlic Bread Soup and Sweet Shrimp alla Busara, 125
    Spaghetti with Dungeness Crab and Jalapeños, 59

Crespelle d'Auttuno, 190

Croquettes, Baccalà, with Red Pepper Jelly, 6

Crostatas
    Eggplant and Chocolate, 196
    Mini Lobster and Corn, 11
    Pineapple, with Pistachio Butter and Candied Pistachios, 193
    Polenta–Polenta Mini, 221

crudo
    Live Large Scallop Crudo with 'Nduja, Asparagus, Mushrooms, and Grilled Scallions, 27
    Veal Tartar and Potato Chip Clubs, 10

D

Del Posto Tomato Sauce, 102

desserts (dolci)
    about, 167
    Amor Polenta with Corn Gelato, Blueberry Compote, and Tarragon Sauce, 173
    Butterscotch–Mascarpone Semifreddo with Dulce "Milk Jam" and Fresh Fruit, 185
    Crespelle d'Auttuno, 190
    Eggplant and Chocolate Crostata, 196
    Grappa Panna Cotta with Sour Raisins and Green Grapes, 188
    Lidia's Chestnut Cakes with Red Wine Plums, Roasted Chestnuts, and Yogurt Sorbetto, 171
    Lidia's Pea Cakes with Strawberry Sauce and Gelato, 168
    Pecorino Cake with Honey-Vinegar and Caramelized Pears, Honey Gelato, and Preserved Walnuts, 179
    Pineapple Crostatas with Pistachio Butter and Candied Pistachios, 193
    Ricotta–Chocolate Tortino, 176
    Slow-Roasted Nectarines with Grilled Lemon Pound Cake and Basil Gelato, 182
    Zabaglione Classico, 199

Dindarello, 181

duck
    Apicius Duck with Savor, 135
    Bigoli with Duck Liver Ragù, 95

Dulce "Milk Jam" and Fresh Fruit, Butterscotch-Mascarpone Semifreddo with, 185

ABOUT THE AUTHORS

MARK LADNER

MARK LADNER is the executive chef of Del Posto Restaurant
in New York City, which he opened in 2005. The restaurant
received a four-star rating from the *New York Times* in 2010,
and was more recently honored with a Michelin star and
a Relais & Châteaux Grand Chef distinction. In 2015, Mark
was the recipient of the James Beard Award for Best Chef:
New York City, and an honorary doctorate from his alma
mater, Johnson & Wales University. Mark cooks a sensible
interpretation of modern and regional cuisines, which
he calls "Cucina New Yorkese." In 2017, he will open Pasta
Flyer, a quick-service pasta restaurant.

MICHAEL R. WILSON

MICHAEL R. WILSON is an editor, producer, and writer
in New York City. He was the editor-in-chief of the American
edition of *La Cucina Italiana* magazine.